ATLAS of ANCIENT
and MEDIEVAL WARFARE

ATLAS of

by ARTHUR BANKS

*with an Introduction
by Lord Chalfont*

ANCIENT and MEDIEVAL WARFARE

HIPPOCRENE
BOOKS, INC.

Hippocrene Books, Inc.
171 Madison Avenue
New York, N.Y. 10016

First published in Great Britain in 1973 by
Seeley Service & Co Ltd.
196 Shaftesbury Avenue
London WC2H 8JL

Previously published as
A World Atlas of Military History: Volume I – to 1500

First published in the United States in 1973
Reprinted 1975, 1982

ISBN 0-88254-698-8

Printed in the United States of America

CONTENTS

viii

PREFACE

For twenty years I have been fighting to impress upon publishers, authors and cartographical draughtsmen the need and value of clear maps in text-books. I became an historical cartographer largely because so many of the maps I saw in books and atlases were difficult to understand. Maps are visual aids: they do not supersede text-books. What are required are simple, clear drawings that one can assimilate with ease.

The greatest drawback to historical maps is that historians are not usually good draughtsmen and cartographers are not usually well-read in history. Furthermore, there is an important difference between a *cartographer* (who can devise and plan a map) and a *cartographical draughtsman* who can only draw the final result from a cartographer's draft. And whereas authors obviously want as many maps as possible in their books, publishers try to keep these to a minimum for economic reasons.

This atlas is an attempt to produce a book of clear and simple maps printed in black and grey with a 'story' line attached. One cannot satisfy everyone's requirements within 154 pages and I can only hope that it proves useful and informative to the reader. In this volume I have included 'general' maps in addition to 'war' maps since one cannot readily grasp military campaigns in early times unless one has a background map to assist one.

ARTHUR BANKS
Oxshott
June, 1972

ACKNOWLEDGEMENTS

During the preparation of this volume I consulted some six hundred reference works, examined innumerable maps and general atlases and had the good fortune to be advised on various items by friends, colleagues and associates.

I should like to thank Dr R. A. Banks (my brother) for his expert suggestions on the Vikings and Alfred the Great maps in particular, and for his inspection of the various story panels.

Mr I. Baxter of the India Records Office supplied details on the maps dealing with India and Asia, and Mr Lim and Mr Freeberne of the School of African and Oriental Studies meticulously checked my spellings in the Chinese, Indian and Asian maps and proffered detailed advice on Far Eastern geography and history in general.

Mr A. Henderson checked my ancient and classical sections with diligence and vigour, and suggested much information to assist my work throughout. Mr R. B. Welsh, my friend since childhood, nobly read extensive notes I supplied, and researched much material for me, notably on Egypt, India, China and Asia. General Sir James Marshall-Cornwall supplied details on guns, rocketry and gunpowder items.

I must also thank Mr I. Rudd, Miss J. Gibbs and Mr J. Watkins for their assistance with the cartographical draughtsmanship on certain maps.

The Chief Librarian and Staff of the Study and Information Department of the Surrey County Library Headquarters and the Branch Library at Leatherhead, Surrey went to great lengths to assist me in my research. To them also I proffer my thanks.

Before the maps were printed Mr Alan Palmer and his wife Veronica gave them a detailed scrutiny for which I am indebted.

INTRODUCTION

BY LORD CHALFONT

I am particularly pleased to have been invited to write the introduction to this volume. The project is one of immense interest and value.

Arthur Banks' technique, which seems to me altogether admirable, is especially suited to the extremely challenging task of explaining in clear and easily understood terms campaigns, strategies and developments in military history which are often regarded as complicated and difficult to understand.

War is one of the most profoundly important manifestations of the human condition. From the first tentative experiments in the organisation of society disputes have been resolved, insults avenged and goods and territory seized or defended by violence, by force of arms, by war. It has been condemned as an obscenity; justified by theological scholars as the last resort against intolerable tyranny; and even, from time to time, glorified as the status symbol of the sovereign nation state. To the civilized mind it is astonishing that men are capable of inflicting upon each other the appalling cruelty and suffering of war; but so far no-one has been able to devise any other way of settling international quarrels or achieving political aims against determined opposition. There have been attempts to bring about disarmament by international agreement; to achieve peaceful settlement of disputes by arbitration; and to impose order on chaos by the establishment of such ambitious institutions as the League of Nations and its successor, the United Nations. None of them has succeeded. Organised violence remains the ultimate sanction in international affairs; it is still considered legitimate for a government in the pursuit of its foreign policy to indulge in the killing or maiming of thousands of human beings, and the destruction of their homes, their crops and their possessions. And it is arguable that the situation will remain unchanged so long as the nation state remains the basic unit of the structure of world society.

The phenomenon of war permeates every aspect of human behaviour. Its vocabulary fills our everyday language with vivid metaphors—the war on want, the battle for survival, the population explosion. It has inspired unforgettable music, immortal painting and some of our greatest literature. It has produced men of greatness and compassion; and others of indescribable evil. Napoleon called it "a simple art, consisting entirely of execution". For Erasmus it was the one human activity which "it is encumbent on every man, by every lawful means, to avoid, to deprecate, to oppose". But perhaps the most perceptive, if possibly the most cynical reflection was that of Thomas Hardy—"My argument is that War makes rattling good history; but Peace is poor reading."

The history of war, then, is at least as old as the recorded history of man. Most military historians divide it into periods roughly corresponding with the principal developments in the technology of war. The primitive, or ancient period of warfare is generally regarded as beginning in about 5,000 BC, when the Sumerians, who lived in the fertile lands between the Tigris and the Euphrates, became the targets of attack by the desert and mountain tribes. One of the earliest Sumerian sculptures shows soldiers carrying spears and shields; and on the ivory handle of a flint-bladed knife, found at Gebel el-Arak in Egypt and dated about 3,000 BC, there is a carving depicting soldiers fighting on a beach. Historic, or medieval warfare dates roughly from AD 500 to 1500, and modern warfare from then on.

Until about 3,000 BC it is probable that war was mainly a highly formalised method of avenging insults between one tribe and another—it was only rarely a matter of economic gain or political conquest. It was the transition from man's hunting and collecting period to that of primitive agriculture which almost certainly brought with it the military organisation designed to further political and economic aims. The ability of some tribes to till fertile lands and to establish reserves of food—the beginnings of organised society—aroused the envy of others, who sought by violence to acquire what they had been unable to provide for themselves. As the nomadic life gave way to the development of permanent communities and villages, the phenomenon later to be described as the "territorial imperative" began to emerge in a recognizable form, and success in war began to confer a hierarchical title to pleasant living space and productive lands. The development of primitive military technology was at first a matter almost entirely of the manufacture of new weapons—swords, shields, spears and bows and arrows. The first significant innovation was the introduction of the horse and the impact of cavalry on military tactics, a development which enabled the Hyksos, a warlike Indo-European people, probably nomads, to conquer Egypt in 1750 BC and to occupy the country for a century and a half.

Much of our knowledge of early military history is indeed identified with Ancient Egypt and its Asiatic Empire, although China and India too provide essential evidence of the various stages in the development of warfare. The Egyptians created one of the greatest and most enduring civilisations in history. It lasted 3000 years and passed through three great eras—the Old and Middle Kingdoms, from 2700 to 1500 BC, when the Egyptians consolidated and improved their occupation of the valley of the River Nile; and the New Kingdom, or Empire, when they occupied lands outside the boundaries of present day Egypt. This period, between 1560 and 1085 BC, represents the summit of Egyptian military power. It opened with the expulsion of the Hyksos ('the desert charioteers') by the Pharaoh Amosis (or Ahmose) I, who also reorganised northern Nubia (originally occupied by Sesostris II about 1850 BC). The successor of Ahmose, Thutmosis (or Thutmose) I, carried on the expansion of Egypt both to the south, beyond the fourth and fifth cataracts of the Nile, and north-eastwards through Palestine and Syria to the banks of the Euphrates. This was, in effect, the cradle of military history.

For almost five hundred years the Egyptians maintained a regular army to secure its great new Empire. Although the basic arm was infantry, much use was made now of the horse-drawn chariot, a weapon adapted from the Hyksos; and the pikes and spears of the Old and Middle Kingdoms were augmented by bows, swords, battle-axes and daggers. At this time also there began to appear the first signs of cohesive military organisation. A quartermaster corps was formed to take care of logistical supplies, and as the Empire developed the traditional skirmishing and head-on pitched battles gave way to more sophisticated tactical methods. The technique of the battle square emerged and the two-man chariots were used as a primitive cavalry, either in massed charges or individually in support of infantry operations.

After 1085 BC the Egyptian Empire began to decline as the power of the military caste grew and the generals began to set themselves up, together with the priests, as the feudal overlords of independent regions. Eventually Egypt collapsed under the invasion of the Assyrians, a cruel and warlike people under whose dominion there were further developments in organisation and tactics. Larger chariots, each drawn by two horses and driven by three men, made their appearance. The foot soldiers were organised into heavy and light infantry, and a corps of engineers was established. Some of the first signs of total war began to emerge, with the massacre of prisoners, mass deportations and the plundering and pillaging of enemy towns and villages. The Assyrians in their turn were expelled with the aid of Greek mercenaries, but in 525 BC Egypt was once again invaded and occupied, this time by the Persians under King Cambyses. The Persians made comparatively little impact on the science of war and the only interesting military innovations of this period were the introduction of the elephant and the development of flexible tactical doctrines which allowed for operations both by large massed formations and by small detachments of troops. Meanwhile the size of armies had grown substantially. Whereas in the early Sumerian period the typical city state had perhaps 1000 foot soldiers, some estimates put the strength of Darius's Persian Army at the Battle of Arbela, against Alexander the Great, in 331 BC, at a million foot soldiers and 40,000 horsemen. The most conservative estimate suggests that the strength was certainly not less than 300,000. In 332 BC the conquest of Egypt by Alexander brought to an end the long supremacy of the Egyptian Empire. The centre of power had moved decisively to Greece.

The Greek civilisation, later to become the Greco-Roman, had already, in the fifth century BC, entered a period of almost continuous warfare which was to last nearly four hundred years. Before the Greco-Persian wars, military operations in the Greek peninsula had been primitive affairs; the early Minoan civilization on the island of Crete had been conquered by the Achaeans in 1600 BC and for the next eight hundred years the Greek mainland and islands were subjected to a series of invasions from the north—the Dorians, Ionians and eventually the Aeolians. There then arose the city states of Classic Greece, dominated by Athens and Sparta. It was the liberal, civilised Athens which rose first to pre-eminence, principally through its leading part in the wars with Persia. At the beginning of the fifth century Darius sent his army to invade Greece and was defeated in 490 by the Athenians at Marathon. Ten years later the Persians returned in greater numbers under Xerxes, but were again defeated. This time the Persians came within striking distance of Athens, and attempts to halt them in a naval battle off Artemisium and a land battle at Thermopylae were unsuccessful, in spite of a heroic Greek stand at Thermopylae under a Spartan—Leonidas. The way to Athens was now open, but an Athenian-Spartan coalition inflicted a heavy defeat on the Persians at Plataea in 479 BC. Thirty years later, in 449 BC, the Persians finally admitted defeat and abandoned the Aegean to the Greeks.

As has so often been the case throughout history, the disappearance of the external threat meant the beginning of internal struggles in Greece. The Peloponnesian War of 431-404 BC led to the defeat of Athens by Sparta and the establishment of over half a century of Spartan hegemony. This was followed by a brief period of Theban predominance, during which there emerged a tactical development of some significance—the device employed by Epaminondas of Thebes in his battle with the Spartans at Leuctra in 371 BC. The Spartan commander, King Cleumbrotus, formed his Army of 1,000 cavalrymen and 10,000 *hoplites* in traditional phalanx formation, with his élite troops, as usual, on the right flank. Instead of doing the same, Epaminondas concentrated his numerically inferior force in great strength on his *left* flank, in a striking phalanx, four times as deep as the enemy immediately to their front. They smashed into the Spartan ranks like a battering ram—the first recorded example of a commander exerting irresistible force at a chosen point of attack.

A little later in the fourth century BC Macedonia began to emerge as a significant military power, and in 338 BC Philip II of Macedonia defeated the Greeks, who had succeeded in forming a coalition of their warring city states in an attempt to meet this new threat at Chaeronea. It was a battle in which his son, Alexander, played a decisive part when he massacred the 'Sacred Band' (a battalion of élite Theban troops) on the right flank of the Greek United Armies, and then wheeled behind the Greek lines in a classic cavalry manoeuvre.

With the makeshift coalition of Greek city states crushed, Alexander, who had succeeded Philip in 336 BC, proclaimed Greek unity and required each of the City States to provide troops for his Asian campaigns. There followed, over a period of twelve years, one of the greatest military campaigns in history, as Alexander the Great set out to punish the Persians for their earlier invasions of Greece and to create an Empire extending over most of the known world. He defeated the Persians in three great battles at Granicus (334 BC), Issus (333 BC) and Arbela (331 BC), and swept on to the frontiers of India where, on the River Hydaspes (now the Jhelum River) a tributary of the Indus, he fought one of his most brilliant battles against the Indians in 326 BC. This was, however, the last of his great victories. Three years later he died, at the age of 32, in Babylon, and his Empire gradually disintegrated.

Technically the art and science of war had advanced considerably during this period. The main weapon of the Greek city states was the thrusting spear carried by the *hoplites* or heavy infantrymen, who were formed in compact masses of up to 5,000—the phalanx—which formed the centre of the basic battle formation, with cavalry and light infantry on the flanks and the *psiloi*—special skirmishing forces—out in front. The Athenian armies also had well organised auxiliary services, including a medical corps of a rudimentary kind. Their tactics were fairly simple, often involving no more than a head-on confrontation between phalanxes.

When Alexander the Great succeeded his father, however, his impact on the military art was dramatic. Tactically he refined the rudimentary but original ideas of Epaminondas of Thebes, developing a system in which the individual phalanx did not advance 'in line'—that is to say in a straight battle front—but roughly in the shape of a V pointing at the enemy. This created a dent in the opposing line and enabled the *hoplites* to pin down the opposing infantry, allowing the cavalry to sweep in on the flanks. The cavalry thus became the decisive arm in battle instead of being used principally as a protection for the infantry. At the same time new engines of war began to make their appearance, the siege tower, the catapult or *ballista*, and the *testudo*, a battering ram under a protective covering of shields. The artillery began to emerge as an organised arm. But the principal factor in the military developments of the era was Alexander the Great himself—one of the greatest generals in history. He showed an extraordinary and precocious skill in combining and manoeuvring forces of all arms; his mastery of tactics was complete and he was able to adapt his method to any form of warfare with which he was confronted, from guerilla warfare to the investing of fortified villages. He was a strategist of remarkable skill and imagination; yet he did not hesitate to lead his own cavalry on the battlefield. Although his basic instincts were aggressive, he never moved on to a new phase in a campaign without first consolidating his gains. In the course of the great twelve year campaign which took him to the borders of India, he never outran his lines of communication or his administrative support. He brought a new dimension to the military art.

Alexander's vision of an Empire encompassing the known world was, however, achieved not by the Greeks, but by the Romans, who had become the masters of Italy in 275 BC after four centuries of war—principally against the Etruscans in the North and the Greek colonists in the south. There followed the period of the Punic Wars, in which Rome and Carthage fought for the control of the Mediterranean. When the First Punic War began in 264 BC, Carthage dominated the north coast of Africa, the south coast of Spain and most of the Mediterranean islands, including part of Sicily. After destroying the Carthaginian fleet at Mylae in Sicily in 260, the Romans landed in Africa but were defeated at Tunis in 255 by Xanthippus. The Second Punic War, which lasted from 218-201 BC, began when Hannibal, crossing the Pyrenees from Spain, defeated the Romans at the River Trebia, Lake Trasimene and Cannae; but after the defeat of Hannibal's brother, Hasdrubal, at the Metaurus River in 207 BC, the Romans sent Scipio to Africa. Hannibal, having returned to Carthage in 203, was defeated by Scipio at the Battle of Zama and Carthage was reduced to the status of a trading port. The defeat of Carthage was finally completed in the Third Punic War (149-146 BC) and by 100 BC the Roman Empire had been extended to cover Spain, Cisalpine Gaul, Illyria, Macedonia, Greece, Tripolitania, and Proconsular Africa.

The principal contribution of the Romans to military organisation and tactics was the legion. It consisted of 4,000 to 6,000 men in three ranks, the first of *hastati*, the second of *principes* and the third of *triarii*. Each rank was divided into 10 *maniples*, each of 120 to 160 men, organised into two *centuries* of 60-80. In the third rank of *triarii* this was varied—each maniple consisting of only one century. Each legion had horsemen in support on the flanks, and *velites* for skirmishing in front. The main advantage over the phalanx was tactical flexibility. With each maniple operating on a 20 yard front, with a similar distance between maniples, it was possible to adapt quickly to uneven terrain or to change formation and pass units rapidly through each other's positions as the tactical situation required. This flexibility was reflected in the equipment of the legion, the *hastati* in the front rank carrying shields, swords and javelins; the *principes* and *triarii* carrying pikes instead of javelins; and the *velites* carrying light javelins or *iacula*. The Romans also developed siege engines, mobile bridging equipment, catapults designed to fire huge arrows and bolts, and the technique of the fortified camp. Administrative arrangements became relatively elaborate and signalling and communications systems were comparatively highly organised.

It was upon this military basis that the great campaigns of Julius Caesar, Pompey, Augustus and Mark Antony were fought. From 61 to 51 BC Caesar's Gallic Wars extended the Roman Empire through Spain and Gaul as far as Britain. He then returned to Rome and a period of civil war followed, in which he defeated his rival Pompey. Caesar's successor Octavian (later the Emperor Augustus) defeated *his* main rival Mark Antony and then began a series of campaigns in Germany and Central Europe from 15 BC to 10 AD.

The reign of Augustus was the beginning of the end of the military power of Rome. He reduced the professional army to just over 300,000 men and disarmed the free civilians. For the next four hundred years the Roman Army underwent fundamental changes. The size of the legion was progressively reduced and large numbers of barbarians were enlisted to protect the Empire from external attack. When, in the third century, the Gothic frontier invasion began, the Army was reorganised into the Palatine Army—a campaign force of shock troops, and *limitani* or border troops. Meanwhile two factors had combined to consolidate the superior status of the cavalry; the need for a high degree of mobility in an Army used mainly for dealing with border raids, and the generally low calibre of the infantry which required them to be massed together for the purpose of improving their morale, thus allowing horsemen to predominate as the offensive arm. There were corresponding changes in arms, and by the 4th century the bow and the sling were beginning to rival the sword and the javelin. At the same time a vast complex of defensive works (the *limes*) had been built up by Rome in Europe, Africa and the Middle East.

There were persistent attacks on this, notably by the Goths and Visigoths in the 2nd, 3rd and 4th centuries; by the Vandals over the same period; and finally by the Huns under Attila, in the 5th century. At the same time the Angles, Picts and Jutes had invaded Britain and the Herulians had established a kingdom in Italy, only to be defeated by the Ostrogoths under Theodoric. Under these repeated assaults the Roman Empire, for all practical purposes, disintegrated. It was split up into barbarian kingdoms ruled by *foederati*, the leaders of Roman auxiliary troops raised from the barbarian peoples.

In 481, as the Roman Empire withered away, Europe came under the Merovingian dynasty; the Frankish King, Clovis, extended his rule through most of Gaul and he and his successors expanded their Empire gradually until in 771 Charlemagne inherited the Frankish Kingdom from his father Pepin III, and rapidly pushed south and east into Italy, Bavaria and Carinthia, south-west into Spain and north-east to the River Elbe. In 800 Charlemagne was crowned Emperor by the Pope in Rome, but in 843 the Treaty of Verdun divided the Empire into three kingdoms. The Carolingian Army was surprisingly small—6,000 to 10,000 men, of whom more than half were mounted troops. Heavy chariots carried supplies in convoys. It was a cumbersome, unimpressive Army, but Charlemagne commanded it in person and his intelligence and boundless energy enabled him to make the best of his limited resources.

When the Carolingian Empire came to its end the feudal system began its period of domination in European history and warfare moved into its historic or medieval phase of development. For more than two hundred years the Vikings from Scandinavia ranged over most of England, Ireland and Northern France. They were a fierce, well-disciplined fighting force, who landed in their shallow-draft long ships, seized horses and weapons from their enemies and used them in marauding cavalry tactics. Their most effective series of campaigns were those against Britain throughout the 9th century.

Meanwhile there began that great period of history, lasting from the end of the Carolingian Empire to the Italian Renaissance in the 15th century, which saw the birth of modern Europe. In the military sense it was not at first a period of dramatic change. The basic fighting unit was the knight, or armoured horseman. The manufacture of armour was raised almost to the level of an art; and there were impressive developments in the techniques of fortification and siege warfare; but tactics remained basically simple. A typical battle would begin with the cavalry formed up within a wall of infantry, which at a given signal would open, allowing the cavalry to charge upon the enemy. The infantry were generally either pikemen or bowmen, armed with either the crossbow or the longbow—the latter enthusiastically adopted by the English armies fighting against the Welsh and the Scots in the 13th century. It was a weapon which was later to have a decisive effect at the Battle of Crécy on August 26th, 1346, the first great English victory over the French in the Hundred Years' War.

Meanwhile William the Conqueror had invaded Britain in 1066 and transformed the structure of English society; and from 1096 to 1192 the Crusades had taken armies from Western Europe on three great expeditions to the Middle East. A number of military lessons emerged from the Crusades—including the importance of sea-power and the value of being able to manoeuvre rapidly with mixed forces of infantry and cavalry. But possibly the most important lesson affected the construction of fortifications and defence systems. The Middle Ages was the great era of fortification, although it was not until the end of the twelfth century that true castles and fortified cities began to replace the feudal residence with its rudimentary protective wall. With the development of strongly fortified areas, siege machinery began to play an increasingly important role. Explosives were still unknown, but it was possible to hurl huge projectiles, at first with giant catapults mounted on towers and later with the *trebuchet*, a counter-weighted sling. The arts of sapping and mining were refined and an early example of 'artificial moonlight' appeared when the trees surrounding medieval fortresses were soaked in oil and set alight to illuminate the surrounding countryside and so discourage night attacks.

While these developments in military science and technology were taking place in Europe, there had been a remarkable century of conquest by the Arabs from 632-732. Within this period they had conquered territory from the Syrian border in the east, across Egypt and North Africa, and north through Spain to the Pyrenees. This extraordinary interlude, however, had little impact on the development of warfare. The campaigns were fought by tribes using camel-borne cavalry and infantry armed with bows and arrows. The Bedouin techniques of surprise attack and rapid movement were fully exploited. Battles usually began with a volley from the archers followed by a cavalry charge with sabre and lance. Even against the comparatively unsophisticated feudal militia their success was predictably short-lived.

The Middle Ages, in spite of the apparent pre-occupation with invasion and counter-invasion, was in fact a period characterised by certain obvious limitations on the scope and scale of warfare. As the Roman Empire gave way to Christendom, the moral authority of the Church increased, and with it the inhibitions against organised violence. Even the great battles of medieval history were trivial affairs by modern standards (at Poitiers and Agincourt, for example, fewer than 30,000 men were engaged) and even long bitter campaigns could be conducted without great hardship to the general population or serious disruption of society. It was not until the 14th and 15th centuries that this situation began to change, leading to the vastly different all pervading experience of modern war. The crucial period of transition was the Hundred Years' War from 1337 to 1453. While it raged in France, the Anglo-Scottish conflict which had begun in 1297 ended when the Scots were defeated at Homildon Hill in 1402; and Owain Glyndwr's brief but brave attempt to achieve independence for Wales finally failed in 1412. Meanwhile, in Europe, Switzerland had emerged as a substantial military power, with a special reputation for effective infantry, highly disciplined and meticulously trained. Military organisation during this period was totally transformed and for the first time there appeared the 'regular Army'—a paid Army owing allegiance to the Crown and not to a feudal lord. Tactically the infantry became once again the Queen of Battles, ending a thousand years of cavalry predominance; gunpowder artillery appeared to change irrevocably the nature of war.

The great battles of the Hundred Years' War were at Crécy (1346), Poitiers (1356) and Agincourt (1415)—all decisive victories for the English. In 1429, however, the French resurgence began with Joan of Arc, and by 1453 the English had been driven from France, their only territorial gain after over a century of war being the port of Calais. This was the end of the Hundred Years' War and, by common consent of most historians, the end of the Middle Ages. The Wars of the Roses, between York and Lancaster, ravaged England for another thirty years, but in general Medieval Europe began to give way to the modern Europe of the nation state—a crucial development in political, economic and military history.

It is, however, not only in Europe, North Africa and the Middle East that military history has its origins—China was at one time the most militarily advanced country in the ancient world. The dates of the early Chinese dynasties and the development of their armies are the subject not of history but of legend. It is likely that in the first two dynasties, the Hsia and the Shang (or Yin), the warrior class became predominant. Certainly the third dynasty, the Chou, who defeated the Shang and moved into Anyang, the Shang capital, in about 1028 BC, were basically a military hierarchy. In about 770 BC they established their capital at Loyang, and there followed a period of internal struggle in China. The country split into a series of loose confederations and until 221 BC there was almost continuous civil war, with enormous walls being built after 450 BC to protect the border states from attacks by the Asiatic Huns. In 221 BC one of the fiercest of the warring leaders—Cheng, who at the age of 22 had come to power in the state of Ch'in—succeeded in reuniting China and, as Shih Huang Ti (First Emperor), founded the fourth (Ch'in) dynasty. Under his rule the sections of wall built under the Chou dynasty were linked together to form the Great Wall of China, and the country was divided into 36 regions. In spite of his efforts, however, China again split into kingdoms at the beginning of the third century BC and it was not until 206 BC that the country was reunited again under Wu Ti, who founded the Han Dynasty, which was to last for four centuries (Western Han 206 BC-24 AD and Eastern Han 25-221 AD). Although he was a soldier, Wu Ti established a civil administration; under his rule, however, there was almost continuous fighting against the

Huns, and the military hierarchy achieved great power and prestige. The Chinese cavalry was improved by a systematic horse-breeding policy and iron weapons were widely used. The Huns were not only driven out of the regions of northern China which they had occupied while China was still in a state of internal disorder; they were also driven west from the borders of China in a series of military campaigns between 128 and 36 BC.

In 221 AD, however, the Han dynasty fell, and yet another period of unrest followed. The period of the Three Kingdoms (San Huo) saw renewed attacks by barbarians from the north and under the Western Tsin Dynasty (265-317) the Huns invaded North China and established a Hun Dynasty. There followed a period of division and conflict, with North and South China under separate dynasties for nearly two centuries. It was not until the end of the Sixth century that the Sui dynasty was founded by Yang Chien (also called Wen Ti) who made a determined attempt to reunite China. He had the Great Wall of China extended and repaired and the country began to enjoy a period of comparative tranquility, under which Chinese civilisation began to flower. The barbarians on the frontiers, however, remained a serious threat, and under the T'ang Dynasty (618-907) the Emperor Li Yuan (also called T'ae Tsu) defeated the Turks with an Army which came to be feared and respected all over Asia. It was towards the end of the T'ang dynasty that gunpowder made its first recorded appearance.

In the tenth century there was yet another internal struggle in China, which culminated in the seizure of power in 960 by a general, Chao K'uang-yin (also called Sung T'ai Tsu) who founded the Sung Dynasty. Chao was a great military leader, but like his predecessor Wu Ti, he insisted on the army being subordinated to the civil authority. The Army, however, continued to develop and it soon reached a strength of one million men—mostly volunteers. Arms and equipment, however, were still rudimentary, the cross-bow being still the basic weapon of the Chinese soldier. Gunpowder was now being used for making bombs launched by catapult and China was centuries ahead of Europe in its siege techniques.

Chao K'uang-yin's successors in the Sung dynasty, however, lacked his military talents and in about 1260 after a period of progressive degeneration in the army, the great Mongol invasion of China began.

The Mongol Army was almost exclusively an Army of horsemen, drawn from a barbarian, patriarchal community living on the Eurasian Steppes. Their military organisation and tactics were simple and effective, and military skills were highly regarded in the Mongol tribes. The cavalrymen were mounted on small, tough horses; they wore leather breast-plates, carried leather shields and were armed with bows and arrows, javelins and lances. They were expert archers and ruthless, savage soldiers. Their tactics were based on the exploitation of surprise and mobility, using small numbers of infantry only to pin down an enemy and set the scene for their cavalry attacks. These were terrifying affairs, carried out at first in total silence, messages being sent by flags; in the final charge they terrorised the enemy with battle cries. This implacable, highly disciplined, military hierarchy produced two of the greatest but most terrifying warriors in History—Genghis Khan and Tamerlane. It was Genghis Khan who, in a sustained military campaign between 1219 and 1225 penetrated into Turkestan, Iran and Afghanistan; and reached the banks of the Indus, Azerbaijan, the Caucasus and South Russia. Under his command no method of waging war was too frightful—civilians, men, women and children, were used as a living screen for his attacks; cities were ruthlessly sacked and mutilation, rape and desecration were systematically used as instruments of terror.

When he died in 1227, Genghis Khan's successors were marginally less barbaric and notably less bellicose, and it was not until the middle of the 14th century that the Mongol military tradition was revived under Tamerlane (Timur i leng or Timur the lame), who between 1380 and 1395 overran Khurasan and Eastern Persia, Iraq, Azerbaijan, Armenia, Mesopotamia and Georgia. During his campaigns he proved to be an apt disciple of Genghis Khan, destroying cities, murdering whole populations and building towns out of the skulls of beheaded prisoners. Like Genghis Khan, he organised his soldiers meticulously; his tactics were imaginative and well-planned, and his disciple draconian and rigid.

The Mongol invasion of China reached its peak in 1279, with the establishment of the Yuan dynasty, and ended nearly a century later with the establishment of the Ming dynasty. In the East, as in the West, the scene was set for a new era in military history.

ATLAS of ANCIENT
and MEDIEVAL WARFARE

1

FOUR EARLY VERSIONS OF THE WORLD

❶ As visualised by Hecataeus c. 500 B.C.

Hecataeus of Miletus was a much-travelled Greek historian and geographer who thought the world was round. His works have perishe

❷ As visualised by Herodotus c. 450 B.C.

Herodotus, born in Halicarnassus in 484 B.C., was a much-travelled Greek historian who wrote a detailed account of the ancient world.

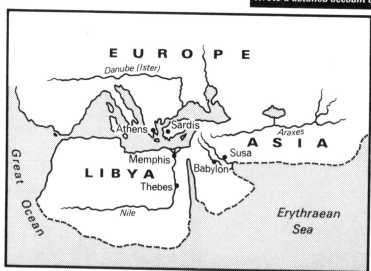

© Arthur Banks

❸ As visualised by Eratosthenes c. 200 B.C.

Eratosthenes, born at Cyrene in 276 B.C., was a scholar of geography, history, astronomy, philosophy, and geometry, and chief librarian at Alexandria. Most of his works have perished.

❹ As visualised by Ptolemy c. A.D. 150

Ptolemy (Ptolemaeus, Claudius) was a geographer, astronomer, and mathematician.

IDENTIFIABLE TRENDS IN EARLY MILITARY HISTORY

NOTE: EARLY HISTORY IS MUCH-DISPUTED BY SCHOLARS

❶ The Fertile Riverine Areas

Early wars (in the sense of organized struggles) appear to have occurred in the area now known loosely as the Middle East and came about due to geography. In about 5000 B.C., people known as Sumerians occupied the area called the Plain of Shinar, and this fertile region became the envy of surrounding desert and mountain tribes.

❷ Early Wars and Invasions

There were three main tribal groupings: Hamites, Semites, and Aryans (or Indo-Europeans). About 3000 B.C., Semitic tribes invaded Akkad-Sumer, and Aryans attacked Assyria. A long struggle ensued, and at one time (c.2320 B.C.), the tribes appear to have occupied the complete area between the rivers Tigris and Euphrates (under Sargon of Akkad).

❸ The Middle East c. 2300–1500 B.C.

KEY
❶ Hittites.
❷ Mitannians.
❸ Assyrians.
❹ Kassites.
❺ Elamites.
❻ Canaanites.
❼ Thebans.

By c.2300 B.C., the main groups had split up into smaller tribes. Fierce struggles continued for the 'land of the two rivers', now known as Babylonia. Raids on the Nile delta were made by desert horsemen (Hyksos) who set up a base at Avaris. They were opposed by the Thebans. An Aryan group from the Black Sea (Hittites) expanded southwards.

❹ The Middle East c.1500–1000 B.C.

KEY
Egyptian Empire c.1450 B.C.
❶ Hittites.
❷ Mitannians.
❸ Assyrians.
❹ Hebrews.
❺ Philistines.
❻ Elamites.
❼ Libyans.
❽ Achaeans.

The Egyptian peoples eventually expelled the Hyksos, and despite attacks from similar border groups, established a great empire. The Phoenicians, a sea-faring people, settled at Tyre and Sidon. The Achaean peoples of Aryan stock advanced southwards from Greece, occupied Minoan Crete, and then expanded eastward into the Middle East.

❺ India before c. 600 B.C.

KEY
- ➤ Aryan invasions.
- ⇨ Further advances.
- ⤍ Mongoloid raids.

0 — 400 Miles

c.2000 B.C., migrations from Asia into India occurred in a pattern similar to the Middle East. Aryan tribal groups advanced over the Hindu Kush to the riverine areas of the Indus and Ganges, and later moved south, even to Ceylon. Infrequent Mongoloid invasions from the north-east were hindered by the Himalayas and Tibetan plateaux.

❻ China before c. 600 B.C.

0 — 300 Miles

c.1766 B.C., the Shang dynastic empire was created in the region of Anyang, its capital. After c.1130 the semi-barbaric Chou from the Wei area moved eastwards, defeated the Shang, and later formed a great empire from the Yangtze to present-day Manchuria. From 800-600 B.C. there were constant feuds between autonomous war-lords.

❼ Italy before c. 600 B.C.

INDO-EUROPEANS

Founded c.700 B.C., possibly as a border post.

0 — 150 Miles

c.900 B.C., the Etruscans arrive by sea from the east and settle here.

KEY
- ➤ Early penetrations.
- ⇨ Etruscan invasions.
- ⇦ Greek colonization.

c.2000 B.C., Indo-European tribes migrated across the Alps and pressed southwards bringing the Bronze Age to Italy and Sicily. c.900 B.C., Etruscans (of different racial origin), arrived by sea and infiltrated north-west Italy. From 750-600 B.C., there were frequent wars between the two groups. Meanwhile, Greeks were colonizing Sicily and southern Italy.

❽ Greece before c. 600 B.C.

0 — 100 Miles

INDO-EUROPEANS

c.1184 B.C., besieged and conquered by the Greeks.

c.1400 B.C., Indo-European people from Achaea in southern Greece (which had been invaded by the Dorians) conquered the highly civilized Minoans of Crete, whose culture had spread over most of the Aegean. From c. 1000 B.C., Sparta became militarily dominant and won two wars against the Messenians (c.700-680 B.C., and c.640-620 B.C.).

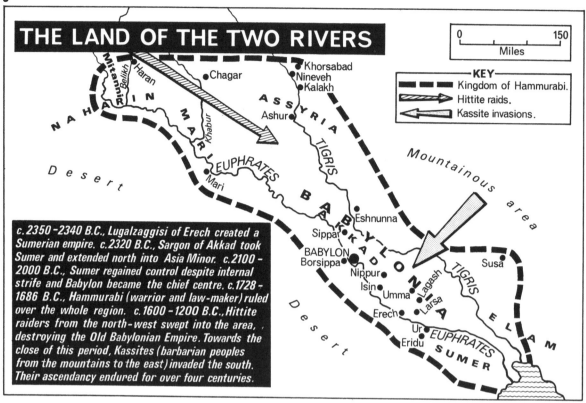

THE LAND OF THE TWO RIVERS

0 — 150 Miles

KEY
- ▬ ▬ Kingdom of Hammurabi.
- ⇨ Hittite raids.
- ⇦ Kassite invasions.

c.2350–2340 B.C., Lugalzaggisi of Erech created a Sumerian empire. c.2320 B.C., Sargon of Akkad took Sumer and extended north into Asia Minor. c.2100–2000 B.C., Sumer regained control despite internal strife and Babylon became the chief centre. c.1728–1686 B.C., Hammurabi (warrior and law-maker) ruled over the whole region. c.1600–1200 B.C., Hittite raiders from the north-west swept into the area, destroying the Old Babylonian Empire. Towards the close of this period, Kassites (barbarian peoples from the mountains to the east) invaded the south. Their ascendancy endured for over four centuries.

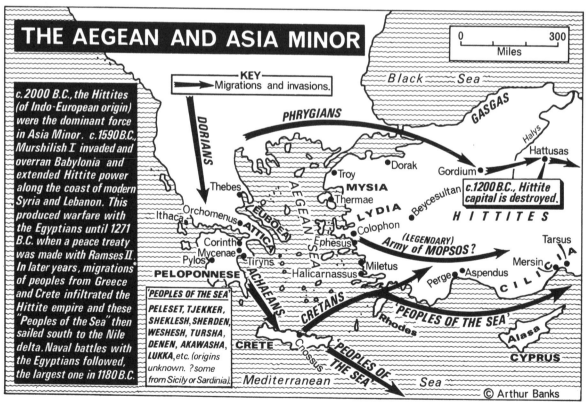

THE AEGEAN AND ASIA MINOR

0 — 300 Miles

KEY Migrations and invasions.

c.2000 B.C., the Hittites (of Indo-European origin) were the dominant force in Asia Minor. c.1590 B.C., Murshilish I invaded and overran Babylonia and extended Hittite power along the coast of modern Syria and Lebanon. This produced warfare with the Egyptians until 1271 B.C. when a peace treaty was made with Ramses II. In later years, migrations of peoples from Greece and Crete infiltrated the Hittite empire and these "Peoples of the Sea" then sailed south to the Nile delta. Naval battles with the Egyptians followed, the largest one in 1180 B.C.

'PEOPLES OF THE SEA'
PELESET, TJEKKER, SHEKLESH, SHERDEN, WESHESH, TURSHA, DENEN, AKAWASHA, LUKKA, etc. (origins unknown. ?some from Sicily or Sardinia).

c.1200 B.C., Hittite capital is destroyed.

© Arthur Banks

ANCIENT EGYPT AND HER ASIATIC EMPIRE

THE WARRIOR PHARAOHS

Menes (c. 3100 B.C.). United 'Two Lands' (Upper & Lower Egypt).
Mentuhotep II (c. 2040 B.C.). Reunited Egypt after chaos.
Sesostris III (c. 1850 B.C.). Established Nubian Empire.
Ahmose I (c. 1567 B.C.). Drove Hyksos from Egypt.
Thutmose I (c. 1515 B.C.). Gained Asiatic Empire.
Thutmose III (c. 1460 B.C.). Regained Asiatic Empire.
Seti I (c. 1310 B.C.). Retained Palestine against strong foes.
Ramses II (c. 1250 B.C.). Retained Palestine against Hittites.
Merneptah (c. 1231 B.C.). Repelled first attack by 'sea people'.
Ramses III (c. 1180 B.C.). Repelled main attack by 'sea' foes.
Sheshonk I (c. 930 B.C.). Libyan pharaoh: sacked Jerusalem.
Piankhi (c. 730 B.C.). First Nubian pharaoh: conquered Egypt.
Necho II (c. 605 B.C.). Led temporary Egyptian resurgence.
Note: there are numerous spelling variations. Examples: Ramses, Rameses, Raamses; Thutmose, Thutmosis, Tuthmosis, etc.

FORTIFIED ZONE BUILT BY RAMSES III

c. 1231 B.C., Egyptians win victory over sea invaders.

Capital of Old Kingdom.

c. 1180 B.C., Egyptians defeat 'Peoples of the Sea' in naval battle.

Hyksos capital.

Egyptian base.

Fortress built by Thutmose III following the battle and siege of Megiddo (c. 1481 B.C.). 'Thutmose-is-the-Binder-of-the-Barbarians'.

CHRONOLOGY OF ANCIENT EGYPT
(all dates are B.C.)

Pre-Dynastic Period	?6000-3100
Archaic Period	3100-2686
Old Kingdom	2686-2160
First Intermediate Period	2160-2133
Middle Kingdom	2133-1786
Second Intermediate Period	1786-1567
New Kingdom	1567-1085
Late Period	1085-332

KEY
▨ Northern extent of Egyptian conquest and influence.
★ Important fortresses.
⊕ Egyptian naval base/docks.
⚔ Important battles.

Note: Hyksos (Hikau-Khoswet) approximates to either 'Princes of the Desert Uplands' or 'Rulers of Foreign Countries'. They can be regarded loosely as 'desert charioteers'.

THE NILE VALLEY TO THE SOUTH

c. 730 B.C. PIANKHI CONQUERS EGYPT
c. 671-661 B.C. ASSYRIANS EXPEL ETHIOPIANS

0 — 100 Miles

First Cataract
Second Cataract
ETHIOPIA (KUSH, NUBIA)
Third Cataract
Fourth Cataract
Napata

Ethiopian capital.

Capital of Middle Kingdom; the main centre of Empire during New Kingdom.

Capital of Menes.

Naval harbour.

FORTIFIED ZONE FROM NORTH TO SOUTH
Fortresses: Faras West, Serra, Buhen, Kor, Meinarti, Dorgonarti, Dabenarti, Mirgissa, Gemai, Murshid, Shelfak, Uronarti, Semna West, Semna East, and Semna South.

Southern limit of Old Kingdom.

Southern limit of Middle Kingdom.

© Arthur Banks

0 — 100 Miles

Map labels: HITTITES, MITANNI, Carchemish, "Height of War", NAHARIN, Niy, Euphrates, Orontes, ALASA, Lake Homs, Kadesh, Shabtuna (Ribleh), Byblos, AMORITES, Damascus, Sidon, Nuges, Yenoam, Tyre, Herenkeru, KODDE, Mediterranean Sea, Megiddo, KHABIRI, Joppa, Jerusalem, Jordan, Dead Sea or MOAB, Gaza, EDOM, SEIR, CANAAN, SHASU (SHOS), Tharu, GOSHEN, Avaris, Buto, Sais, Pi-ye, Naucratis, TEHENU, LIBYANS (LIBU), LOWER EGYPT, Pyramids → Giza, Peru-nefer, Memphis, Sakkara, Lake Moeris, Fayum, (Bahr Yusuf), DESERT, SINAI, MIDIAN, Nile, Tell-el-Amarna, Abydos, Leukos Limen, Red Sea, THEBES, Karnak, Luxor, Hierakonpolis, UPPER EGYPT, Elephantine (island), Aswan, First Cataract, Faras West, Buhen, Semna, Second Cataract, to Punt (Somali coast)

THE BATTLE AND SIEGE OF MEGIDDO 1481 B.C.

The Battle (?15 May)

Note: the king of Kadesh slips away to north.

Asiatics retreat into fortress and siege begins.

MEGIDDO

PLAIN OF ESDRAELON

RIDGE OF CARMEL

night 14-15 May

Brook of Kina

MOUNTAIN PASS

KEY
■ Egyptian dispositions.
▨ Asiatics' dispositions.

Egyptian Pre-Battle Strategy

0 — 3 Miles

RIDGE OF CARMEL

Zefti Road

★MEGIDDO

Aruna Pass

Taanach

ASIATICS' FIRST POSITION

to Damascus

from Yehem Damascus Road

Morning of battle, Asiatics redeploy in great haste west and south of fort.

Egyptians (?20,000) advance in file over narrow mountain pass.

Asiatics expect the Egyptians to attack from this direction.

In May 1481 B.C., the king of Kadesh led a revolt of the Egyptian Empire's Asiatic city kings against the pharoah, Thutmose III. The Egyptian army marched to Megiddo, defeated the insurgents in battle, and besieged the fortress. After a campaign to secure the northern regions, Thutmose III returned to Thebes in October.

THE BATTLE OF KADESH 1288 B.C.

The Egyptian Advance

Hittite army concentrates north of Kadesh. As Ramses II and the Amon division advance, Hittites manœuvre to intercept Re.

Lake Homs

Orontes

Ⓗ ★KADESH

noon ?30 May

Ramses II leads advance

Orontes

Shabtuna
■ Ramses II
■ Amon Division
Aranami
■ Re Division

■ Ptah Division

■ Sutekh Division

KEY
Ⓔ Egyptian encampment at night (?29 May).
■ Egyptian divisions at dawn (?30 May).
Ⓗ Hittites first position at dawn (?30 May).

The Egyptian army was arranged in four divisions: Amon, Re, Ptah, and Sutekh. Ramses II took personal command over Amon and led in front during advance.

0 — 3 Miles

Ⓔ As Egyptians move out, Ptah and Sutekh lag behind.

The Hittite Ambush

Lake Homs

Ramses II and Amon Ⓔ

KADESH

Re survivors flee north to join Amon

Brook of El-Mukadiyeh

Re ■ Ⓗ

Orontes

Hittites allow Ramses II and Amon to pass before emerging to attack Re. The Egyptian advance is cut in two as Ptah is far behind.

The Egyptian 'Victory'

Orontes

RAMSES II

Egyptian troops from coast arriving on scene

El-Mukadiyeh

HITTITES

Brook of

★ KADESH

Ptah (arriving)

Hittites attack Amon; strong Egyptian defence aided by unexpected arrival of 'recruit' troops. Hittites driven back into Kadesh as Ptah arrives.

By 1288 B.C., the Hittites under Metella had swept southwards and made Kadesh their base. Ramses II led his army to engage them and a battle ensued at Kadesh. Each army numbered about 20,000 and despite gaining an early tactical success, Metella was beaten. This battle is notable for the extensive use of chariots in warfare.

© Arthur Banks

8

ANCIENT PALESTINE AND THE ISRAELITES

❶ The Jewish Exodus from Egypt

MEDITERRANEAN SEA

CANAAN

Ai?
Jericho
Gilgal
MT. NEBO

Hebron
Hormah

Egyptian pursuit ends in disaster.

Ramses

GOSHEN
ETHAM

Oboth
MOAB
Zared

Nile

Succoth

SHUR

EGYPT

Marah
Elim

SEA OF REEDS

Kadesh-barnea
(water source)

PARAN

EDOM

▲MT. HOR

MIDIAN

c.1280 B.C., the Hebrews rebel against Pharoah and trek begins.

SIN

Rephidim

Ezion-gaber

▲MT. SINAI

KEY
→ Route followed by Israelites?
--- Israeli scouting groups.
✂ Battle.

0 ——— 100
Miles

❷ Campaigns east of the River Jordan

0 — 5
Miles

BASHAN

Yarnuk
Edrei?

Israelites defeat Og, king of Bashan.

CANAAN

ISRAELITES

Jordan

Jabbok

Adam?

AMORITES

Israelites defeat Sihon, king of the Amorites.

Jericho
Gilgal
Shittim
Heshbon
▲MT. NEBO

❸ Joshua's Conquests

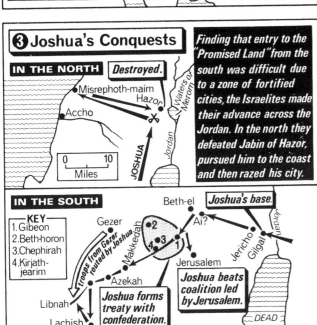

IN THE NORTH   **Destroyed.**

Misrephoth-maim
Hazor

Accho

Waters of Merom

JOSHUA

Jordan

0 — 10
Miles

Finding that entry to the "Promised Land" from the south was difficult due to a zone of fortified cities, the Israelites made their advance across the Jordan. In the north they defeated Jabin of Hazor, pursued him to the coast and then razed his city.

IN THE SOUTH

KEY
1. Gibeon
2. Beth-horon
3. Chephirah
4. Kirjath-jearim

Beth-el
Joshua's base.
Gezer
Ai?
Makkedah
Jericho
Gilgal

Troops from Gezer routed by Joshua

Jerusalem

Azekah

Joshua beats coalition led by Jerusalem.

Libnah

Joshua forms treaty with confederation.

Lachish
Hebron
Eglon
Debir
DEAD SEA
to Gaza

0 — 10
Miles

❹ Settlement of the Tribes

0 — 30
Miles

ASHER
DAN
ZEBULON
NAPHTALI
Waters of Merom
L.Chinnereth (Sea of Galilee)

MEDITERRANEAN SEA

later moves north

ISSACHAR
MANASSEH
MANASSEH
part moves to here
Jordan

EPHRAIM
GAD
DAN first position

BENJAMIN
REUBEN

JUDAH
DEAD SEA

SIMEON

© Arthur Banks

9

CANAAN IN TURMOIL

THE WARRIOR JUDGES OF ISRAEL

OTHNIEL expels invading nomads.
EHUD expels Moabite invaders from Jericho.
SHAMGAR defeats Philistines.
DEBORAH leads northern tribes (under **BARAK**)
to victory over Canaanites.
GIDEON expels Midianites.
JEPHTHAH, exiled, is recalled to fight Ammonites.
SAMSON fights and harries Philistines.

(Note: the book of Judges includes the names of other judges and their periods of service, but no details of their military exploits. They are: **TOLA, JAIR, IBZAN, ELON,** and **ABDON**).

The period between Joshua's death and Saul's crowning was Israel's "Iron Age". The Israelites had to face attacks from the Canaanites, Midianites, Amalekites, and the "Children of the East". As each threat developed, a "judge" came forth to win deliverance for the tribe or area under attack. Consequently, the "judges" were, more properly, military leaders. Later 'sea-peoples' from the Aegean settled along the southern coast, and their commercial expansion brought them into conflict with the Israelites who realised (under Saul) that they must act as a united force to confront this new menace.

Note: the Philistines eventually gave their name to the area because Palestine is a Latinized form of Philistia.

Misrephoth-maim · Hazor · Accho (Acre) · *SEA OF GALILEE* · *MT. CARMEL* Harosheth · *MT. TABOR* · Dor · Megiddo · Jezreel · Spring of Harod · Taanach · *MT. GILBOA* · Jabesh-gilead · Bezek · Thebez · Beth-shittah · Shechem · Arumah · Pirathon · Shiloh · Aphek · Ramah · Mizpah of Gilead · Jordan · Ekron · Gezer · Mizpah · Jericho · Rabbah of the Ammonites · Ramah · Gilgal · Heshbon · Eshtoal · Jerusalem · Zorah · Azekah · Socoh · Tekoa · Ashkelon · Gath · Hebron · Aroer · Gaza · Jezreel · Horesh · Ziglag · Eshtemoa · *DEAD SEA* · Beersheba · Arad · Hormah

PHILISTINES (Sea-peoples or 'Peleset')

KEY
Expulsion of invaders by the Judges of Israel (named).
Israelite offensives mentioned in the two books of Samuel.
Campaigns of the enemies of Israel.

0 10 20 Miles

© Arthur Banks

ISRAEL'S GOLDEN AGE UNDER DAVID AND SOLOMON 1000 - 926 B.C.

David reigned for thirty-three years during a period of almost unbroken success. He cleared the Philistines from the land (containing them in the coastal plain), and he created a great empire, only Phoenicia remaining outside his control. By creating an army with allegiance to himself alone, he became independent of tribal levies. His power was personal rather than national, but he failed to unite the northern and southern sections of his kingdom. Solomon extended Israel's influence by alliances and treaties, and he fortified cities and introduced chariots to his armies. However, his introduction of Israelite forced labour led to the collapse of the empire after his death.

SYRIA

ASSYRIA

Euphrates

Hamath

HAMATH

Orontes

Arvad

ARAM

Emesa

Kadesh

Tadmor

Gebal

ZOBAH

Baalbek

Rehob

Sidon

Damascus

BETH-REHOB

Tyre

Dan

Cartan

BETH-MAACAH

Hazor

Solomon joins with Hiram to finance his building and military projects.

Acre (Accho)

Mt. Carmel

GESHUR

Dor

Megiddo

JOB

Taanach

Beth-shean

Shiloh

I S R A E L

A M M O N

Joppa

Rabbath-Ammon

David's seaport.

Beth-el

Gezer

Ashdod

JERUSALEM

Gaza

P H I L I S T I A

Hebron

DEAD SEA

Beersheba

M O A B

David captures this from Jebusites and makes it the capital of his Israelite kingdom. This is a wise choice as no tribal feuds are caused. He installs the Ark of the Covenant with great ceremony.

AMALEK

EGYPT

E D O M

DESERT

David's original capital when King of Judah.

DESERT

Note: Solomon's army is given as 1,400 war-chariots and 12,000 cavalry in the book of Kings.

Solomon builds docks and naval base after subduing Edomites.

Ezion-gaber

0   50

Miles

KEY

Extent of David's empire, consolidated by his chosen son, Solomon.

David's campaigns.

© Arthur Banks

ANCIENT CHINA

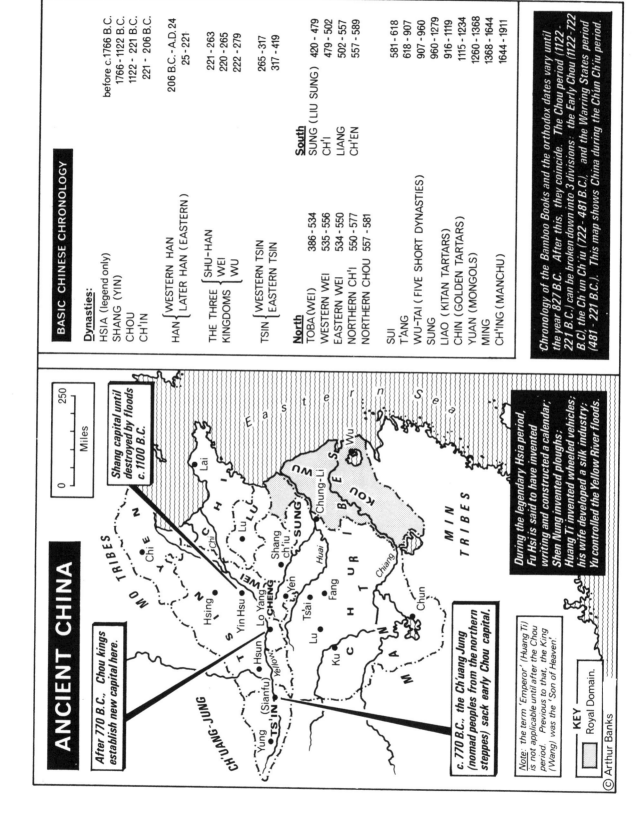

After 770 B.C., Chou kings establish new capital here.

Shang capital until destroyed by floods c. 1100 B.C.

c. 770 B.C., the Ch'uang Jung (nomad peoples from the northern steppes) sack early Chou capital.

0   250
Miles

During the legendary Hsia period, Fu Hsi is said to have invented writing and constructed a calendar. Shen Nung invented ploughs; Huang Ti invented wheeled vehicles; his wife developed a silk industry; Yu controlled the Yellow River floods.

Note: the term 'Emperor' (Huang Ti) is not applicable until after the Chou period. Previous to that, the King (Wang) was the 'Son of Heaven'.

KEY
Royal Domain.

© Arthur Banks

BASIC CHINESE CHRONOLOGY

Dynasties:

HSIA (legend only)	before c.1766 B.C.
SHANG (YIN)	1766 - 1122 B.C.
CHOU	1122 - 221 B.C.
CH'IN	221 - 206 B.C.

HAN	WESTERN HAN	206 B.C. - A.D. 24
	LATER HAN (EASTERN)	25 - 221

THE THREE KINGDOMS	SHU-HAN	221 - 263
	WEI	220 - 265
	WU	222 - 279

TSIN	WESTERN TSIN	265 - 317
	EASTERN TSIN	317 - 419

North

TOBA (WEI)	386 - 534
WESTERN WEI	535 - 556
EASTERN WEI	534 - 550
NORTHERN CH'I	550 - 577
NORTHERN CHOU	557 - 581
SUI	581 - 618
T'ANG	618 - 907
WU-TAI (FIVE SHORT DYNASTIES)	907 - 960
SUNG	960 - 1279
LIAO (KITAN TARTARS)	916 - 1119
CHIN (GOLDEN TARTARS)	1115 - 1234
YUAN (MONGOLS)	1260 - 1368
MING	1368 - 1644
CH'ING (MANCHU)	1644 - 1911

South

SUNG (LIU SUNG)	420 - 479
CH'I	479 - 502
LIANG	502 - 557
CH'EN	557 - 589

Chronology of the Bamboo Books and the orthodox dates vary until the year 827 B.C. After this, they coincide. The Chou period (1122 - 221 B.C.) can be broken down into 3 divisions: the Early Chou (1122 - 722 B.C.), the Ch'un Ch'iu (722 - 481 B.C.), and the Warring States period (481 - 221 B.C.). This map shows China during the Chun Chiu period.

11

ANCIENT INDIA

IMPORTANT: SEE MAPS ON PAGE 42.

① c. 500 B.C.

Annexed to the Persian Empire under Darius.

Area populated by following clans in sixth century B.C.:
SAKIYAS, BULIS, KALAMAS, BHAGGAS, KOLIYAS, MORIYAS, MALLAS OF PAVA AND KUSINARA, VIDEHAS OF MITHILA, LICCHAVIS OF VESALI.

KEY

MAGADHA etc. — Main powers of northern India.

MALLA etc. — Other powers or tribes.

☐ — Area linked with history of Persian Empire under Cyrus and Darius.

The bow was the primary weapon employed by foot-soldiers. Cavalry and chariots were employed by the early Hindu princes, and later (c. 500 B.C.) war-elephants were introduced. The first military commander of note was Chandragupta I (c. 350 - 297 B.C.) who was thought to have met Alexander the Great during his campaign in north-west India.

Labels on map 1: ACHAEMENID EMPIRE, KAMBOJA, KAPISA, GANDHARA, Indus, old course of Indus?, Sutlej, Jhelum, Chenab, Ravi, Beas, Indus, Ganges, KURU, MATSYA, SURASENA, PANCHALA, KOSALA, VATSA, KASI, CHEDI, Jumna, Son, Narbada, MALLA, ANSA, MAGADHA, Ganges, Brahmaputra, Tsangpo, VIDARBHA, BHOJAS, MULAKA, ASMAKA, Godavari, ANDHRA, DAKSHINAPATHA, KALINGA, Mahanadi, Krishna, AVANTI

0 — 400 Miles

© Arthur Banks

② c. 250 B.C.

This area ceded to Chandragupta Maurya by Seleucus Nikator.

KEY

☐ Mauryan Empire. ● Settlements, rock or pillar edicts.

1 Shahbazgarhi.
2 Mansera.
3 Topra.
4 Mirath.
5 Indraprastha.
6 Mathura.
7 Prayaga.
8 Sravasti.
9 Kapilavastu.
10 Rummindi.
11 Lalita Patan.
12 Rampurwa.
13 Lauriya Nandangarh.
14 Lauriya Araraj.
15 Sahasram.
16 Champa.
17 Tamralipti.
18 Rupnath.
19 Sanchi.
20 Sopara.
21 Tosali.
22 Jaugada.
23 Kopbal.
24 Siddapura.
25 Nellore.

Asoka's capital.

Rock edict mentions Asoka.

① 326 B.C., Alexander at R. Beas.

② 323 B.C. Nanda (Magadha ruler) overthrown by Chandragupta.

③ 323 - 297 B.C., Chandragupta expanded his domains.

④ 305 B.C., Chandragupta obtained concessions from Seleucus Nikator.

⑤ 297 - 274 B.C., Bindusara expanded empire to the south.

⑥ 274 - 232 B.C., Asoka brought Mauryan Empire to its greatest power and extent.

MILITARY KEY

→ Asoka's campaign against Kalinga.

Labels on map 2: PAROPANISADAE, Beas, KALINGA, SURASHTRA, AVANTI, PUNDAS 261 B.C., ANDHRA, PITINIKAS, RASHTRIKAS, Maski, SATIYAPUTRA 25, CHOLAS, KERALAPUTRA, PANDYAS, TAMRAPARNI, Pataliputra, MAGADHA, VAMSA

13

ANCIENT GREECE

Note: place-names are in traditional Latinized form. Thus, island names end in -os and mainland names in -us.

PAEONIA

THRACIA

Epidamnus

ILLYRIA

PELAGONIA

CRESTONIA

EDONES

Strymon

Nestus

Abdera

L.Lychnidus

Cellae ALMOPIA

Pella

Amphipolis

Eion

ANTHEMUS

Thasos

Apsus

O R E S T I S

Pelium

Aegae

Therma

Apollonia

CHALCIDICE

ACTE

Apsus

M A C E D O N I A

BOTTIAEA

Methone

Pydna

Olynthus

Acanthus

Dium

MT.ATHOS

Aous

Oricus

ELIMEA

Philace

Haliacmon

Petra

MT.OLYMPUS

Potidaea

Singus

Torone

SITHONIA

Cassiope

Buthrotum

E P I R U S

Chalcis

Aeginium

PIERIA

Heracleum

Mende

Scione

PALLENE

Corcyra

Dodona

ATHAMANIA

Tricca

THESSALY

MT.OSSA

Corcyra

Peneus

Crannon

Polyaegos

Paxos

Ithome

Pherae

Pagasae

Sciathos

Icos

Thebes

Peparethos

Scyros

AMBRACIA

Pharsalus

PHTHIOTIS

(ACHAEA)

Pteleum

Artemisium

Nicopolis

Argos

Amphilochicum

MALIS

Oreus

Cerinthus

Cyme

Leucas

ACARNANIA

Achelous

E. LOCRIS

E U B O E A

C.Chersonesus

Leucas

AETOLIA

Thermum

Heraclea

Thermopylae

Elatea

PHOCIS

Chalcis

Eretria

Ithaca

Naupactus

W. LOCRIS

Delphi

Cirrha

BOEOTIA

Delium

Cephallenia

Bulis

Thebes

Plataea

C. Caphereus

GULF OF CORINTH

Patrae

Aegium

Marathon

Dyme

A C H A E A

Eleusis

ATHENS

ATTICA

Helena

Cyllene

Tritaea

Sicyon

Megara

Andros

Elis

Clitor

Corinth

Salamis

Piraeus

Phlius

Mycenae

Aegina

Ceos

ELIS

Olympia

ARCADIA

ARGOLIS

Cythnos

Zacynthos

Mantinea

Argos

Tiryns

Syros

Phigalia

Tegea

Troezen

CYNURIA

Hydrea

Seriphos

Alpheus

Eurotas

Prasiae

MESSENIA

Pylus

Pharae

SPARTA

LACONIA

Zarax

Siphnos

Methone

Epidaurus

Limera

Melos

C.Acritas

C.Malea

Pholegandros

C.Taenarum

Cythera

c.700 B.C., under Lycurgus, Sparta became an entirely military society. Its army dominated the whole area of the Peloponnese, being noted for its iron discipline, unit manoeuvrability, and higher organization.

c.560 - 500 B.C., the city state of Athens rose to challenge the supremacy of Sparta. Occupied by Spartans Athens expelled them in 507 B.C.

ANCIENT CRETE

0   40
Miles

Cydonia

Rhithymna

Cnossus

Lappa

Mallia

MT.IDA

Gortyna

Phaestus

Myrtos

Hierapytna

0   50
Miles

© Arthur Banks

ANCIENT ITALY

KEY

Greatest extent of Etruscan power and influence in Italy.

Rome began as a small settlement of pastoral peoples but later grew to be the centre of a great empire. Often known as "the City of the Seven Hills", the two most important hills were the Palatine and Aventine. Nearby was the Quirinal Hill inhabited by the Sabines. Fights were common between the Romans and the Sabines until the two groups made peace and became allies.

0 100 Miles

15

THE SPREAD OF GREEK AND PHOENICIAN INFLUENCE

There was no state of Phoenicia. A string of small towns along a stretch of coast (roughly where modern Lebanon is situated) constituted "Phoenicia". The Phoenicians were great sailors, and their towns were often situated on small islands just off the coast (example: Tyre), or on headlands or promontories (example: Sidon). They were basically traders and colonizers, rather than warriors, but one of their settlements, Carthage, later became a great military power to challenge Rome itself.

KEY

Phoenician colonies.

a Soluntum.
b Panormus.
c Motya.

Greece and Greek colonies.

1 Tarus (Tarentum).
2 Metapontum.
3 Sybaris–Thurii.
4 Crotona.
5 Locri.
6 Rhegium.
7 Acragas (Agrigentum).
8 Hippo Zarytus.
9 Hippo Regius.

© Arthur Banks

0   300
Miles

THE ASSYRIAN SUPREMACY

Assyrian capital.

The Assyrians were essentially a warrior race. First, as a Semitic tribe, they settled at Ashur, but in the ninth century B.C., they commenced upon a course of conquering a huge area of the Middle East which eventually reached Egypt. Their main advantage lay in their reputation for bestowing savage retribution on their defeated adversaries, and sheer terror always preceded their advances. They utilised iron weapons on a huge scale for the first time in warfare, and employed organized siege forces specially equipped with movable towers to protect their battering-ram contingents. Their armies sometimes totalled 50,000 men. Finally, they over-extended themselves and in 614 B.C. the Medes (led by Cyaxares) captured Ashur. The Medes joined with the Chaldaeans (led by Nabopolassar) and in 612 B.C. the combined force obliterated Nineveh, thus destroying the base of the Assyrian Empire.

THE FEROCIOUS WARRIOR RULERS

Tiglath-pileser I (c.1110 B.C.). Expanded Assyrian influence into Anatolia and northern Syria.

Ashurnasirpal II (c. 880 B.C.). Conquered Babylonia and Syria.

Shalmaneser III (c. 830 B.C.). Carried Assyrian power into Kurdish mountains and extended influence in Syria.

Tiglath-pileser III (c.730 B.C.). Organised a regular standing army, improved weapons, and undertook expeditions at the periphery of Assyria's frontiers.

Sargon II (c. 715 B.C.). Subdued northern revolts, and suppressed Babylonia.

Sennacherib (c. 690 B.C.). Destroyed Babylon following setback at Jerusalem.

Essarhaddon (c.670 B.C.). Repelled Cimmerians and conquered Egypt.

Ashurbanipal (c.650 B.C.). Crushed Babylon, Arabs, and Elamites.

THE ASSYRIAN ARMY

1 **Main strike force. Horse-drawn two-wheeled chariots.**

2 **Infantry. Archers, spearmen, slingers.**

3 **Supply-train. Rudimentary: composed of camels and asses.**

KEY

Greatest extent of Assyrian Empire (c. 670 B.C.).

0   200

Miles

© Arthur Banks

MEDIA

ELAM

Susa

Ecbatana

Amardus

URARTU (ARARAT)

Persian Gulf

Nisibis

Dur Sharrukin

Arbela

Kalakh (Nimrud)

NINEVEH

ASHUR

ASSYRIA

Ashur

Tigris

Bagdada

Babylon

Nippur

Ur

BABYLONIA

CHALDAEA

Sippar

Melid

Haran

Khabur

Euphrates

ARAMAEANS

ARIBI (ARABS)

Arpad

Hamath

Damascus

Orontes

Cimirra

KIDRI (KEDAH)

Aribua

Karkar (854 B.C.)

AHAB

Lachish (700 B.C.)

Citium

CYPRUS

Acre

Joppa

Ascalon

Gaza

Pelusium

Sinai

Sarus

Halys

CIMMERIANS

Tarsus

Mediterranean Sea

Nile

EGYPT

Thebes

Memphis

LIBYA

Nile

THE EMPIRES OF CHALDAEA, MEDIA, AND LYDIA

KEY

Chaldaean Empire.
Median Empire.
Lydian Empire.

400

0   Miles

CHALDAEANS

c. 1500 - 700 B.C., a Semitic desert people infiltrated Babylonia.   c. 612 B.C., following the overthrow of Assyria, the Chaldaeans dominated all of previous Assyria west of the Tigris.   c. 612 B.C., Nabopolassar defeated the Egyptian pharaoh Necho II at Carchemish.   c. 600 B.C., Nebuchadnezzar conquered Syria, Palestine, and Phoenicia, but failed to take Tyre.

MEDIANS

c. 800 - 625 B.C., descendants of Asiatic Scythians occupied present-day Persia (Iran).   c. 625 - 593 B.C., Cyaxares joined with Nabopolassar (of Chaldaea) to overthrow Assyria, and expanded his empire in the east, almost to the river Indus.   A war with Lydia (c. 600 - 580 B.C.) ended in the establishment of the river Halys as a frontier line.

LYDIANS

The kingdom of Phrygia was destroyed c. 676 by the Cimmerians (migrating barbarians), who were driven south by the horse - archer Scythians.   Lydia was a successor-state: it drove out the Cimmerians and destroyed Smyrna.   c. 678 - 648 B.C., Gyges founded the Lydian military dynasty.   c. 585 - 560 B.C., Lydia shared an uneasy balance of power with Chaldaea, Media, Egypt, and Persia.   c. 546 B.C., Cyrus (of Persia) defeated Croesus (of Lydia) at the Battle of Thymbra and captured Sardis.

Capital of Median Empire.

Capital of Chaldaean Empire.

Capital of Lydian Empire.

Unconquered by Lydia.

INDUS

ARACHOSIA

GEDROSIA

SOGDIAN

BACTRIA

Bactra

MARGIANA

DRANGIANA

Oxus

Jaxartes

Aral
Sea

ARIA

PARTHIA

Carmana

CARMANIA

HYRCANIA

Pasargadae

Persepolis

PERSIS

SCYTHIANS

Caspian   Sea

Rhagae

MEDIA

ECBATANA

Araxes

SUSIANA

Susa

Persian Gulf

Arbela

Tigris

Amida

BABYLONIA

BABYLON

Ur

Carchemish

Euphrates

Hamath

SYRIA

Trapezus

Amisus

Sinope

Byzantium

Halys

CIMMERIANS

SARDIS

Thymbra

Smyrna

Miletus

Crete

Athens

Cyprus

Citium

Sidon

Tyre

Gaza

Mediterranean   Sea

Naucratis

Memphis

EGYPT

Nile

© Arthur Banks

THE PERSIAN EMPIRE

KEY
— Persian Empire at its greatest extent.
═ Royal Road.

c.560 B.C., the Persians, an Aryan people related to the Medians, deposed Astyages (of Media). Their leader, Cyrus (the first great captain of recorded history) fought the Lydians at the indecisive Battle of Pteria (c. 547 B.C.), and followed this by winning the Battle of Thymbra (c. 546 B.C.), and capturing Sardis. Cyrus then conquered the lands as far as the River Indus and subsequently defeated King Nabonidus at Babylon after a long siege (during which he diverted the waters of the River Euphrates). His son, Cambyses, conquered Egypt. c.512 B.C., Darius subdued internal revolts and invaded south eastern Europe to confront the Scythians and Greeks. c.486 B.C., the Persian Empire commenced a slow decline under Xerxes.

0 — 500
Miles

Note: c. 512 B.C., Darius constructed a boat-bridge across the Bosporus to transport his armies from Asia to Europe. In October 1973 A.D. a new road-bridge (non-military) across the Bosporus is due for operation.

Persian capital.

Note: the Macedonians regarded Persepolis (capital of Persis) as the Empire's capital. Greek historians mention Susa, Babylon, and Ecbatana.

© Arthur Banks

19

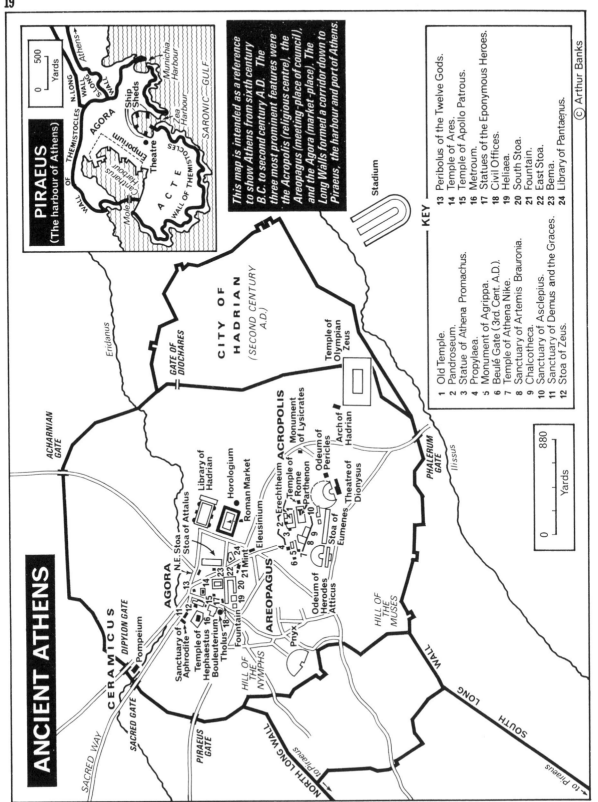

ANCIENT ATHENS

PIRAEUS (The harbour of Athens)

This map is intended as a reference to show Athens from sixth century B.C. to second century A.D. The three most prominent features were the Acropolis (religious centre), the Areopagus (meeting-place of council), and the Agora (market-place). The Long Walls formed a corridor down to Piraeus, the harbour and port of Athens.

KEY

1 Old Temple.
2 Pandroseum.
3 Statue of Athena Promachus.
4 Propylaea.
5 Monument of Agrippa.
6 Beulé Gate (3rd. Cent. A.D.).
7 Temple of Athena Nike.
8 Sanctuary of Artemis Brauronia.
9 Chalcotheca.
10 Sanctuary of Asclepius.
11 Sanctuary of Demus and the Graces.
12 Stoa of Zeus.
13 Peribolus of the Twelve Gods.
14 Temple of Ares.
15 Temple of Apollo Patrous.
16 Metroum.
17 Statues of the Eponymous Heroes.
18 Civil Offices.
19 Heliaea.
20 South Stoa.
21 Fountain.
22 East Stoa.
23 Bema.
24 Library of Pantaenus.

© Arthur Banks

20

ANCIENT ROME

THE FOUR REGIONS

1 Suburana.
2 Esquilina.
3 Collina.
4 Palatina.

Via Nomentana
Via Tiburtina
Via Labicana
Porta Esquilina
Porta Caelimontana
Porta Collina
Via Latina
Via Appia
Porta Capena
VIMINAL
QUIRINAL
CARINAE
CAELIAN
ESQUILINE
WALL OF SERVIUS
Forum
PALATINE
AVENTINE
Via Ostiensis
Via Appia
Porta Fontinalis
Circus Flaminius
Capitol
CAMPUS MARTIUS
Via Triumphalis
Circus Maximus
Via Flaminia
Tiber
Via Aurelia
JANICULUM
Quays

0   500
Yards

ANCIENT PERSEPOLIS

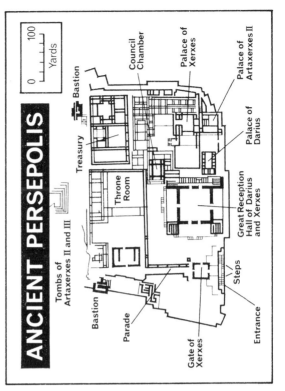

0   100
Yards

Bastion
Council Chamber
Palace of Xerxes
Palace of Artaxerxes II
Palace of Darius
Treasury
Throne Room
Great Reception Hall of Darius and Xerxes
Tombs of Artaxerxes II and III
Bastion
Parade
Steps
Gate of Xerxes
Entrance

ANCIENT SPARTA

Eurotas
Roman Bridge
Holy Shrines
LIMNAI
Temple
Market Place
CYNOSURA
Temple
Treasury
Theatre
Roman buildings
MESOA
Aqueduct
Musga
PITANE
CITY WALL (200 B.C.)
Magula
to Amyclae (2 miles)

0   500
Yards

ANCIENT CARTHAGE

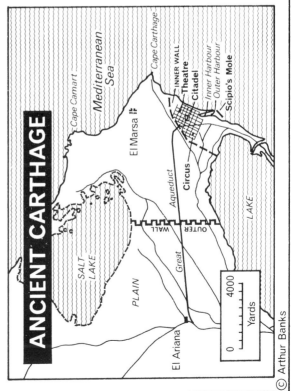

Cape Carthage
Cape Camart
Mediterranean Sea
INNER WALL
Theatre
Citadel
Inner Harbour
Outer Harbour
Scipio's Mole
El Marsa
Circus
Aqueduct
OUTER WALL
LAKE
SALT LAKE
PLAIN
Great
El Ariana

0   4000
Yards

© Arthur Banks

21

RIVAL WAR PLANS AND PREPARATIONS OF PERSIANS AND GREEKS 483 – 480 B.C.

KEY

■ Persian plans and preparations for war.
□ Greek plans and preparations for war.

0 ___ 100
Miles

480 B.C., Persian naval base. Xerxes assembles 1,207 warships and 3,000 transports.

481 B.C., Greek engineer Harpalus constructs two boat-bridges across Hellespont. 314 ships are used for western bridge and 360 for eastern bridge. Linked by cables of flax and papyrus, two wooden roadways complete scheme.

483 – 481 B.C., remembering previous Persian naval disaster in 492 B.C., Xerxes constructs canal across isthmus for safe passage of Persian fleet. Workers on canal are protected by Persian ships operating from a base at Elaeus.

480 B.C., Headquarters of Xerxes. Army formed from all of Persian dominions totals 180,000 troops.

482 B.C., silver vein discovered here. Themistocles urges Greek League to denote money for constructing a modern navy. Keels of 100 triremes laid down in 482 – 481 B.C.

482 – 480 B.C., Greek land force commanders consider defending passes of Tempe and Thermopylae. Themistocles disagrees, arguing that with limited Greek troops available, strategy should be naval and battles should be fought in confined seas or narrow straits to offset Persian numerical superiority.

481 B.C., Greeks try unsuccessfully to enlist aid of Gelo of Syracuse. He refuses on grounds that an invasion of Syracuse by Carthaginians is imminent. (Successful Persian diplomacy?).

ASIA MINOR

Sardis
Abydus
Hellespont
Elaeus
MT. ATHOS
Cape Sunium
Athens
GREECE
Sparta
Tempe
Thermopylae
ITALY
SICILY
Syracuse
Carthage

© Arthur Banks

PERSIAN MILITARY AND NAVAL EXPEDITIONS AGAINST GREECE

© Arthur Banks

0 30 Miles

The Persians launched three assaults against the Greeks: all of them ended in failure. In 492 B.C., a gale wrecked the Persian fleet; in 490 B.C., they were defeated at Marathon; in 480 B.C., the largest invasion of the three ended in the defeats at Salamis and Plataea, and in 479, at Cape Mycale.

PERSIAN EMPIRE

PROPONTIS (Sea of Marmara)

THRACE

MACEDONIA

THESSALY

PHRYGIA

TROAS

HELLESPONT (Dardanelles)

Abydos

MYSIA

LYDIA

SARDIS

IONIA

CARIA

Ephesus

C. Mycale
Miletus

Rhodes

AEGEAN SEA

MT. ATHOS

Canal

Artemisium

EUBOEA

Eretria

Marathon

BOEOTIA

Athens

Plataea

Salamis

Corinth

Troezen

Delphi

Thermopylae

Sparta

Naxos

KEY

- ⇨ Persian army invasion 492 B.C.
- ↓ Persian naval invasion 492 B.C.
- ⇣ Persian naval invasion 490 B.C.
- ⇦ Persian army invasion 480 B.C.
- ⇩ Persian naval invasion 480 B.C.
- ✗ Important battle.
- ✳ Persian naval disaster due to gale.
- ▨ The Persian Empire.
- ▦ Persian vassal-state from 492 B.C.
- ▫ Allied with Persia in 480 B.C.

THE GREEK VICTORY AT MARATHON 490 B.C.

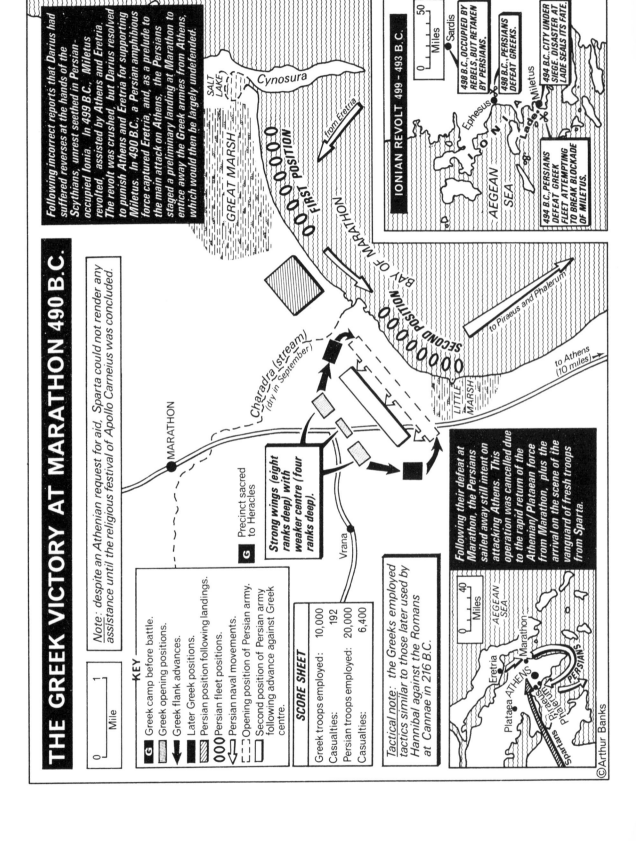

Note: despite an Athenian request for aid, Sparta could not render any assistance until the religious festival of Apollo Carneius was concluded.

Following incorrect reports that Darius had suffered reverses at the hands of the Scythians, unrest seethed in Persian-occupied Ionia. In 499 B.C., Miletus revolted, assisted by Athens and Eretria. The revolt was crushed, but Darius resolved to punish Athens and Eretria for supporting Miletus. In 490 B.C., a Persian amphibious force captured Eretria and, as a prelude to the main attack on Athens, the Persians staged a preliminary landing at Marathon to entice away the Greek armies from Athens, which would then be largely undefended.

IONIAN REVOLT 499 - 493 B.C.

498 B.C. OCCUPIED BY REBELS, BUT RETAKEN BY PERSIANS.

498 B.C. PERSIANS DEFEAT GREEKS.

494 B.C. CITY UNDER SIEGE. DISASTER AT LADE SEALS ITS FATE.

494 B.C. PERSIANS DEFEAT GREEK FLEET ATTEMPTING TO BREAK BLOCKADE OF MILETUS.

Sardis

Ephesus

Miletus

Lade

AEGEAN SEA

50 Miles

SALT LAKE

Cynosura

GREAT MARSH

from Eretria

FIRST POSITION

BAY OF MARATHON

SECOND POSITION

LITTLE MARSH

to Piraeus and Phalerum

to Athens (10 miles)

MARATHON

Charadra (stream) (dry in September)

Vrana

G Precinct sacred to Heracles

Strong wings (eight ranks deep) with weaker centre (four ranks deep).

Following their defeat at Marathon, the Persians sailed away still intent on attacking Athens. This operation was cancelled due to the rapid return of the Athenian/Plataean force from Marathon, plus the arrival on the scene of the vanguard of fresh troops from Sparta.

Eretria

Plataea ATHENS Marathon

Piraeus

Phalerum

Spartans

PERSIANS

AEGEAN SEA

0   40 Miles

KEY

- G Greek camp before battle.
- Greek opening positions.
- Greek flank advances.
- Later Greek positions.
- Persian position following landings.
- Persian fleet positions.
- Persian naval movements.
- Opening position of Persian army.
- Second position of Persian army following advance against Greek centre.

0   1 Mile

SCORE SHEET

Greek troops employed:	10,000
Casualties:	192
Persian troops employed:	20,000
Casualties:	6,400

Tactical note: the Greeks employed tactics similar to those later used by Hannibal against the Romans at Cannae in 216 B.C.

© Arthur Banks

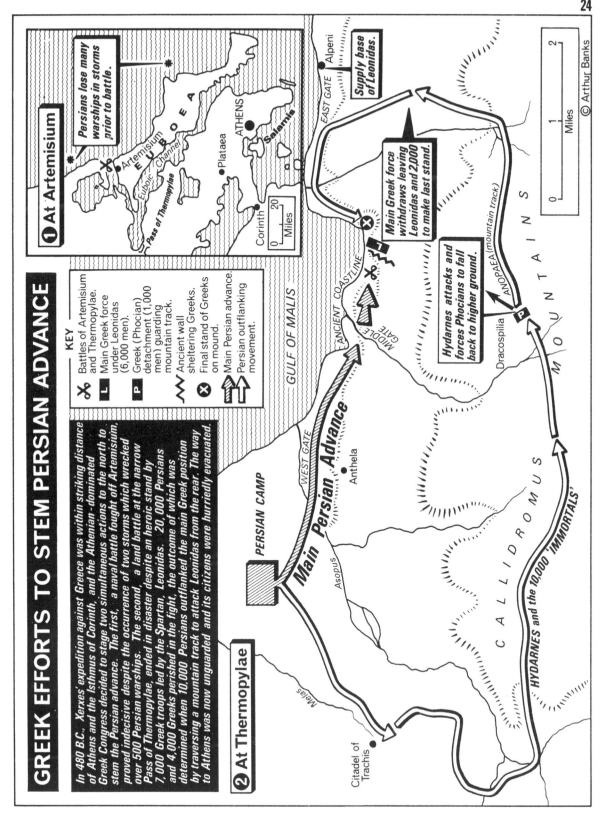

GREEK EFFORTS TO STEM PERSIAN ADVANCE

In 480 B.C. Xerxes' expedition against Greece was within striking distance of Athens and the Isthmus of Corinth, and the Athenian-dominated Greek Congress decided to stage two simultaneous actions to the north to stem the Persian advance. The first, a naval battle fought off Artemisium, proved indecisive despite the occurrence of two storms which wrecked over 500 Persian warships. The second, a land battle at the narrow Pass of Thermopylae, ended in disaster despite an heroic stand by 7,000 Greek troops led by the Spartan, Leonidas. 20,000 Persians and 4,000 Greeks perished in the fight. the outcome of which was determined when 10,000 Persians outflanked the main Greek position by traversing a mountain track to attack Leonidas from the rear. The way to Athens was now unguarded and its citizens were hurriedly evacuated.

KEY

- ⚔ Battles of Artemisium and Thermopylae.
- **L** Main Greek force under Leonidas (6,000 men).
- **P** Greek (Phocian) detachment (1,000 men) guarding mountain track.
- 〰 Ancient wall sheltering Greeks.
- ⊗ Final stand of Greeks on mound.
- ⇧ Main Persian advance.
- ⇧ Persian outflanking movement.

① At Artemisium

Persians lose many warships in storms prior to battle.

EUBOEA
Artemisium
Euboic Channel
Pass of Thermopylae
ATHENS
Salamis
Plataea
Corinth
Miles 0 20

② At Thermopylae

Citadel of Trachis
Melas
Asopus
Anthela
PERSIAN CAMP
WEST GATE
Main Persian Advance
Asopus
MIDDLE GATE
ANCIENT COASTLINE
GULF OF MALIS
EAST GATE
Alpeni
Supply base of Leonidas.
Main Greek force withdraws leaving Leonidas and 2000 to make last stand.
Hydarnes attacks and forces Phocians to fall back to higher ground.
Dracospilia
ANOPAEA (mountain track)
MOUNTAINS
CALLIDROMUS
HYDARNES and the 10,000 'IMMORTALS'

Miles 0 1 2

© Arthur Banks

THE GREEK NAVAL VICTORY AT SALAMIS 480 B.C.

❷ The Battle (?23 September)

0 1 2 3
Miles

MEGARIS

Eleusis

Bay of Eleusis

Corinthian detachment heads north to deceive Persians who believe Greeks are fleeing. After Persian armada is within strait, detachment wheels to the south and joins battle.

NERA

S A L A M I S (populated by evacuees from mainland).

Xerxes, seated upon a specially-erected golden throne, views the battle from high ground.

THE BATTLE AREA

STRAIT OF SALAMIS

G
G
G

Salamis

Cynosura Promontory

PSYTTALEIA

Recaptured by hoplites under Aristides and held as a haven for damaged Greek ships.

ADVANCING IN THREE LINES AT OUTSET, LATER BECOMING TWO, DUE TO NARROWNESS OF CHANNEL (IONIANS ON LEFT, PHOENICIANS ON RIGHT)

Former Athenian naval base.

A T T I C A *(under Persian occupation)*

Piraeus

BAY OF PHALERUM

Ⓟ

Phalerum

The Greek naval strength was approximately 380 ships as opposed to the Persian armada of some 800 (excluding the 200 blockading the western channel) and both fleets used triremes. The battle (basically a mêlée) lasted for 8 hours, the Persians losing 200 ships, the Greeks 40. The Persians fled back to Phalerum and never again engaged the Greeks at sea.

❶ Persian Pre-Battle Movements

0 5
Miles

BAY OF ELEUSIS

Eleusis

PERSIAN LAND ARMY

Strait

Ⓟ

Piraeus

Phalerum

S A L A M I S

Salamis

OCCUPIED

200 ships (Egyptian) detached to blockade western channel

KEY
← Persian dispositions (night preceding action).
▵▵ Persian naval blockades.
Ⓟ Island of Psyttaleia.

THE GREEK PLAN

1 To lull enemy into believing Greeks would not fight stout-heartedly and would attempt to escape from Salamis via the western sea channel.
2 To restrict manœuvrability of enemy ships by making them fight in the confined strait.

THE PERSIAN PLAN

1 To block two main "escape" routes of Greeks, thus forcing them to fight or surrender.
2 To annihilate Greeks by employing huge superiority of both ships and men.
3 To go on to invade Isthmus of Corinth before autumn.

KEY
Ⓟ Concentration area of Persian armada (at night).
◄ Advance of Persian armada (at dawn).
G Greek naval dispositions (at night).
⇨ Greek naval advances (at dawn).
▨ Greek local attack (during day).

© Arthur Banks

THE GREEK MILITARY VICTORY AT PLATAEA 479 B.C.

0 — Mile — 1

to Thebes →

to Thebes

ASIATICS   PERSIANS

Asopus

PHASE TWO

BOEOTIANS and others

Asopus

ATHENIANS   ALLIES   SPARTANS

P

Cavalry raid to poison Greek water source

Cavalry sortie ends in disaster as Persian commander Masistius is slain

Successful raid on Dryocephalae Pass

PHASE ONE

Moloeis

BOEOTIANS and others

ATHENIANS

PHASE THREE

Gargaphia (spring)

Oeroe

PERSIANS and ASIATICS

the 'Island'

ALLIES   SPARTANS

Erythrae?

DRYOCEPHALAE PASS   to Athens →

Greek supply column surprised and massacred.

PLATAEA

Important note: the locations of passes are disputed by historians. Consequently, the Persian sorties, for example, might have occurred here ———→

? PLATAEA-MEGARA PASS

PASS TO ATHENS

MT. CITHAERON

KEY

- Greek position on arrival.
- P Persian camp within stockade.
- Persian cavalry sorties in sequence.
- Greek opening dispositions.
- Persian opening dispositions.
- Greek final positions.
- Persian final positions.

©Arthur Banks

Following the disaster at Salamis, Xerxes withdrew his main force to Asia Minor (especially to protect his Hellespont bridges). 50,000 troops under Mardonius remained in Greece to continue the war. The Persians fired Athens and then withdrew into Boeotia to entice the new Greek army (led by Pausanias) to fight in country favourable to Mardonius. The two forces clashed near Plataea, and victory went to the Greeks despite their numerical inferiority (39,000 men). Of the Persians, all but 3,000 died (Mardonius was killed), and the Greek casualties numbered 1,360. Thirty days later, after a siege, the Persian base of Thebes surrendered to the victorious Greek army. The loss of Persian prestige was enormous and the Athenians went on to take Sestus.

THE PELOPONNESIAN WAR 431 - 404 B.C.

0   50
Miles

422 B.C., Athenian defeat. Both Brasidas and Cleon (opposing commanders) are killed. Athenians lose 600 men, Spartans lose 7.

435 B.C., Corcyra appeals for Athenian aid in her quarrel with Corinth.

IMMEDIATE CAUSES OF THE WAR

432 B.C., Potidaea revolts from Athens.

426 B.C., Athenian victories under Demosthenes.

424 B.C., Athenian defeat. Hippocr_ and 1,200 troops are slain by Boeotia under Pagondas of Thebes. This is _ battle of war where full army of Athe_ is employed, and she realises that se_ power, not land-power, is her strong_

429 - 427 B.C., Archidamus besieges city. Finally, every inhabitant is killed and city razed to ground.

429 B.C., three important Athenian naval victories.

431 B.C., captured by Athenian fleet.

418 B.C., during the period of uneasy "peace", Spartans defeat army of Argive coalition.

425 B.C., Spartan attempt to blockade Athenians is repelled. Spartans themselves are blockaded on island of Sphacteria. Cleon and Demosthenes eventually take island and capture 300 Spartans. Pylus fortified.

424 B.C., Nicias takes Methone and Cythera.

416 B.C., Athenian expedition rest_ in murder of all men with women an_ children sold into slavery.

Epidamnus

MACEDONIA

Amphipoli_

CHALCIDICE

Potidaea

THESSALY

EPIRUS

to Syracuse

Corcyra

EUBO_

Cephallenia

AETOLIA

Naupactus

Delium

Oropu_

Plataea

Decelea

ATHENS

ACHAEA

Corinth

Piraeus

ELIS

Mantinea

Pylus

Sparta

Methone

Melos_

ATHENIAN EXPEDITION TO SYRACUSE

Cythera

415 B.C.

_ B.C., Athenian victory. _loponnesians lose 21 ships _ainst 15 of Athenians. _e latter sail up Hellespont, _ture Cyzicus, and take _yzantine warships._

405 B.C., final defeat of Athenian sea-power. Lysander captures 171 ships out of a total of 180, following which he sails to blockade Piraeus.

The war was in two parts: 431-421 B.C., and 416-404 B.C., with a period of uneasy "peace" from 421-416 B.C. It was essentially a conflict between the land-power of Sparta and the sea-power of Athens. Sparta controlled most of the Peloponnese while Athens controlled the Aegean and the coast of Asia Minor. The war itself was a drawn-out affair with a number of indecisive actions taking place. The Athenian expedition to Syracuse in Sicily (415-413 B.C.) was the main military cause of Athens being defeated even though the Athenians held out for a further nine years before surrendering to the Spartans.

Byzantium

Cyzicus

Aegospotami

Cynossema

410 B.C., Alcibiades defeats 60 ships of Peloponnesian fleet, lands troops and captures Cyzicus. Peloponnesians unable to assemble a new large fleet for 3 years.

PEACE TERMS

1 Long Walls and Piraeus fortifications to be destroyed.

2 Athens to surrender all foreign possessions.

3 Athens to become allied with Sparta.

4 Athenian fleet, with the exception of twelve triremes, to be destroyed.

5 All exiles to be recalled.

Mytilene

_B.C., Euboea _lts._

Arginusae

Delphinium

Chios

428-427 B.C., rebellion against Athens suppressed, and city surrenders to Paches. 1,000 men killed.

_ fortifying this post, _artans prevent _henians working _eir silver mines in _dition to cutting _eir communications._

Notium

Ephesus

406 B.C., Athenian victory. 75 Peloponnesian ships are sunk, but later, 25 Athenian ships are lost in storm.

406 B.C., Athenian naval defeat. Lysander sinks 22 Athenian ships and goes on to capture Delphinium.

Syme

411 B.C., Athenian naval defeat.

Rhodes

KEY
Athens and close allies.
Other states in alliance with Athens.
Sparta and allies.
✂ Battles.

_0-429 B.C., plague ravages Athens. One in four of _ulation dies including her war leader Pericles._

THE DISASTROUS SICILIAN EXPEDITION 415-413 B.C.

SICILY

Himera

Segesta
Allied with Athens.

Rhegium

414 B.C. GYLIPPUS LEADS 3,000 TROOPS TO AID SYRACUSANS

Naxus

Athenian bases.

Selinus

Catania

Agrigentum

Allied with Syracuse.

Thapsus

Gela

SYRACUSE

Assinarus

Megarian colony allied with Syracuse.

413 B.C., ATHENIAN ARMY (IN RETREAT) IS CAUGHT AND BUTCHERED AT RIVER.

0   30
Miles

GREECE

By fortifying Decelea, Sparta severed communications to Athens, forcing her to fight a war on two fronts.

Naupactus

★Decelea

Corinth

Athens

25 Corinthian triremes engage Athenian fleet to cover the departure of a force sent to relieve Syracuse.

Sparta

0   50
Miles

SYRACUSE

0   1
Mile

Megarian Plain

to Thapsus

Leon

Trogilius

ATHENIAN NAVAL BLOCKADE

Labdalum

THE EXPEDITION WAS THE LARGEST UNDERTAKEN BY ANY GREEK STATE TO DATE, AND INCLUDED 30,000 TROOPS AND 134 TRIREMES.

Euryalus

EPIPOLAE PLATEAU

The expedition against Syracuse was an utter disaster caused by inept leadership, bad execution and defection of Alcibiades to Sparta. If Athens had been successful, her enemies (Sparta and Corinth) might have been defeated by lack of food, thus compensating for Athens' lack of military man-power. Of 45,000 Athenian and allied troops, some 7000 survived, only to die as Syracusan slaves.

TEMENITES

Q

Q

ACHRADINA

Agora

LITTLE HARBOUR

Anapus

mole

ORTYGIA ISLAND

413 B.C., naval action results in Athenian victory, but Syracusans gain forts.

GREAT HARBOUR

KEY

- **A** First Athenian encampment, winter 415 B.C.
- Main Athenian attack, summer 414 B.C.
- ⊛ Athenian round fort.
- ▲▲▲ Athenian north wall.
- ∘∘∘∘∘∘ Athenian north wall extension (under construction).
- △△△ Athenian south walls.
- ━━━ Foundations of old wall built by Dionysius I.
- ⊔⊔⊔⊔ Syracusan walls before siege.
- ■■■■ Wall completed during siege.
- ⊓⊔⊓ First Syracusan counterwork (wall).
- ⋯⋯⋯ Second Syracusan counterwork (trench & palisade).
- ─ ─ ─ Third Syracusan counterwork (built by Gylippus).
- ★ Forts on Plemmyrium.
- Swamp or marsh.
- Ⓠ Syracusan quarries.

A

413 B.C., Athenian fleet is destroyed in battle. Her army tries to escape southwards but troops are caught and slain at ford over R. Assinarus.

PLEMMYRIUM

© Arthur Banks

30

THE ASCENDANCY OF SPARTA 404-380 B.C.

CHALCIDICE

PHRYGIA

To defeat Athens, Sparta had sold the Asiatic Greeks to Persia, thus restoring Persia's influence in the Greek world. Sparta's strength rested upon Persia, and thus her attempt to build her own empire failed. Also there was not in Sparta the spirit that had made Athens great.

381 B.C., league of cities suppressed by Sparta.

396 B.C., overrun by Agesilaus who collects much booty.

PERSIAN EMPIRE

394 B.C., Spartan Agesilaus wins victory.

Athenians under Thrasybulus hold out against rule of the 'Thirty' in Athens. 403 B.C., Spartan king Pausanias makes peace.

Coronea

382 B.C., seized by Sparta.

Thebes • Phyle

Elis

Corinth

• Athens

387 B.C., Artaxerxes of Persia makes 'King's Peace' settlement. States of Greece are independent but Asiatic Greeks left subject to Persia.

Mantinea

• Argos

Destroyed by Sparta.

SPARTA

Successes won by Iphicrates and his peltasts (light-armed troops).

394 B.C., Persians (under Athenian Conon) crush Spartan navy.

0   50
Miles

Cnidus

MARCH OF THE 'TEN THOUSAND' AGAINST PERSIA 401-400 B.C.

• Sinope

KEY

Byzantium

Perinthus

Chalcedon

Trapezus

City friendly to the expedition.

Gymnias

Advance of the 'Ten Thousand'.

Retreat of the 'Ten Thousand'.

Erzerum

ARMENIA

P E R S I A N

Pergamum

Sardis

401 B.C.

• Celaenae

Iconium

Tyana

0   100
Miles

Euphrates

Tigris

E M P I R E

Nineveh

Larissa

Tarsus

• Issus

401 B.C.

400 B.C.

To oust his brother Artaxerxes from the Persian throne, Cyrus formed an army to invade Persia, among whom were 10,000 Spartan hoplites. The advance electrified Greece; never had a Greek army penetrated the very heart of the Persian Empire and escaped.

Thapsacus

Erzi

401 B.C., Cyrus is killed in battle and further advance of the expedition is abandoned.

Cunaxa

© Arthur Banks

THE ASCENDANCY OF THEBES 379–362 B.C.

Thebes rose for a short time to be the ruling state in Greece due to two main factors.
☐1 The war-weariness of Sparta and Athens.
☐2 Thebes possessed two leaders of great stature, Epaminondas and Pelopidas. The former fortified Thebes and created a cadre of 300 élite warriors – the Sacred Band.

364 B.C., Thebans fight a drawn battle against the Athenian ally, Alexander of Pherae, but lose Pelopidas.

375 B.C., Sacred Band of Thebes defeat two units of Spartans (600 men) plus killing both generals.

371 B.C., Epaminondas forms military ties with Jason of Pherae, who commands force of 8,000 cavalry, 20,000 hoplites, and peltasts.

362 B.C., Thebans out-manoeuvre opposing army of Arcadians, Spartans, Athenians. Each army consists of 25,000 troops. Utilising the tactics successful at Leuctra, Thebans gain victory, but Epaminondas is killed during battle.

376 B.C., Chabrias (of Athens–allied with Thebes at this time) defeats 60 Spartan warships in naval battle.

369 B.C., founded by Epaminondas. Became capital of new state hostile to Sparta.

THE BATTLE OF LEUCTRA 371 B.C.

SPARTANS

Strong left wing.

THEBANS

THEBAN VICTORY. SPARTANS NUMBERED 1,000 CAVALRY AND 10,000 HOPLITES (1,000 MEN SLAIN). THEBANS NUMBERED 600 IN CAVALRY AND 6,000 HOPLITES. FIRST INSTANCE OF DEEP COLUMN ATTACK AND REFUSED FLANK.

KEY

Thebes and allies.
Athens and allies.
Sparta and allies.
Chalcidian League.
Neutral states.
☓ Important battles.
⟶ Theban attacks against the Spartans, with dates.
➡ Theban naval expedition to Byzantium (100 ships).

0   50
Miles

© Arthur Banks

THE BATTLE OF MANTINEA JUNE 362 B.C.

MANTINEA

Epaminondas entered Arcadia to "assert Boeotia's interests." This split the Arcadian League into two camps. In the first were Mantinea, Sparta, Athens, Achaea, and Elis: in the second were Thebes, Boeotia, Locris, Euboea, Malis, Aeniania, and Thessaly. The rival armies fought a major battle on the plain between Mantinea and Tegea which the Thebans all but won. The Mantinean force had 20,000 infantry and 2,000 cavalry against the Thebans' 30,000 infantry and 3,000 cavalry. Under cover of a dust cloud raised by their cavalry, the Thebans launched a major attack on their left, broke through the enemy's lines and then halted—paralysed by the death of Epaminondas, their commander-in-chief. The enemy escaped and later concluded a peace, causing even greater confusion and indecision in Greece than existed hitherto.

KEY

INFANTRY CAVALRY

Defensive positions of Mantinean-dominated Arcadian League forces (**M** = Mantineans, **S** = Spartans, **A** = Athenians).

Morning positions of Theban-led forces.

Noon positions of Theban-led forces.

Final positions of Theban-led forces before attack commenced.

Theban-led advances.

0   1
Mile

PLAIN

Wood

St. Mitikas

St. Elias

HIGH GROUND

HIGH GROUND

M S   A

road

PLAIN

dust cloud

Tegea is utilised as a supply base by Thebans.

to Tegea

© Arthur Banks

33

MACEDONIA'S GROWTH AS A MILITARY POWER 359 – 336 B.C.

0   50
Miles

357 B.C., Philip besieges town and secures gold mines, thus making Macedonia the richest state in Greece.

Renamed as Philippi by Philip.

340-339 B.C., Philip besieges seaports without success. Only serious military setbacks in his career.

Macedonian capital.

PAEONIA

THRACE

Strymon

Hebros

Axios

Nestos

Crenides

Maronea

Perinthus

Bosporus

PELLA

Aegae

Amphipolis

Byzantium

Methone

Stagirus

Pydna

Olynthus

Potidaea

Abydus

THESSALY

PERSIAN EMPIRE

352 B.C., Philip gains victory of the 'Crocus Field'. Phocian general Onomarchus is killed.

Pherae

Sardis

Ambracia

Oreus

Pass of Thermopylae

Delphi

Elatea

338 B.C., Philip becomes master of Greece by defeating Athens, Thebes and allies. Alexander plays important part in battle.

Naupactus

Chaeronea

Thebes

346 B.C., during Pythian Games, Isocrates calls on Philip to unite Greece and fight Persia.

Corinth

Athens

Miletus

338 B.C., Philip creates Hellenic League. Parmenion is later sent to Asia to carry out a reconnaissance in force (336 B.C.).

Sparta

Halicarnassus

KEY

Macedonia in 359 B.C.

The Persian Empire.

✗ Important battles.

PHILIP'S AIMS

❶ To establish his base of operations (wars to the west, north, and east of Macedonia).
❷ To gain control of Thessaly (wars to the south of Macedonia).
❸ To establish his dominion over Thrace and gain command of the Bosporus.
❹ To impose Macedonian authority over the whole of Greece south of Thermopylae.

Philip organized the Macedonian army into the finest fighting force the world had yet seen.

Note: In 359 B.C., Amyntas (infant son of Perdiccas) was elected king by the people of Macedonia, with Philip nominated as regent. Following the defeat of Illyria in 358 B.C., Philip was made King Philip II of Macedon.

© Arthur Banks

THE MACEDONIAN VICTORY AT CHAERONEA 338 B.C.

MT. ACONTIUM

Cephissus

'THEBAN
'SACRED
BAND.'

BOEOTIANS

UNITED ARMIES OF
CENTRAL GREECE

ALLIES mercenaries

ATHENIANS

Cavalry
(held in reserve).

Haemon

ALEXANDER

PHALANX

PHILIP

PHILIP

Light-armed units

Light-armed troops

Walled acropolis
of CHAERONEA

STRENGTHS and CASUALTIES

MACEDONIANS	
Infantry :	30,000
Cavalry :	2,000
Casualties :	5,000
GREEKS	
Infantry :	35,000
Cavalry :	2,000
Casualties :	15,000

© Arthur Banks

— KEY —

	INFANTRY	CAVALRY	
			Macedonian opening positions.
			Macedonian second positions.
			Macedonian advances.
			Greek opening positions.
			Greek second positions.

Realising that the Athenians were the weakest section of the enemy, Philip advanced his personal battalions, the 'Hypaspists.' The Greeks stood firm, whereupon Philip organized a step by step 'orderly withdrawal, meanwhile advancing his phalanx and Alexander's cavalry. (Note: This "withdrawal" was notable for Macedonian discipline). Seeing Philip's apparent retreat, the whole Greek front (except the 'Sacred Band') advanced, veering to its left to concentrate on Philip. This manoeuvre created a gap in the Greek lines into which Alexander's cavalry charged, first massacring the 'Sacred Band', then turning right to attack the Greek rear. Philip ordered a general advance and the Greeks were trapped, their cavalry (in reserve) retreating in panic. This battle is not dissimilar in tactics to those of Leuctra in 371 B.C.

0 — 500 — 1000
Yards

THE CAMPAIGNS OF ALEXANDER THE GREAT
336–323 B.C.

ALEXANDER'S OBJECTIVES

1 To secure his home base.
2 To establish a stable overseas base.
3 To gain command of the seas.
4 To defeat the Persians on land.

ALEXANDER'S ARMY OF INVASION
(Total: 40,000)

INFANTRY
12,000 Macedonians.
7,000 Greek League hoplites.
6,000 Agrianian javelin-men, Thracians, Cretan archers.
5,000 mercenary hoplites.

CAVALRY
2,000 Companions.
2,000 Thessalians.
1,000 Thracians, Paeonians, Greek allied horse, lancers.

MISCELLANEOUS
5,000 artillerists, sapp
surveyors, siege-engine
transport-drivers, serv
camp-followers, etc.

The aim of the invasion
ideological: to avenge w
done to Hellas by Xerxe

②Alexander's Foreign Campaigns

1 Spring 334 B.C., Alexander commences his great journey- never to return.

2 With the capture of city, Alexander now has an overseas base.

3 By conquering eastern area of Mediterranean, Alexander ensures his naval command. ✳

Note: in winte
324 B.C., Alexa
fought in a sm
campaign aga
the Cossaei.

4 Roy
Acade
captur

✳*Naval note: at the start of Alexander's campaign, he had 160 warships as opposed to the Persians' total of 400.*

MACEDONIA — Pella — 334 B.C. — THRACIA — Black Sea — Sestus — Arisbe — Lampsacus — Granicus — PHRYGIA — Gordium — Ancyra — Halys — CAPPADOCIA — ARMENIA — Athens — Sardis — Sparta — Ephesus — Miletus — Celaenae — 333 B.C. — CILICIAN GATES — Halicarnassus — Side — CILICIA — Tarsus — Issus — Myriandrus — Gaugamela — 331 B.C. — Tigris — Arbela — LIBYA — Paraetonium — 332 B.C. — Aradus — Byblus — Sidon — 332 B.C. Marathus — Thapsacus — Euphrates — Ammonium — Rhacotis — Pelusium — Gaza — Tyre — 331 B.C. — Babylon — 323 B — 331 — Memphis — EGYPT — 331 B.C. — Nile — Red Sea

KEY
→ Routes of Alexander's army.
←- - Sea route of Nearchus.
←•••• Route of Craterus.
✂ Important battles.

0 ———— 500
Miles

ALEXANDER'S FURTHER PLANS

1 He intended to remodel the Macedor phalanx in brigade form (more suita for occupation purposes).
2 He intended to explore the Caspian S to ascertain if it were a lake or a gu
3 He ordered a harbour to be construc at Babylon capable of accommodatir to 1,000 ships, which were to be us to explore the Arabian Sea.

© Arthur Banks

Securing the Home Base

100 200 Miles

KEY
European Empire of Alexander the Great.
Dependent states.
Independent states.

With great speed, Alexander marched south against the rebellious Thessalians and Athenians who were quickly beaten. He then quelled the wild tribes on his northern and western borderlands, returning south to crush a Theban revolt. Having put Antipater in command to observe Sparta, Alexander was then ready to confront Persia, his main enemy.

Alexander lived from 356 B.C. to 323 B.C. Son of Philip II of Macedonia (who was murdered in 336 B.C.), he became king at the early age of 19, and in the following twelve years created by conquest a large empire extending from Greece eastwards across Asia to the borders of India. After first establishing his authority in Greece in the early years of his reign between 336 B.C. and 334 B.C., he recruited and led an army against the Persian Empire, whose armies he defeated in a long series of battles and sieges. Following a number of small wars in the east, he returned to Babylon to consolidate his empire. There he died of malaria at the age of 33.
As well as being a great military captain, Alexander was a statesman, diplomat and explorer. He founded at least seventeen "Alexandrias" during his career.

NOTE: SEE MAPS ON PAGE 42 FOR ALTERNATIVE RIVER NAMES.

7 Bessus is tried and condemned: sent to Ecbatana for execution.

6 Darius is murdered by Bessus. Though Darius was his enemy, Alexander resolves to punish Bessus.

5 Palace of Xerxes burnt

8 Craterus detached to quell disturbances in Arachosia and in Drangiana.

9 Nearchus detached with naval force to explore coastline for settlements, islands and possible harbours.

ALEXANDER'S GREAT BATTLES AND SIEGES

Army strengths and losses are estimates only.

① Battle of the Granicus 334 B.C.

MACEDONIANS
Total strength: 40,000
Casualties: 250

PHILIP
CALAS
AGATHON
CRATERUS
MELEAGER
PHILIP
AMYNTAS
COENUS
PERDICCAS
NICANOR
AMYNTAS
PHILOTAS
CLEARCHUS
ATTALUS
ALEXANDER
Parmenion

River Granicus
to Sea of Marmara
RHEOMITHRES
ARSITES
SPITHRIDATES
ARSAMENES
Greek mercenaries
OMARES
MEMNON
MEMNON OF RHODES

Lake

0   1000
Yards

PERSIANS
Total strength: 15,000
Casualties: 2,000
Captured: 2,000

KEY
- ■ Macedonian infantry.
- ▨ Macedonian cavalry.
- ➤ Main Macedonian attacks, numbered in sequence.
- ▭ Persian infantry.
- ▨ Persian cavalry.

Persian movements in this battle have been omitted for clarity. They were mainly defensive, for the Macedonians made the first attack.   In early warfare it was essential to kill or capture the opposing commanders since panic among their soldiers invariably followed. Thus the Persians were intent on eliminating Alexander, but he survived.   On the other hand, the Persians lost a number of their own unit commanders, a factor of some significance in all the battles to come. In view of the importance of the leaders, units are shown with the names of their respective commanders.

② Siege of Halicarnassus 334 B.C.

0   500
Yards

to Myndus
from Myndus
WALL
B
WALL
1
road to Mylasa
(25 mls.)
C
HALICARNASSUS
road to Myndus
(12 miles)
A
WALL
HARBOUR
WALL
2
3
ARCONNESUS ISLAND
GULF OF COS
MOAT
(45 feet wide
22 feet deep)
M

Persians reinforce and supply citadels by sea.

GULF OF COS

KEY
- ▨ Citadels of Halicarnassus.
  - 1 Acropolis.
  - 2 Fortress of Salmacis.
  - 3 King's Castle.
- ⊏⊐ Gates of Halicarnassus.
  - A Myndus Gate.
  - B Triple Gate.
  - C Mylasa Gate.
- M Macedonian encampment.
- ⊏⇨ Sortie by the garrison.
- ◄— Macedonian reconnaissance of the walls.
- ◄••• Alexander's abortive march to subdue Myndus.
- ➤ Main Macedonian attack.
- ⇦ Garrison's abortive counter-attack.
- ◄-- Garrison's attempt to fill in the breached wall.
- ⇦ Garrison's retreat into the citadels.   Despite the Macedonian land blockade, citadels resisted for a year.

© Arthur Banks

3 Battle of Issus 333 B.C.

BATTLEFIELD APPROACH ROUTES OF ALEXANDER AND DARIUS

```
0        20
    Miles
```

Darius
Alexander
Islahiya
Pinarus
ISSUS
GULF OF ISSUS
Jonah Pass
Payas
Sochoe
Jonah Pass
Mallus
Myriandrus

Alexander marched from Issus en route for Myriandrus, just missing Darius who reached Issus twenty-four hours later. On his arrival at Myriandrus, Alexander was surprised to learn that Darius was advancing *behind* him. Realising that his line of retreat had been cut, Alexander resolved to surprise Darius in return by reversing his line of advance and resting his men, then launching a rapid attack on the weary Persians.

PERSIANS
Total strength: 100,000
Killed: 50,000
Escaped: 8,000

DARIUS
Pinarus
ALEXANDER
Parmenion
Gulf of Issus

MACEDONIANS
Total strength: 40,000
Killed: 450
Wounded: 4,500

```
0              1000
     Yards
```

KEY

- ■ Macedonian infantry.
- ◢ Macedonian cavalry.
- ◀ Macedonian thrusts.
- ▭ Persian infantry.
- ◿ Persian cavalry.
- vvvv Persian archers.
- ⇨ Persian advances.

MACEDONIANS
A Allied Greek cavalry.
B Thessalian cavalry.
C Thracian javelin-men.
D Cretan archers.
E Phalanx (Amyntas).
F Phalanx (Ptolemy).
G Phalanx (Meleager).
H Phalanx (Craterus).
I Phalanx (Perdiccas).
J Phalanx (Coenus).
K Hypaspists.
L Companion cavalry.
M Macedonian archers.
N Agrianians.
O Greek mercenaries.
P Lancers.
Q Paeonian light horsemen.
R Agrianians.
S Light horse squadron.

PERSIANS
A Cavalry (Nabarzanes).
B Asiatic levies.
C Cardaces.
D Greek mercenaries.
E Bodyguard (Darius).
F Archers.
G Light troop detachment.

4 Siege of Tyre 332 B.C.

```
0              500
     Yards
```

CYPRIANS
Sidonian Harbour
to Sidon (18 miles)
MOLE
~(200 feet wide)~
MAINLAND
Shrine of Agenor
NEW TYRE
Egyptian Harbour
PHOENICIANS
to Old Tyre (Palaetyros) (1 mile)

1 Alexander's first task is to construct a mole from the mainland to New Tyre. The work is hindered by Tyrian attacks, including a fire-ship's sortie.

2 Alexander decides to blockade the two Tyrian harbours with two fleets.

3 Tyrian navy sorties out from Sidonian Harbour, but despite initial success, it is thwarted by Alexander sailing round west coast of island to reinforce his Cyprian contingent.

4 Alexander finally breaches city wall south of Egyptian Harbour and advances into city. Simultaneously his naval contingents storm the two harbours.

5 Tyrians make final stand at Shrine of Agenor but are overwhelmed.

The siege lasted for seven months. 8,000 Tyrians were killed and 30,000 sold into slavery. During the various assaults, 400 Macedonians were killed.

ALEXANDER'S BATTLES–continued

⑤ Battle of Arbela (Gaugamela) 331 B.C.

PERSIAN KEY

▨ Cavalry	▭ Infantry
	⊏⊐ Asiatic levies
○ ○ ○ ○ ○ Chariots (total: 200)	
● ● ● ● ● Elephants (total: 15)	

1 Sacesinians.	10 Cappadocians.	19 Carians.
2 Albanians.	11 Armenians.	20 Cadusians.
3 Hyrcanians.	12 Mardians (archers).	21 Susians.
4 Tapurians.	13 Indians.	22 Persians.
5 Sacians.	14 Greeks (mercen's).	23 Arachosians.
6 Parthians.	15 Persians (horse).	24 Dahaeians.
7 Medians.	16 Persians (foot).	25 Bactrians.
8 Mesopotamians.	17 Persians (horse).	26 Scythians.
9 Coelo-Syrians.	18 Greeks (mercen's).	27 Bactrians.

PRE-BATTLE DISPOSITIONS

MACEDONIAN KEY (arranged under commanders)

▨ Cavalry	■ – Infantry

1 Andromachus.	6 Clearchus.	11 Polyperchon.	16 Attalus.	21 Aretes.
2 Agathon.	7 Philip.	12 Meleager.	17 Briso.	22 Ariston.
3 Coeranus.	8 Erigyius.	13 Perdiccas.	18 Balacrus.	23 Attalus.
4 Sitalces.	9 Craterus.	14 Coenus.	19 Philotas.	24 Briso.
5 (mercenaries).	10 Simmias.	15 Nicanor.	20 Menidas.	25 Cleander.

Mazaeus (right wing) — DARIUS (centre) — Bessus (left wing)

The Macedonian strength totalled 47,000 against the Persian total of 250,000. Consequently, Alexander's deployment needed to be flexible to allow for any possible contingency.

Parmenion · ALEXANDER

(left wing) | (right wing)

Rear Phalanx

Right flank-guard stronger than left.

THE BATTLE–PHASE ONE

PERSIANS (whole line moving to left) ②

MACEDONIANS (advancing obliquely)

① Without physical features (such as hills or rivers) upon which to position his flanks, Alexander moves in an oblique direction towards the Persian line (twice the length of his own) veering to the right.

② Persians commence moving to left to keep abreast of Alexander, their left-wing cavalry racing ahead to intercept Macedonian advance.

③ Persian right-wing cavalry moves forward to envelop Macedonians from rear.

④ Macedonian left flank-guard closes to main body to prevent Persian breakthrough.

THE BATTLE–PHASE TWO

Mazaeus · Darius · Bessus

SCORE SHEET
Persians killed:	50,000
Macedonians killed:	1,000

① Rapidity of Persian cavalry advance creates gaps in Persian main line. ② and ③ Macedonian right flank-guard engages Persian cavalry. ④ Alexander advances into gap between Bessus and Darius; fierce fighting in mêlée-style ensues. ⑤ Persian right-wing nearly breaks through, but ⑥ is intercepted by Alexander answering Parmenion's call for help. ⑦ Macedonians attack Persian cavalry in strength. ⑧ Darius flees.

© Arthur Banks

❻ Battle of the Hydaspes* 326 B.C.

Note: modern name is Jhelum.

MACEDONIANS (Alexander)

Light-armed Infantry
Cavalry (Coenus)
(Seleucus) Phalanx
Companion Cavalry
ALEXANDER
Hypaspists
Horse-archers
① ④ *feint attack* ③ *(veering)* ② ⑥ ⑤

Chariots o o o o
Cavalry
PORUS
Elephants ● ● ● ● ● ● ● ● ● ● ● ● Chariots o o o o
Infantry
Cavalry

INDIANS (Porus)

KEY
◄─○─ Main attacks, numbered in sequence.

STRENGTHS		CASUALTIES	
MACEDONIANS		**MACEDONIANS (killed)**	
Infantry:	10,000	Infantry:	700
Cavalry:	5,000	Cavalry:	280
Horse-archers:	1,000	Horse-archers:	10
INDIANS		**INDIANS**	
Infantry:	30,000	Killed:	12,000
Cavalry:	4,000	Captured:	9,000
Chariots:	200	Elephants captured:	80
Elephants:	200		

Prior to the main battle, Alexander fought an Indian delaying-action with the son of Porus (who was killed). Following this, he undertook a massive task in transporting his army across the River Hydaspes.

ALEXANDER'S TACTICS

In his major battles, Alexander positioned himself on the right wing and opened his attack from that side. This avoided a 'centre' confrontation at the outset and compelled his foes to rearrange their dispositions.

ALEXANDER'S "ALEXANDRIAS"

Note: there is no evidence of an Alexandria at Kandahar.

Alexander founded at least seventeen "Alexandrias" and promised an eighteenth (Alexandria Troas) which was never built. Six are "certain," in that they are represented by modern towns. A further seven existed well down into Greek history. The remaining four were built but the precise location of Alexandria in Babylonia is unknown.

Oxus
Alexandria Eschate (CHODJEND)
Alexandria on the Oxus (TERMEZ)
Alexandria in Margiane (MERV)
⊙ Alexandria Bactra
Indus
Alexandria Nicaea ⊙
Alexandria Iomousa
Alexandria of ⊙ the Caucasus
Alexandria by Issus
Alexandria in Aria (HERAT)
Alexandria in Arachosia (GHAZNI)
Alexandria Bucephala
Tigris
Euphrates
Alexandria in Babylonia / (site unknown) ?
Alexandria Prophthasia ⊙
Alexandria by Egypt (ALEXANDRIA)
⊙ Alexandria in Susiana
Alexandria in Carmania ●
Alexandria in Makarene ⊙
Indus
Nile

332 B.C., first Alexandria is founded here.

0 ——— 400
Miles

KEY
● The six foundations where towns remain.
⊙ The seven foundations confirmed in the writings of Greek historians.
● The four foundations agreed by scholars.

THE EFFECT ON WORLD HISTORY OF AN ARMY 'MUTINY' IN 326 B.C.

① Alexander's Campaigns in North-West India

Following his victory over Porus at the river Hydaspes (Jhelum), Alexander built Nicaea and Bucephala, stormed Sangala (capital of the Cathaei), and then advanced to the river Hyphasis (Beas). At this point his army staged a "mutiny." Exhausted and homesick after eight years of campaigning, during which they had marched 17,000 miles, the troops refused to go on, and returned to Nicaea.

© Arthur Banks

② Two Rivers and Two Civilizations

Alexander knew of the existence of the River Ganges and wished it to be the line of his eastern frontier. If the 'mutiny' had not occurred, he could not have failed to collide with the tribes of northern India, consequently affecting future world events. Sandracottus (Chandragupta), India's first great military leader, was in Alexander's camp at this particular period.

PROBLEMS OF CHANGING NOMENCLATURE IN HISTORY: THE "LAND OF THE FIVE RIVERS"

❶ Greek Historians' Versions of Indian Names

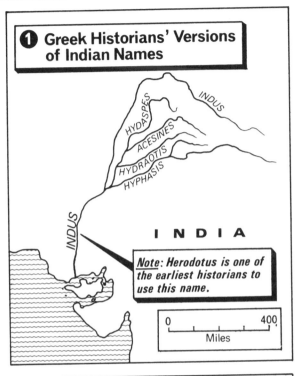

Note: Herodotus is one of the earliest historians to use this name.

❷ Ancient Indian Names

❸ Names Current in Medieval and Modern History

Note: the course of the Indus is different.

Just as one city may be famous in history under different names (for example, Byzantium - Constantinople - Istanbul), so other changes of name at different periods present a problem to historical cartographers.

The area of north - west India shown on these three sections illustrates this problem, and touches upon another: rivers may change their courses (for example, the Yellow River or Huang Ho in China), and coastlines alter at different periods of history. Often, as at Thermopylae, these changes affect the tactical characteristics of an area.

Side by side with changing nomenclature, goes the additional problem of transliteration (for example, Rheims - Reims).

The Indus (Sindhu in Sanskrit) is the origin of the name India, as well as of Sind.

© Arthur Banks

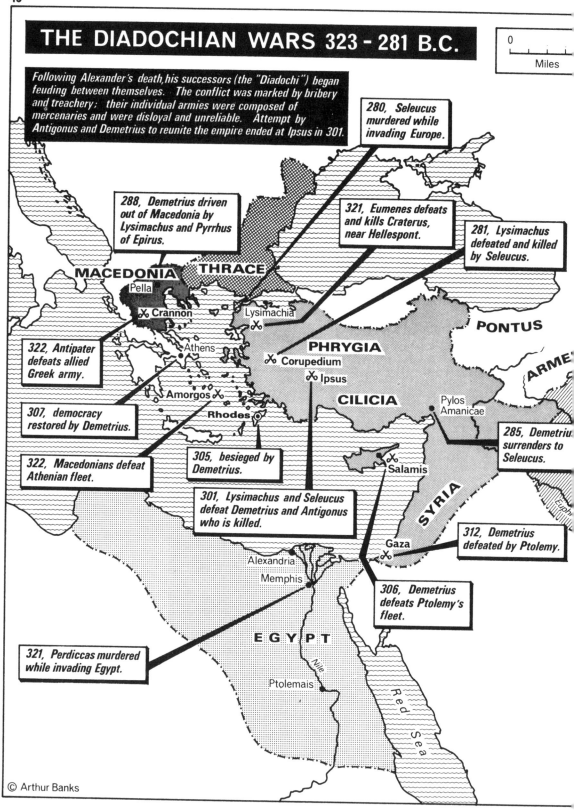

43

THE DIADOCHIAN WARS 323 - 281 B.C.

0
Miles

Following Alexander's death, his successors (the "Diadochi") began feuding between themselves. The conflict was marked by bribery and treachery; their individual armies were composed of mercenaries and were disloyal and unreliable. Attempt by Antigonus and Demetrius to reunite the empire ended at Ipsus in 301.

280, Seleucus murdered while invading Europe.

288, Demetrius driven out of Macedonia by Lysimachus and Pyrrhus of Epirus.

321, Eumenes defeats and kills Craterus, near Hellespont.

281, Lysimachus defeated and killed by Seleucus.

MACEDONIA
Pella
Crannon

THRACE

Lysimachia

PONTUS

322, Antipater defeats allied Greek army.

Athens

PHRYGIA

Corupedium

ARME

Ipsus

CILICIA

Pylos
Amanicae

285, Demetriu surrenders to Seleucus.

307, democracy restored by Demetrius.

Amorgos

Rhodes

322, Macedonians defeat Athenian fleet.

305, besieged by Demetrius.

Salamis

SYRIA

301, Lysimachus and Seleucus defeat Demetrius and Antigonus who is killed.

Gaza

312, Demetrius defeated by Ptolemy.

Alexandria
Memphis

306, Demetrius defeats Ptolemy's fleet.

E G Y P T

321, Perdiccas murdered while invading Egypt.

Nile

Ptolemais

Red Sea

KEY

///// Kingdom of Seleucus.

····· Kingdom of Ptolemy.

▦ Kingdom of Antigonus.

▓ Kingdom of Cassander.

▨ Kingdom of Lysimachus.

• Important battle.

• Important siege.

THE MAIN CONTESTANTS AND THEIR FATES

Perdiccas (killed by Ptolemy-bribed mutineers in 321 B.C.).
Craterus (killed by Eumenes 320 B.C.).
Antipater (died 319 B.C.).
Eumenes (killed by his own men, bribed by Antigonus 316 B.C.).
Antigonus (killed at Battle of Ipsus 301 B.C.).
Demetrius (son of Antigonus, died in captivity of Seleucus 301 B.C.).
Cassander (son of Antipater, died 300 B.C.).
Ptolemy (died 283 B.C.).
Lysimachus (killed by Seleucus at Battle of Corupedium 281 B.C.).
Seleucus (murdered by Ptolemy Keraunos 280 B.C.).

*founded by Seleucus
is capital.*

SOGDIANA

*311-302, Seleucus unites
eastern provinces under
his rule. Indian provinces
ceded to Sandracottus
(Chandragupta).*

PARTHIA

BACTRIA

ARIA

GABENE

*316, after indecisive battle, Eumenes is
betrayed to Antigonus and put to death.*

Paraetacene

DRANGIANA

PERSIS

ARACHOSIA

CARMANIA

KINGDOM OF SANDRACOTTUS
(CHANDRAGUPTA)

Indus

*Seleucus, expelled
Antigonus, recovers
lon.*

GEDROSIA

*317, indecisive battle between
Antigonus and Eumenes.*

Caspian Sea

Tigris

CELTS, SCYTHIANS, SARMATIANS, AND EARLY GERMANS c. 700 - 50 B.C.

SETTLEMENTS — KEY — MIGRATIONS

Early Celts before 600 B.C.
Celtic diffusion 600 - 400 B.C.
Celtic diffusion 400 - 300 B.C.
Celtic diffusion 300 - 200 B.C.
Scythian settlement 600 - 200 B.C.
Sarmatian settlement 200 B.C.
Early Germanic settlement.

Celts.
Scythians.
Sarmatians.
Early Germans.
Important battles.

Celts west of Byzantium annihilated by Thracians, soon after 220 B.C.

Before 230 B.C., Attalus I of Pergamum wins crushing victory over Celts (Galatians).

279 B.C., Celtic raid on Delphi turned back by Greeks.

c. 512 B.C., Scythians beat off invasion of Darius.

113 B.C., Cimbri defeat Romans.

222 B.C., Marcellus defeats Celtic army at Clastidium.

390 B.C., Gauls defeat Romans at river Allia and sack Rome.

101 B.C., Cimbri wiped out by Marius at Vercellae.

105 B.C., Cimbri defeat Romans at Arausio.

102 B.C., Marius defeats Teutones at Aquae Sextiae.

© Arthur Banks

45

THE WARRING STATES IN CHINA 481 - 221 B.C.

KEY TO STATES

CHOU	CH'I	HAN	T'ENG
CH'U	WEI	YEN	T'SOU
CHAO	CH'IN	SUNG	LU

BARREN WASTE

HSIUNG - NU
(HUNS)

TUNG - HU

Although the main bulk of the Great Wall was not constructed until the period immediately following the Warring States, it is shown on this map because sections of walls were built between 450 - 221 B.C. in efforts to prevent raids into central China by the Asiatic Huns (Hsiung - nu). Also, Cheng (ruler of Ch'in 247 - 222 B.C.) was responsible for the Great Wall's construction when, in 221 B.C., he became Shih Huang Ti and commenced to link together parts of earlier walls.

SECTIONS BUILT c. 300

SECTIONS BUILT c. 290

CHAO-HSIEN

HU

Tai

Chi

JUNG

BUILT 353

237

SECTIONS BUILT c. 300

300

Chin-yang

Han-tan

Lin-tzu

Ho

c. 450

NOMADS

376

Hsien-yang

Yeh

Wei

Yung

An-i

Lo-yang

Yang-cho

Nan-cheng

Wan

Ts'ai

Huai

333

H

Yu-fu-ch'eng

SHU PA

Chiang

Ying

Chiang

E

Wu

Kuei-chi

NOMADS

U
(481-334 B.C.)

Y

MILITARY KEY

Chinese inter-state conquests.

Attacks by nomads.

Fortifications.

0	200

Miles

This period marked an increase in feudal anarchy. The Ch'in and Ch'u emerged as leading military powers.

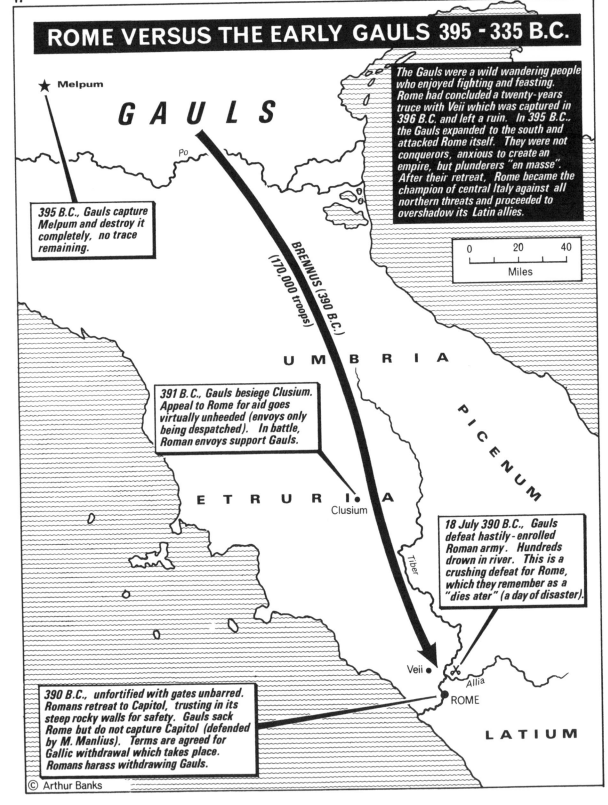

47

ROME VERSUS THE EARLY GAULS 395 - 335 B.C.

Melpum

G A U L S

Po

The Gauls were a wild wandering people who enjoyed fighting and feasting. Rome had concluded a twenty-years truce with Veii which was captured in 396 B.C. and left a ruin. In 395 B.C., the Gauls expanded to the south and attacked Rome itself. They were not conquerors, anxious to create an empire, but plunderers "en masse". After their retreat, Rome became the champion of central Italy against all northern threats and proceeded to overshadow its Latin allies.

395 B.C., Gauls capture Melpum and destroy it completely, no trace remaining.

0   20   40
Miles

BRENNUS (390 B.C.)
(170,000 troops)

U M B R I A

P I C E N U M

391 B.C., Gauls besiege Clusium. Appeal to Rome for aid goes virtually unheeded (envoys only being despatched). In battle, Roman envoys support Gauls.

E T R U R I A

Clusium

18 July 390 B.C., Gauls defeat hastily-enrolled Roman army. Hundreds drown in river. This is a crushing defeat for Rome, which they remember as a "dies ater" (a day of disaster).

Tiber

Veii

Allia

ROME

390 B.C., unfortified with gates unbarred. Romans retreat to Capitol, trusting in its steep rocky walls for safety. Gauls sack Rome but do not capture Capitol (defended by M. Manlius). Terms are agreed for Gallic withdrawal which takes place. Romans harass withdrawing Gauls.

LATIUM

© Arthur Banks

THE SAMNITE WARS 343 - 290 B.C.

295 B.C., Romans defeat Samnites and Gauls combined, losing 9,000 troops. Umbria is now in Roman hands.

The Samnites were Rome's most powerful neighbours. They ruled over southern Italy but dreamed of ruling the whole land. Although their territorial extent was larger than Rome's, this was a factor in Samnite weakness, as much of the territory was feebly-held. In 343 B.C., war broke out to decide whether Rome or Samnium was to be the first power in Italy. The struggle lasted for 57 years, with two short interludes of peace, and at its conclusion, Rome emerged as the dominant power. To become complete mistress of Italy, Rome now had only to conquer "Magna Graecia" in the south.

341 B.C., Roman victory.

306 B.C., Roman victory.

309 B.C., Lucius Papirius (the elder) defeats Samnites.

338 B.C., Roman victory.

305 B.C., Samnite capital is taken by storm.

321 B.C., Caius Pontius traps a Roman army, compelling it to "pass under the yoke" (a very great dishonour).

Constructed by Rome to facilitate transport of troops. Trade also passes along it.

343 B.C., Roman victory.

293 B.C., Lucius Papirius (the younger) defeats Samnites.

341 B.C., Romans gain victory, but lose Decius.

UMBRIA • Tifernum • Sentinum • Mevania • PICENUM • ETRURIA • Vadimonian Lake • Tiber • ROME • Allia • Pedum • LATIUM • Liris • APPIAN WAY • Astura • Volturnus • Bovianum • Saticula • CAUDINE FORKS • Capua • Suessula • Veseris • Maleventum (Beneventum) • Aquilonia • APPIAN WAY • Aufidus • SAMNIUM • CAMPANIA • LUCANIA • ADRIATIC SEA • Mt. Gaurus

0 20 40 Miles

© Arthur Banks

ROME VERSUS PYRRHUS 280-274 B.C.

0 — 50
Miles

279 B.C., nearest town to Rome conquered by Pyrrhus during his northward advance.

"WHAT A BATTLEFIELD I AM LEAVING FOR CARTHAGE AND ROME!" *Prophetic words of Pyrrhus upon leaving Italy for home.*

<u>Note:</u> *Hannibal rated Pyrrhus as second to Alexander The Great in his estimation of great captains.*

ROME
Praeneste
Anagnia

279 B.C., captured by Pyrrhus.

LATIUM

Fregellae
Maleventum (Beneventum)
Asculum
APULIA

CAMPANIA

279 B.C., Pyrrhus wins a two-day battle during which he is wounded. He cannot follow up his victory and is compelled to await the arrival of reinforcements from Epirus.

275 B.C., Pyrrhus is defeated by Romans. His army has a too large admixture of Italians by now, his elephants fall into disorder, and his phalanx is handicapped by rough ground. Pyrrhus falls back to Tarentum.

Tarentum
CALABRIA
LUCANIA
Heraclea
GULF OF TARENTUM
Siris

Thurii

BRUTTIUM

277 B.C., Pyrrhus captures Carthaginian bases.

280 B.C., Pyrrhus wins his first battle against Romans. Seven times the infantry clash before Pyrrhus sets free his elephants (which Romans have never seen before now). Romans flee in panic but Pyrrhus loses 4,000 men and comments that a further victory such as this will spell disaster. (Hence the term "a Pyrrhic victory").

Eryx   Panormus
Lilybaeum

Rhegium

SICILY

277-276 B.C., Pyrrhus conducts unsuccessful siege of one year's duration.

Syracuse

Pyrrhus was killed during a street brawl at Argos in 272 B.C.

278 B.C., Pyrrhus breaks Carthaginian investment.

Tarentum
0 — 80
Miles
EPIRUS

Capital city.

Thurii

The Lucanians quarrelled with the coastal Greeks and in 282 B.C. they attacked Thurii. Rome (in breach of treaty) sailed ten ships into Gulf of Tarentum whereupon four were sunk by Tarentines. Rome declared war on Tarentum which appealed to Pyrrhus of Epirus for help. Despite a series of victories against Romans and Carthaginians (in alliance against common foe), Pyrrhus never conquered Rome, which went on to become mistress of Italy.

Ambracia

280 B.C., Pyrrhus sails to aid of Tarentum with elephants, archers, 20,000 Macedonian infantry, and 3,000 cavalry.

Argos

© Arthur Banks

CARTHAGINIAN POWER IN THE WESTERN MEDITERRANEAN

SPAIN
Corsica
ROME
Malaca
Balearic Is.
Sardinia
Ilici
Panormus
Gades
Rusaddir
Tingis
Sicily
CARTHAGE
Hadrumetum
Leptis (minor)
NUMIDIA
Leptis
Magna
Aspis
Charax

KEY
■ Extent of Carthaginian power.
▨ Extent of Roman power.

The forthcoming struggle between Rome and Carthage (the "Punic city") was to decide which power was to rule the world. In the event, Rome emerged victorious, with its subsequent influence on history. Two great commanders were involved: Hannibal (for Carthage) and Scipio (for Rome).

ROMAN ITALY

0   80
Miles

Where colonists kept their full rights, the colony was known as 'Roman'. If only part of their rights were kept, it was known as 'Latin'.

ROME

KEY
✳ Roman-franchised colonies.
■ Latin-franchised colonies.

THE TWO GIANTS COMPARED

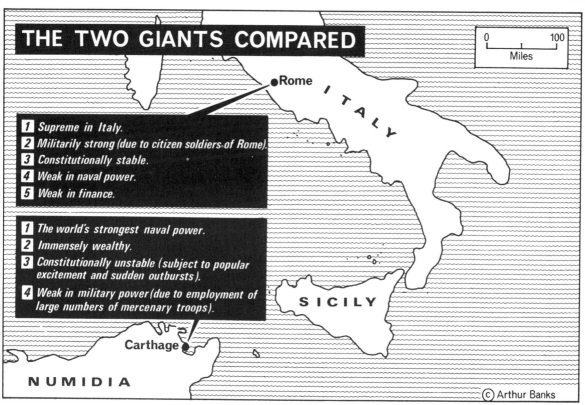

0   100
Miles

●Rome   ITALY

1 Supreme in Italy.
2 Militarily strong (due to citizen soldiers of Rome).
3 Constitutionally stable.
4 Weak in naval power.
5 Weak in finance.

1 The world's strongest naval power.
2 Immensely wealthy.
3 Constitutionally unstable (subject to popular excitement and sudden outbursts).
4 Weak in military power (due to employment of large numbers of mercenary troops).

Carthage●

SICILY

NUMIDIA

© Arthur Banks

THE FIRST PUNIC WAR 264 - 242 B.C.

❶ The General Scene

0 — 400 Miles

Ally of Rome; rival of Carthage.

Massilia
Corsica
ROME
Ebro
Tagus
Sardinia
WAR and RIVALRY
Sicily
Tingis
Rusaddir
CARTHAGE
REGULUS (256 B.C.)

Carthaginian influence is more commercial than political.

KEY

■	Under Roman rule 264 B.C.
▢	Under Carthaginian rule 264 B.C.
✗	Important battles.

Two battles near Carthage (Adys, 256 B.C., and Tunes, 255 B.C.).

CAUSES OF THE WAR

1 The Mamertines (Campanian mercenaries) seized Messana but were defeated by Hiero II of Syracuse at Mylae (270 B.C.), whereupon they appealed to Carthage for help.

2 Hanno arrived from Carthage and occupied citadel at Messana.

3 Romans ousted Hanno and made treaty with Hiero II.

4 Thus, the war was to decide whether Rome or Carthage was to be paramount in Sicily.

THE NAVAL WAR

1 The Carthaginians were supreme at the outset, so the Romans started a programme of naval construction.

2 Battles apart, the Romans unfortunately lost 700 ships and 200,000 troops in four sudden storms during war.

3 Roman tactics were to row their vessels next to the enemy crafts, secure them together with 'corvi'(crows), and fight a semi land–battle across the decks.

❷ Sicily: Main Area of Operations

2 *260 B.C., Carthaginians defeat Roman naval squadron under C.Cornelius Scipio.*

7 *249 B.C., Carthaginians defeat Romans who lose 93 ships and 8,000 men killed. 20,000 Romans captured.*

3 *260 B.C., Roman naval victory wrests sea mastery from Carthaginians.*

ITALY
Liparae
Mt. Hercte
Drepanum
Messana
Mylae
Rhegium

Finest harbour in Sicily.

Eryx
Panormus
• Segesta
Aegates Islands
Lilybaeum

Carthaginians transfer their naval base to here from Panormus.

6 *251 B.C., Marcellus defeats Hasdrubal.*

S I C I L Y

Halycus

8 *242 B.C., Romans win decisive naval victory over Carthaginians who lose 50 ships sunk and 70 captured.*

1 *262 B.C., falls to Romans after siege lasting seven months.*

Agrigentum
C. Ecnomus
Gela
Syracuse

ROMAN PEACE TERMS

① *Carthaginians to evacuate Sicily.*

② *Carthaginians to pay war indemnity of 3,000 talents (about £720,000).*

③ *Carthaginians to undertake not to attack Syracuse nor allies.*

5 *255 B.C., Roman expedition returning from Africa caught in storm. 284 ships wrecked and 100,000 men drowned.*

4 *256 B.C., Roman naval victory ensures safe conduct of forces to Africa. 30 Carthaginian ships sunk and 64 captured. Romans lose 24 ships.*

0 — 50 Miles

THE GENERAL SCENE BETWEEN FIRST AND SECOND PUNIC WARS

The First Punic War had been fought for possession of Sicily. the Second Punic War was to be for possession of Spain. Between the two main wars, a number of smaller wars and skirmishes occurred. In 229 B.C., the Greek states requested Roman aid in suppressing Illyrian piracy and this assistance was forthcoming. 225–222 B.C., a Gallic invasion of Italy forced the Romans to extend their existing military road (between Rome and Spoletium) to Ariminium and to fight a number of battles with the Boii. Meanwhile, as Rome prepared Sicily as a new base for possible operations against Spain and Africa, Hannibal had a fresh plan in mind — to invade Italy itself!

HANNIBAL'S STRATEGY

1 To circumvent Roman sea-mastery by an overland advance on Italy via the Alps.

2 To force Rome to fight a two-front war by allying Carthage with Macedonia.

Romans are invited to citizenship and to an initiation in Eleusinian mysteries.

ATHENS

─KEY─
⊙ Roman colonies 220 B.C.
⊕ Roman garrisons 220 B.C.
▨ Aetolian League.
↑ Raids by Gauls, Ligurians.
✗ Battles, with dates.
Achaean League.

229 B.C., Illyrians promise Romans that no warships will sail south of this line.

Lissus
Epidamnus

"Friend and ally" of Rome.

Corcyra

Blockade by Queen Teuta of Illyria broken by Rome. Illyria is invaded and crushed during 229–228 B.C.

229 B.C., occupied by Romans.

228 B.C., Romans are invited to participate in Isthmian Games.

ILLYRIA
PIRATE COAST
Issa

ILLYRIAN PIRATE RAIDS

I T A L Y

Syracuse

222 B.C., Romans defeat Gauls.

Clastidium
Cremona
Placentia
Mutina
Parma
Bononia
Ariminium

VIA FLAMINIA
Spoletium
Rome

✗ Faesulae
Telamon

225 B.C., Gauls defeat Romans.

224 B.C., Romans defeat Gauls but lose Regulus.

241 B.C., following the First Punic War, becomes Roman province (except Syracuse).

S I C I L Y

241 B.C., annexed to Rome.

to Spain

238 B.C., insurrection quelled by Rome. Becomes Roman province in 225.

C O R S I C A

S A R D I N I A

Carthage

241–239 B.C., aided by Libyan cities, mercenaries mutiny against Carthage. Ringleaders Spendius and Mathos are killed and Carthage survives.

238 B.C., HAMILCAR TO SPAIN

© Arthur Banks

0   50   100
Miles

HANNIBAL AND THE SECOND PUNIC WAR 218-201 B

Son of Hamilcar, at the age of nine Hannibal was made to swear undying hatred of Rome, Carthage's rival in the Mediterranean. He trained as a soldier in Carthaginian Spain, and at the age of 26 he commanded the entire army in that territory. His greatest feat was to attack the Romans on their home ground by transporting a huge army (including elephants) by an overland route across the southern Alps, and then down in to Italy itself where he defeated large enemy armies, one after the other. His weakness was at sea; reinforcements could not reach him due to Roman naval supremacy in the western Mediterranean. He refrained from a direct attack upon Rome itself, and the defeat of brother Hasdrubal's reinforcing army at Metaurus (207 B.C.) meant that he was isolated without help in southern Italy.

6 218 B.C., Hannibal crosses Pyrenees

5 Hannibal subdues the Ilergetes, the Bargusii, the Ausetani, and part of Lacetania.

Greek colony allied with Rome.

Hanno, Hannibal's distr commander, surveils Emporium; Carthaginia prefer not to invade i

1 221 B.C., Hannibal strengthens Punic hold on Spain by subduing the Vaccaei and Olcades.

2 221 B.C., Hannibal wins decisive victory over the Carpetani.

Although no treaty existed, relations between Saguntum and Rome were on a friendly basis.

3 219 B.C., Hannibal attacks Saguntum. Siege lasts eight months, but ends in victory for the Carthaginians. The Romans regard this as an act of war.

4 218 B.C., Hannibal commences hi great march to Italy with 90,000 fo soldiers, 12,000 cavalry, and 37 eleph

BATTLE OF THE METAURUS 207 B.C.

Hasdrubal, Hannibal's brother, withdrew to more favourable ground during the night preceding the action, after being deserted by his Italian guides. At dawn, Livius engaged his right while Nero outflanked the Spanish infantry and attacked from their rear. Hasdrubal's army, completely demoralised by Nero's attack, became panic-stricken. The Carthaginian army was completely beaten, losing 10,000 men (including Hasdrubal). Roman losses amounted to some 2,000 men.

After first charge, elephants roam aimlessly across the battlefield.

Nero's rear attack forces Spaniards on to Ligurians, thus creating confusion.

KEY

Hannibal's great march from Spa Italy (Cannae).
[Sections of his ro disputed by histor

Campaigns afte
Battle of Canna

Roman moveme

Territory contro or influenced b Carthage.

Important battl

Mountainous la

KEY

Carthaginians' first positions.

Hasdrubal's elephants.

Romans' first positions.

Nero's outflanking movement.

0   1
Miles

8 Hannibal storms Taurini stronghold.

Hannibal battles with Allobroges.

9 218 B.C., Scipio loses first clash with Hannibal.

10 December 218 B.C., Hannibal defeats both Scipio and Sempronius at Battle of Trebia.

Unaware of Roman defeat at Lake Trasimene, Servilius sends 4,000 cavalry to intercept Hannibal. Maharbal's smaller force kills half of them, and remainder are captured.

207 B.C., Hasdrubal defeated.

12 Late summer 217 B.C., Hannibal rests at Picenum. Later he moves south, ravaging the countryside. Romans use "delaying" tactics.

13 Spring 216 B.C., Hannibal defeats Romans at Battle of Cannae. Romans lose 70,000 men, and never again oppose Hannibal in massed battle on their own soil.

Col de Grimone
Taurini
"the island"
Greek colony allied with Rome.
Massilia
R. Ticino
R. Trebia
R. Po
Ariminum
R. Metaurus
Umbria
Etruria
Corsica
Picenum
APENNINES
Rome
Latium
Samnium
Capua
Campania
Beneventum
Apulia
Tarentum
Calabria
Lucania
Bruttium
Sardinia
Sicilia

209 B.C. Roman fleet of 60 ships arrives with P. Scipio's legion. Learning of Hannibal's march, P. Scipio dispatches Gnaeus to attack remaining Carthaginian military forces in Spain, while he returns to northern Italy to intercept Hannibal.

11 June 217 B.C., Battle of Lake Trasimene, where Flaminius loses 15,000 men, and is killed.

Following Cannae, Capua goes over to the Carthaginians; however, Hannibal does not go on to attack Rome.

14 216 - 203 B.C., Romans refrain from another massed battle with Hannibal. The Carthaginian forces are whittled down by small localised actions. Hannibal takes Tarentum, and uses Apulia as his base area. Capua is reconquered by the Romans (211 B.C.) despite march towards Rome by the Carthaginians, and in 209 B.C. Tarentum is retaken.

15 203 B.C., Hannibal is recalled to Carthage.

ROMAN SEA MASTERY

Carthage
Zama
Hadrumetum
Leptis (minor)

16 Hannibal arrives at Leptis, marches to Hadrumetum, and then on to Zama.

203 B.C. Hannibal returns to Africa by sea

17 202 B.C., Battle of Zama ends Second Punic War. Hannibal is defeated. He retires to Carthage until 195 B.C. when he leaves for Syria and Asia Minor, still trying to obtain allies for yet another fight with Rome. When Bithynia comes under the Romans, he takes poison to avoid arrest.

Note: there were several Roman commanders named Scipio. The Scipio shown at Massilia and northern Italy on this map, was the father of Scipio (Africanus), the victor of Zama.

0   100
Miles

© Arthur Banks

HANNIBAL'S GREAT BATTLES.

0	1	2	3	4	5	6	7
			Miles				

❶ Trebia: December 218 B.C.

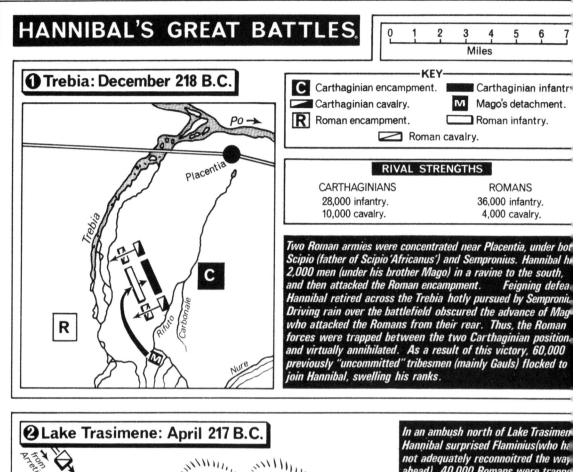

KEY

- **C** Carthaginian encampment.
- ◣ Carthaginian cavalry.
- **R** Roman encampment.
- ▨ Roman cavalry.
- ▰ Carthaginian infantry.
- **M** Mago's detachment.
- ▱ Roman infantry.

RIVAL STRENGTHS

CARTHAGINIANS	ROMANS
28,000 infantry.	36,000 infantry.
10,000 cavalry.	4,000 cavalry.

Two Roman armies were concentrated near Placentia, under bot[h] Scipio (father of Scipio 'Africanus') and Sempronius. Hannibal h[id] 2,000 men (under his brother Mago) in a ravine to the south, and then attacked the Roman encampment. Feigning defea[t] Hannibal retired across the Trebia hotly pursued by Semproniu[s]. Driving rain over the battlefield obscured the advance of Mag[o] who attacked the Romans from their rear. Thus, the Roman forces were trapped between the two Carthaginian position[s] and virtually annihilated. As a result of this victory, 60,000 previously "uncommitted" tribesmen (mainly Gauls) flocked to join Hannibal, swelling his ranks.

❷ Lake Trasimene: April 217 B.C.

In an ambush north of Lake Trasimen[e] Hannibal surprised Flaminius (who ha[d] not adequately reconnoitred the way ahead). 40,000 Romans were trappe[d] in a four-mile defile and attacked fro[m] three directions simultaneously. 15,000 Romans were killed (including Flaminius and another 15,000 capture[d]. A 4,000-strong cavalry force sent o[n] by Servilius was likewise annihilated.

KEY

- ◣ Carthaginian cavalry.
- ▰ Carthaginian heavy infantry.
- ▨ Carthaginian light infantry.
- ▱ Roman troops (under Flaminius).
- ◪ Roman cavalry (sent by Servilius).

0	1	2	3
		Miles	

©Arthur Banks

❸ Cannae: 2 August 216 B.C. (Hannibal's greatest victory)

KEY

CARTHAGINIANS

- **C** Carthaginian encampment.
- Spanish and Gallic heavy cavalry.
- Numidian light cavalry.
- **a** African infantry.
- **s g** Spanish and Gallic infantry.

ROMANS

- **R** Roman encampment.
- Roman cavalry.
- Allied horsemen.
- Allied infantry.

Phase 1 Hannibal's infantry was drawn up in convex formation with cavalry on the wings. As the Romans advanced, the centre was withdrawn to a concave line.
Phase 2 Hannibal's cavalry defeated the Roman cavalry.
Phase 3 Roman front and flanks were now engulfed and encirclement was completed by Hannibal's cavalry units. Of Roman army of 89,600, 70,000 were killed (according to Polybius). Carthaginian losses were only 5,700.

---

❹ Zama: 19 October 202 B.C. (Hannibal's defeat by Scipio)✱

✱ Later known as 'Africanus' by the Romans. (Full name: PUBLIUS CORNELIUS SCIPIO AFRICANUS).

KEY

HANNIBAL

- Main Carthaginian force (Bruttians).
- Ligurian and Gallic infantry.
- Carthaginian and African infantry.
- Cavalry.
- ●●● 80 elephants (disposed in advance).
- Advances and retreats.

SCIPIO

- Main Roman force (triarii).
- First line of velites (hastati).
- Second line of velites (principes).
- Cavalry.
- Advances.

Phase 1 Hannibal advanced his elephants; most were diverted by Roman horn blasts. Masinissa advanced his Numidian cavalry.
Phase 2 Scipio's infantry engaged Hannibal and initially the Carthaginians held firm. Cavalry attacks by Laelius and Masinissa on the rear ultimately proved decisive. Carthaginian losses were 20,000; Romans lost 1,500. Hannibal fled to Hadrumentum.

ROMAN OPERATIONS AGAINST CARTHAGE DURING AND AFTER SECOND PUNIC WAR

KEY

▨ Roman-controlled territory in 218 B.C.
→ Roman offensives.
Ⓡ Roman overseas bases.
✗ Roman victories.

Scipio 'Africanus' ③ was the greatest Roman general of the Second Punic War (218–202 B.C.). By capturing the Carthaginian base in Spain and then invading Africa, he drew Hannibal away from Italy and his prime objective, the destruction of Rome.

THE SCIPIO FAMILY TREE

Lucius Cornelius Scipio
① Publius Cornelius Scipio ② Gnaeus Cornelius Scipio
③ Publius Cornelius Scipio 'Africanus'
Publius Cornelius Scipio
④ Publius Cornelius Scipio Aemilianus Africanus (adopted)

(The numerals denote which Scipio is involved on map)

Roman navy in actions against Philip V of Macedon.

215 B.C., Hiero II dies and Syracuse sides with Carthage. 211 B.C., captured by Marcellus.

146 B.C., destroyed by Scipio ④ after three years' siege.

215 B.C., reinforced by Carthage.

Masinissa assists Scipio ③ in defeating Hannibal 202 B.C.

215 B.C., raided by Carthage.

216 B.C., attacked by Scipio ②. Balearic Islands come under Roman control.

203 B.C., Romans defeat Syphax (ally of Carthage).

Hannibal's elephants are 'recruited' from this region.

Romans establish 'New Rome' here in opposition to New Carthage.

133 B.C., conquered by Scipio ④.

211 B.C., Scipios ① and ② are killed in battle.

208 B.C., Scipio ③ defeats Hasdrubal who escapes.

209 B.C., captured by Scipio ③.

206 B.C., Scipio ③ wins decisive victory.

206 B.C., captured by Scipio ③. Mago sails for Italy.

ILLYRICUM

Apollonia Ⓡ

Adriatic Sea

Brundisium
Tarentum
Capua ✗
Metaurus ✗
Rome ●
Ostia ⚓
ITALY

Genua

Corsica

Sardinia

Sicily
Lilybaeum
Syracuse

Utica
Carthage ●
✗ Zama
Cirta ✗

GAUL

Massilia Ⓡ
Emporiae
Ⓡ
Tarraco Ⓡ

Balearic Is.
Ebusus

SPAIN

Numantia ●

Saguntum Ⓡ

New Carthage

Baecula ✗

Ilipa ✗

Gades
Tingis ●
Rusaddir

ATLAS MTNS.

0 — 150
Miles

© Arthur Banks

ROMAN CONSULAR ARMY IN THE TIME OF HANNIBAL c. 220 B.C.

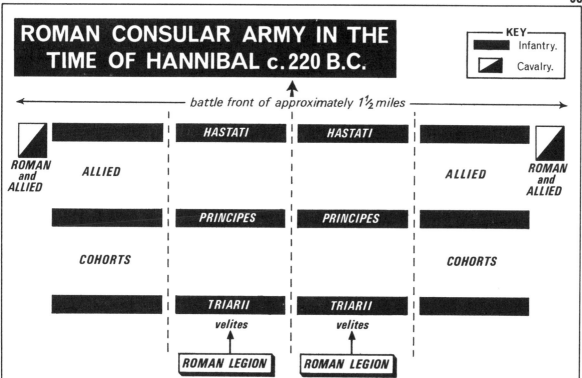

KEY
Infantry.
Cavalry.

battle front of approximately 1½ miles

ROMAN and ALLIED — ALLIED — HASTATI — HASTATI — ALLIED — ROMAN and ALLIED

COHORTS — PRINCIPES — PRINCIPES — COHORTS

TRIARII — TRIARII
velites — velites

ROMAN LEGION — ROMAN LEGION

A consular army comprised some 17,500 men of Romans and "auxilia". A Roman legion contained some 3,000 heavy infantrymen arranged in three main classifications or groupings according to experience and age. The hastati (20-30 age range) were the front line troops; the principes (30-35 age range) were veterans and the backbone of the legion; the triarii were the oldest men. In addition, velites (young light infantry) and cavalry were utilised. Each legion contained ten cohorts of 300 heavy infantry and these were broken down in to manipuli (maniples). In battle, the principes covered gaps in the ranks of the hastati and the triarii covered gaps in the ranks of the principes. The cavalry (total 600) was positioned on the wings and the velites, initially skirmishing in front, withdrew to take up a rear position.

ROMAN LEGION

HASTATI — maniples
each maniple consisted of 120 men, 12 in width and 10 in depth.
COHORT
PRINCIPES
each maniple consisted of 120 men, 12 in width and 10 in depth.
TRIARII
each maniple consisted of 60 men, 6 in width and 10 in depth.

© Arthur Banks

A ROMAN SOLDIER'S WEAPONS IN THE PUNIC WARS

HASTATI
Helmet (bronze) with purple and black 18 inch plume.
Bronze breastplate.
Greaves (leg-armour).
Shield (scutum) about 2½ by 4 feet: two layers of wood glued together, leather-covered and bound with iron. Iron boss (umbo) in centre, with handgrip inside.
Two javelins (pila) 4 feet long with 9 inch iron head (neck bent on impact to prevent use by enemy).
Sword (Spanish gladius) 2 foot blade, 2 inches wide, for cut and thrust work.
PRINCIPES and TRIARII
As hastati, but triarii carry pike (hasta) instead of two javelins.
VELITES (light missile troops)
(Probably operating in front. then withdrawing to rear. May have been administratively attached to triarii, who had only 600 men, as opposed to 1200 hastati and principes).
Helmet without crest.
Light circular shield (parma) 3 feet in diameter. Light javelins (iacula).

59

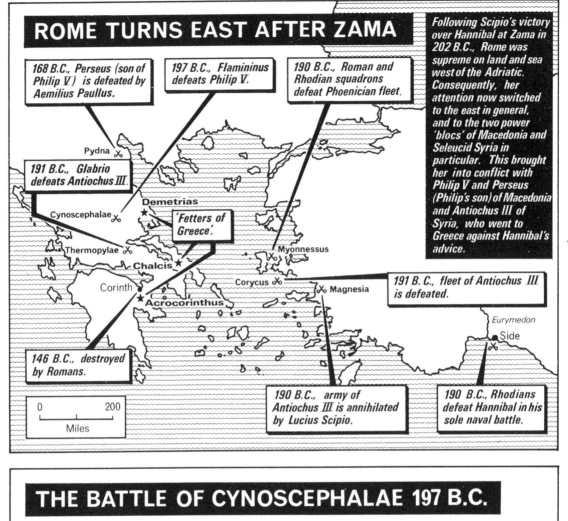

ROME TURNS EAST AFTER ZAMA

168 B.C., Perseus (son of Philip V) is defeated by Aemilius Paullus.

197 B.C., Flamininus defeats Philip V.

190 B.C., Roman and Rhodian squadrons defeat Phoenician fleet.

191 B.C., Glabrio defeats Antiochus III.

'Fetters of Greece'.

191 B.C., fleet of Antiochus III is defeated.

146 B.C., destroyed by Romans.

190 B.C., army of Antiochus III is annihilated by Lucius Scipio.

190 B.C., Rhodians defeat Hannibal in his sole naval battle.

Following Scipio's victory over Hannibal at Zama in 202 B.C., Rome was supreme on land and sea west of the Adriatic. Consequently, her attention now switched to the east in general, and to the two power 'blocs' of Macedonia and Seleucid Syria in particular. This brought her into conflict with Philip V and Perseus (Philip's son) of Macedonia and Antiochus III of Syria, who went to Greece against Hannibal's advice.

Pydna

Cynoscephalae

Demetrias

Thermopylae

Chalcis

Corinth

Acrocorinthus

Myonnessus

Corycus

Magnesia

Eurymedon

Side

0   200
Miles

THE BATTLE OF CYNOSCEPHALAE 197 B.C.

MACEDONIAN CAMP   PHILIP V

RIGHT-WING   LEFT-WING
FIRST POSITIONS

HILLY COUNTRY

LEFT-WING

RIGHT-WING

LEFT-WING   RIGHT-WING
FIRST POSITIONS

FLAMININUS   ROMAN CAMP

Note: the two armies met unexpectedly during a fog. The terrain did not suit the orderly Macedonian phalanx.

① Macedonian right-wing attacks and forces back Roman left.
② Macedonian left-wing commences deployment, but
③ is attacked and scattered by Roman right-wing.
④ Roman right swings round to attack and rout Macedonian right, which flees in panic.

SCORE SHEET	
ROMANS	MACEDONIANS
Strength: 26,000	Strength: 26,000
Casualties: 300	Casualties: 13,000

© Arthur Banks

THE NEAR EAST IN CONFLICT c.200 – 125 B.C.

This period was marked by a number of wars and struggles involving Seleucid Syria, Ptolemaic Egypt, and the Maccabees in Palestine. Meanwhile, Rome (heavily engaged in Greece) became increasingly involved as her power continued to expand eastwards.

KEY

- ✂ Important battles.
- ⬇ Antiochus IV's two invasions of Egypt, 171 and 168 B.C.
- ⬆ Broad lines of Roman expansion and involvement.
- ⊚ Victories of Judas 166 - 161 B.C.

0 ___ 200
Miles

Caspian Sea

Araxes

129 B.C., Phraates II of Parthia defeats and kills Antiochus VII.

141 B.C., Mithridates I of Parthia captures city.

Ecbatana ✂

Tigris

Babylon

Euphrates

198 B.C., Antiochus III wins victory, making Palestine a dependency of the Seleucids.

SELEUCID SYRIA

145 B.C., Ptolemy VI of Egypt defeats Alexander Balas of Syria but is killed.

Oenoparus ✂

Orontes

160 B.C., Bacchides of Syria defeats and kills Judas.

165 B.C., Judas captures most of city including temple. Seleucid garrison holds out in citadel.

Paneion ✂

Ptolemais ●
Elasa ✂
Adasa 161 B.C.
Jerusalem ⊚⊚

Beth Horon 166 B.C.
Emmaus 166 B.C.
Beth Zur 165 B.C.

143 B.C., Jonathan is ambushed and captured by Syrians and some dissident Jews. Later, killed.

ASIA MINOR

Black Sea

Halys

Pergamum ●

PTOLEMAIC EGYPT

Mediterranean Sea

Alexandria

168 B.C., Antiochus IV is warned by Rome to restore Egypt to the Ptolemies.

© Arthur Banks

61

ROMAN EXPANSION IN THE NEAR EAST

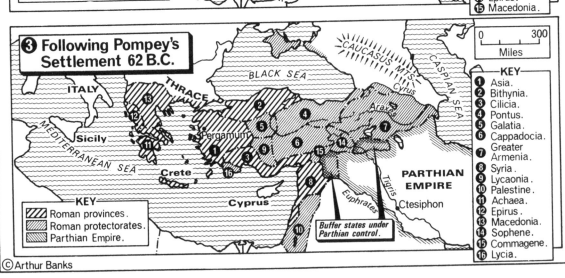

❶ Following Battle of Magnesia 190 B.C.

KEY
- ❶ Rhodes.
- ❷ Bithynia.
- ❸ Paphlagonia.
- ❹ Pontus.
- ❺ Galatia.
- ❻ Cappadocia.
- ❼ Armenia.
- ❽ Syria.

KEY
- Kingdom of Pergamum (Eumenes II).
- Greek free states and dependencies.
- Achaean League (280–146 B.C.).
- Aetolian League (220–146 B.C.).

Peace treaty (188) between Rome and Antiochus III.

❷ Prior to Mithridatic Wars 89 B.C.

KEY
- ❶ Asia.
- ❷ Bithynia.
- ❸ Paphlagonia.
- ❹ Pontus.
- ❺ Galatia.
- ❻ Cappadocia.
- ❼ Greater Armenia.
- ❽ Commagene.
- ❾ Syria.
- ❿ Lycaonia.
- ⓫ Pisidia.
- ⓬ Lycia.
- ⓭ Achaea.
- ⓮ Epirus.
- ⓯ Macedonia.

KEY
- Roman provinces.
- Roman protectorates.
- Kingdom of Mithridates VI.
- Allied with Mithridates VI.

PARTHIAN EMPIRE

❸ Following Pompey's Settlement 62 B.C.

KEY
- ❶ Asia.
- ❷ Bithynia.
- ❸ Cilicia.
- ❹ Pontus.
- ❺ Galatia.
- ❻ Cappadocia.
- ❼ Greater Armenia.
- ❽ Syria.
- ❾ Lycaonia.
- ❿ Palestine.
- ⓫ Achaea.
- ⓬ Epirus.
- ⓭ Macedonia.
- ⓮ Sophene.
- ⓯ Commagene.
- ⓰ Lycia.

KEY
- Roman provinces.
- Roman protectorates.
- Parthian Empire.

Buffer states under Parthian control.

PARTHIAN EMPIRE

Ctesiphon

© Arthur Banks

62

THE PARTHIAN EMPIRE

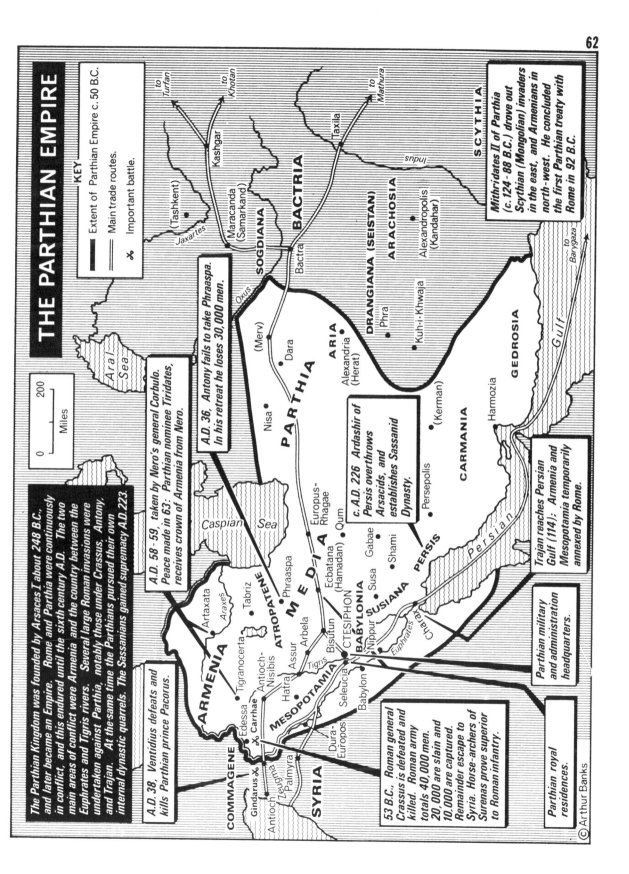

KEY
— Extent of Parthian Empire c. 50 B.C.
═ Main trade routes.
⚔ Important battle.

The Parthian Kingdom was founded by Arsaces I about 248 B.C. and later became an Empire. Rome and Parthia were continuously in conflict, and this endured until the sixth century A.D. The two main areas of conflict were Armenia and the country between the Euphrates and Tigris rivers. Several large Roman invasions were undertaken against Parthia, notably those under Crassus, Antony, and Trajan. At the same time the Parthians pursued their own internal dynastic quarrels. The Sassanians gained supremacy A.D. 223.

A.D. 38, Ventidius defeats and kills Parthian prince Pacorus.

A.D. 58 - 59, taken by Nero's general Corbulo. Peace made in 63: Parthian nominee Tiridates, receives crown of Armenia from Nero.

A.D. 36, Antony fails to take Phraaspa. In his retreat he loses 30,000 men.

c.A.D. 226 Ardashir of Persis overthrows Arsacids, and establishes Sassanid Dynasty.

Mithridates II of Parthia (c.124 - 88 B.C.) drove out Scythian (Mongolian) invaders in north-west. He concluded the first Parthian treaty with Rome in 92 B.C.

Trajan reaches Persian Gulf (114): Armenia and Mesopotamia temporarily annexed by Rome.

53 B.C., Roman general Crassus is defeated and killed. Roman army totals 40,000 men. 20,000 are slain and 10,000 are captured. Remainder escape to Syria. Horse-archers of Surenas prove superior to Roman infantry.

Parthian military and administration headquarters.

Parthian royal residences.

© Arthur Banks

THE EXPANSION OF CH'IN POWER AND INFLUENCE

Cheng took the title of *Shih Huang Ti*, proclaiming himself Emperor of China. (The name *China* is derived from *Ch'in*). He built the Great Wall to prevent raids into China by northern nomads, and made military expeditions south of the Yangtze. His two main generals were Ming T'ien and Chao T'o.

The Great Wall of China (constructed from brick, stone, and earth), was 1,500 miles in length, with watchtowers every few hundred yards. Along the top ran a 12 feet - wide roadway, and at irregular intervals there were gatehouses. Moats protected vulnerable sections of the wall on its northern side.

BARREN WASTE

FU-YU

THESE PEOPLES MOVE LATER TO CENTRAL ASIA.

HSIUNG - NU (HUNS)

GREAT WALL

CHAO-HSIEN

WU - SUN

Liao-tung

YUEH-CHIH

Wang -hsien

N. Chia

c.214 B.C.

Yun-chung

c.228 B.C.

TAI

YU-YANG

c.222 B.C.

Ch'ui

Chao-wu

PEI-TI

T'AI YUAN

CHU-LU

CH'I

LANG-YA

CHIANG

SHANG

c.230 B.C.

c.226 B.C.

T'ai-yuan

Ho

HO-TUNG

Lung-hsi

Han-tan

HAN-TAN

c.225 B.C.

Tsou

TANG

Ho

Lin-t'ao

Hsien-yang

P'eng

CH'IN

HAN-CHUNG

NAN-YANG

T'AN [WU]

Han-chung

Wu

SHU

NAN

CHANG

c.223 B.C.

Shu

Pa

Chiang

(Yangtze)

PA

(Ying) Nan

c.214 B.C.

CH'IEN-CHUNG

Ch'ang sha

YANG-YUEH

TIEN

CH'ANG -SHA

MIN-YUEH

N O M A D S

YEH-LANG

Tien

Kuei-lin

c.214 B.C.

HSIANG?

Hsiang

Nan-hai

LOU-LANG

KEY

⊙ Important centres.

Major routes.

← Ch'in conquests.

0   200

Miles

© Arthur Banks

CHINA UNDER THE HAN (WESTERN) AND LATER (EASTERN) DYNASTIES 206 B.C. – A.D.221

KEY

Frontier of Western Han c. 100 B.C.	
Frontier of Eastern Han c. A.D. 100.	
Major routes.	
Han expansion.	

The reign of Wu Ti (the Martial Emperor) marked a period of great military activity in China with campaigns against the Huns (Hsiung -nu) plus a policy of expansion. The Chinese cavalry was carefully improved by a horse- breeding programme. The modern Chinese often refer to themselves as the "sons of Han" (not in all areas, e.g. Canton).

Han expansion to the west is assisted by building roads, improving cavalry, and the wider use of iron weapons.

© Arthur Banks

0   200
Miles

Eastern Sea

FU - YU / PUYO
Hsuan t'u
KO-KU-RYEI
c. 108 B.C.
Lo-lang

WU-HUAN
c. 119 B.C.
c. 92 B.C.
c. 128 B.C.
c. 119 B.C.
HSIUNG - NU
c. 99 B.C.
Chu-yen
GREAT WALL

Yen
Po-hai
Ho-chien
Tai
Tzu-chuan
Chiao-tung
Tung-hai
Chi-yin
Kuang-ling
Kuei-chi
Hai-yen

YU
Chu
HSU
HUAN

CHI
YEN
PING
Tai-yuan
Chu-lu
Ho-nan (Lo-yang)
Nan-yang
Liu- an
Chiang
Ch'ang-sha
TUNG-YANG
MIN-YüEH
c. 110 B.C.
c. 111 B.C.
Nan-hai

Ho
Shang-ho
Shang
SSU-LI
Tso-feng-i
An-ting
Ching-chao
Wu
CHING
Wu-ling
YEH-LANG
Ling-ling
Ts'ang-wu
(Canton)
c. 109 B.C.
NAN-YüEH

Pei-ti
Wu-tu
P'o
Shu (Cheng-tu)
Chia-ming
TRIBES
Tsang-k'e
TIEN
c. 109 B.C.
Chiao-chih (Cattigara)

Chu-yen
Wu-wei
Sera
TZIU-LU
LANG
INDEPENDENT I (CHOU)
Pai-yai
Ch'en-li
c. 109 B.C.

WESTERN AREA
c. 36 B.C.
W. CH'IANG
CHIANG

Baltic
Sea

Antonine Wall.

Hadrian's Wall.

BRITAIN
Londinium

(GERMANY)

**LOWER
GERMANY**

Rhine

Durocortorum

'Limes' (fortified line).

Danube Vindobona

BELGICA

LUGDUNENSIS

**UPPER
GERMANY**

RAETIA

NORICUM

PANNONIA

*Bay of
Biscay*

GAUL

AQUITANIA

NARBONENSIS

②

⑦

②

⑦

ILLYRICUM

DALMATIA

②
③
⑬

*Adriatic
Sea*

GALACIA

TARRACONENSIS

Ebro

LUSITANIA

SPAIN

Tarraco

Corsica

⑩ ④
⑤ ⑧

Rome
Ostia

① ①
③
⑥

ITALY

⑪
⑥
⑫ ⑨

Saguntum

BAETICA

New Carthage

Sardinia

Port of Rome.

M e d i t e

Carthage

Sicily

Syracuse

AFRICA
(Earliest
province)

r r a n e a

M A U R E T A N I A

NUMIDIA

A F R I C A

Leptis
Magna

In the late Third Century A.D.,
a rampart, ditch, and wall (?)
was constructed. It was known
as "fossatum Africae".

— **KEY TO ROADS IN ITALY** —
①	Via Valeria.	⑧	Via Salaria.
②	Via Postumia.	⑨	Via Popillia.
③	Via Latina.	⑩	Via Cassia.
④	Via Flaminia.	⑪	Via Trajana.
⑤	Via Aurelia.	⑫	Via Domitiana.
⑥	Via Appia.	⑬	Via Julia Augusta.
⑦	Via Aemilia.		

— **KEY TO ALPINE AREAS** —
1. PENNINE, 2. COTTIAN, 3. MARITIME

© Arthur Banks

s map shows some important
ges in the growth of the Roman
pire, together with the road
tem that was so important in
development.

STAGES IN THE DEVELOPMENT OF THE ROMAN EMPIRE

200
Miles

KEY

The Conquest of Italy (to 266 B.C.).
The Supremacy of the Mediterranean area (to 146 B.C.).
The New Frontiers (to 49 B.C.).
The New Frontiers (to A.D. 14).
Extreme extent of Empire (to A.D. 284).
Main Roman roads.
Fortifications.

CIA

Black Sea

Danube

ESIA

THRACE

ARMENIA

Byzantium

BITHYNIA

PONTUS

Tigris

Amida

Ancyra

CAPPADOCIA

PARTHIAN EMPIRE

GALATIA

ASIA

CILICIA

MESOPOTAMIA

Ephesus

Antioch

Sura

Euphrates

Aegean

Athens

Sea

LYCIA

SYRIA

Palmyra

Babylon

CHAEA

Rhodes

Cyprus

Damascus

The "Syrian Limes" was a
string of forts and strongpoints
(double in places) connected by
roads. Mainly the work of
Trajan, and later of Diocletian.

Tyre

Bostra

Crete

Caesarea

JUDAEA

S   e   a

A R A B I A

Alexandria

Aelana

ARABIA
PETRAEA

ENAICA

E G Y P T

Nile

Red Sea

67

ROME'S MAIN ENEMIES, OPPONENTS, AND REBELS c. 200 B.C.–A.D.150

This map is intended to illustrate the names and locations of Rome's main enemies during the Republic, the military dictatorship, and the Empire.

KEY

- Roman Empire (A.D. 100–200).
- Enemies of the Roman Republic (before 100 B.C.).
- Rome's enemies during her military dictatorships (c.100–28B.C.).
- Enemies during the period of Empire (after 27 B.C.).
- **VINDEX** Names of individual enemies.
- *TEUTONS* Names of enemy tribes.

© Arthur Banks

ATLANTIC OCEAN

North Sea

Baltic Sea

Caspian Sea

Black Sea

Mediterranean Sea

Red Sea

PARTHIANS

TIGRANES

ANTIOCHUS

BAR KOCHBA

CLEOPATRA

MITHRIDATES

ANTIOCHUS

HANNIBAL

DEMETRIUS (c.220 B.C.)

PHILIP

PERSEUS

DECEBALUS

REGNUM BOSPORI

MAROBODUS

CIMBRIANS

TEUTONS

BOUDICCA

CIVILIS

AMBIORIX

ARMINIUS

ARIOVISTUS

VINDEX

VERCINGETORIX

CARATACUS

CASSIVELLAUNUS

VIRIATHUS

SERTORIUS

JUGURTHA

TACFARINAS

SPARTACUS

SEXTUS POMPEIUS

ROME

Ural

Volga

Don

Dnieper

Dniester

Dvina

Pripet

Niemen

Vistula

Danube

Tisza

Sava

Drava

Elbe

Rhine

Rhone

Loire

Po

Tiber

Ebro

Tagus

Nile

Tigris

Euphrates

0   300

Miles

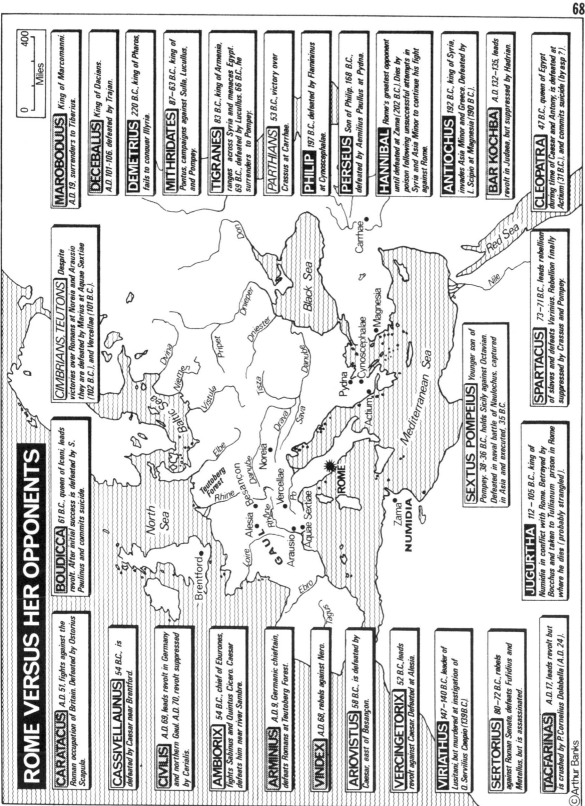

ROME VERSUS HER OPPONENTS

CARATACUS A.D. 51, fights against the Roman occupation of Britain. Defeated by Ostorius Scapula.

CASSIVELLAUNUS 54 B.C., is defeated by Caesar near Brentford.

CIVILIS A.D. 69, leads revolt in Germany and northern Gaul. A.D. 70, revolt suppressed by Cerialis.

AMBIORIX 54 B.C., chief of Eburones. Fights Sabinus and Quintus Cicero. Caesar defeats him near river Sambre.

ARMINIUS A.D. 9, Germanic chieftain, defeats Romans at Teutoberg Forest.

VINDEX A.D. 68, rebels against Nero.

ARIOVISTUS 58 B.C., is defeated by Caesar, east of Besançon.

VERCINGETORIX 52 B.C., leads revolt against Caesar. Defeated at Alesia.

VIRIATHUS 147–140 B.C., leader of Lusitani, but murdered at instigation of Q. Servilius Caepio (139B.C.).

SERTORIUS 80–72 B.C., rebels against Roman Senate, defeats Fufidius and Metellus, but is assassinated.

TACFARINAS A.D. 17, leads revolt but is crushed by P.Cornelius Dolabella (A.D. 24.).

MAROBODUUS King of Marcomanni. A.D. 19, surrenders to Tiberius.

DECEBALUS King of Dacians. A.D. 101-106, defeated by Trajan.

DEMETRIUS 220 B.C., king of Pharos, fails to conquer Illyria.

MITHRIDATES 87–63 B.C., king of Pontus, campaigns against Sulla, Lucullus, and Pompey.

TIGRANES 83 B.C., king of Armenia, ranges across Syria and menaces Egypt. 69 B.C., defeated by Lucullus. 66 B.C., he surrenders to Pompey.

PARTHIANS 53 B.C., victory over Crassus at Carrhae.

PHILIP 197 B.C., defeated by Flamininus at Cynoscephalae.

PERSEUS Son of Philip. 168 B.C., defeated by Aemilius Paullus at Pydna.

HANNIBAL Rome's greatest opponent until defeated at Zama (202 B.C.). Dies by poison following unsuccessful attempts in Syria and Asia Minor to continue his fight against Rome.

ANTIOCHUS 192 B.C., king of Syria, invades Asia Minor and Greece. Defeated by L. Scipio at Magnesia (190 B.C.).

BAR KOCHBA A.D. 132-135, leads revolt in Judaea, but suppressed by Hadrian.

CLEOPATRA 47 B.C., queen of Egypt during time of Caesar and Antony, is defeated at Actium (31 B.C.), and commits suicide (by asp ?).

BOUDICCA 61 B.C., queen of Iceni, leads revolt. After initial success is defeated by S. Paulinus and commits suicide.

CIMBRIANS, TEUTONS Despite victories over Romans at Noreia and Arausio they are defeated by Marius at Aquae Sextiae (102 B.C.), and Vercellae (101 B.C.).

SEXTUS POMPEIUS Younger son of Pompey. 38–36 B.C., holds Sicily against Octavian. Defeated in naval battle of Naulochus, captured in Asia and executed, 35 B.C.

JUGURTHA 112 – 105 B.C., king of Numidia in conflict with Rome. Betrayed by Bocchus and taken to Tullianum prison in Rome where he dies (probably strangled).

SPARTACUS 73–71 B.C., leads rebellion of slaves and defeats Varinius. Rebellion finally suppressed by Crassus and Pompey.

Red Sea

Nile

Carrhae

Black Sea

Don

Dnieper

Dniester

Pripet

Niemen

Dvina

Baltic Sea

Vistula

Tisza

Drava

Sava

Danube

Elbe

Magnesia

Cynoscephalae

Pydna

Actium

Mediterranean Sea

Zama

NUMIDIA

Aquae Sextiae

Arausio

Po

Vercellae

Rhône

Alesia

Besançon

GAUL

Loire

Rhine

Teutoberg Forest

Noreia

Danube

Drava

North Sea

Brentford

Tagus

Ebro

ROME

0   400
Miles

© Arthur Banks

69

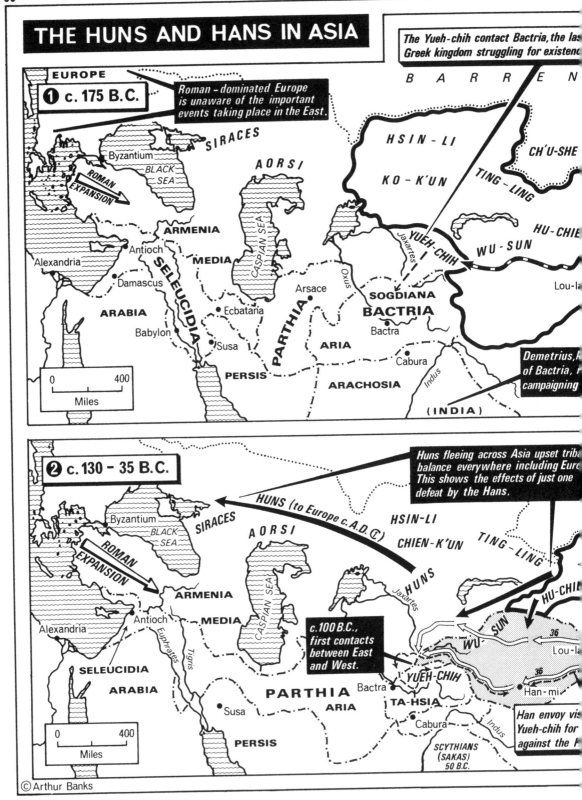

THE HUNS AND HANS IN ASIA

① c. 175 B.C.

The Yueh-chih contact Bactria, the las[t]
Greek kingdom struggling for existenc[e]

Roman-dominated Europe
is unaware of the important
events taking place in the East.

EUROPE

B A R R E N

Byzantium
BLACK SEA
SIRACES
AORSI

HSIN-LI
KO-K'UN
CH'U-SHE
TING-LING
HU-CHIE[H]

YUEH-CHIH
WU-SUN

Lou-la[n]

ARMENIA
Antioch
Alexandria
MEDIA
Damascus
SELEUCIDIA
Ecbatana
Arsace
CASPIAN SEA
Oxus
SOGDIANA
BACTRIA
Bactra

ARABIA
Babylon
Susa
PARTHIA
ARIA
Cabura
Indus

Demetrius,[K]
of Bactria, [i]
campaigning

PERSIS
ARACHOSIA
(INDIA)

0   400
Miles

② c. 130 – 35 B.C.

Huns fleeing across Asia upset trib[al]
balance everywhere including Eur[ope.]
This shows the effects of just one
defeat by the Hans.

Byzantium
BLACK SEA
SIRACES
AORSI
HUNS (to Europe c.A.D. ①)

HSIN-LI
CHIEN-K'UN
TING-LING

ROMAN EXPANSION

HUNS
HU-CHI[EH]

ARMENIA
Antioch
Alexandria
MEDIA
CASPIAN SEA
Jaxartes
WU-SUN

36
Lou-la[n]
36

c.100 B.C.,
first contacts
between East
and West.

Euphrates
Tigris
SELEUCIDIA
ARABIA
Susa
PARTHIA
Bactra
YUEH-CHIH
ARIA
TA-HSIA
Cabura
Indus
Han-mi[ng]

Han envoy vis[its]
Yueh-chih for [?]
against the [Huns?]

PERSIS
SCYTHIANS
(SAKAS)
50 B.C.

0   400
Miles

© Arthur Banks

KEY

.... Southern extent of barren area.

▨ Homeland of the Huns.

▤ Hun-dominated lands.

◄━━ Hun expansion.

━━━ Under threat of Hun rule.

◄═══ Other tribes, fleeing from Huns.

overrun northern China
ing period of anarchy.

W A S T E

TUNG-HU FU-YU

HUN-YU

Lung

U-SUN?

EH-CHIH

H'IANG

FREQUENT HUN-HAN CLASHES

Ho Chi-nan

Ch'ang-an

Wu

EMPIRE OF

THE HAN

Ch'ang-sha

YUEH

AINU

U N E X P L O R E D

O C E A N

KEY

✖ Area where major Han-Hun battles occurred.

━━ Hun-dominated lands c.100 B.C.

◄━━ Huns fleeing from victorious Hans.

▨ Han-dominated territory c.100 B.C.

◄─── Journeys of Chang Ch'ien to the Yueh-chih 138-126 B.C. to enlist military assistance.

HUN-YU

TUNG-HU

THE HUN HOMELAND WU-HUAN

119 78 92

99 119

Shang-ku

H'IANG

Ho Chi-nan

Wu

EMPIRE

Ch'ang-an

OF THE

HAN

Ch'ang-sha

YUEH

U N E X P L O R E D

O C E A N

CHINESE GENERALS AND EXPEDITIONS

◄══ Wei Ch'ing 128 B.C.

◄▥▥ Ho Ch'u-ping and Wei Ch'ing 119 B.C.

◄▬▬ Li Ling 99 B.C.

◄▥▥ Li Kuang-li 92 B.C. (similar to track 128 B.C.).

◄━━ Ch'en T'ang's two campaigns in 36 B.C.

ROMAN DEFENCE SYSTEMS

1 Hadrian's Wall

Wall was built by Hadrian 122 – 128, north of the Stanegate, the road which formed Trajan's frontier. It was 80 Roman miles long, 8 -feet wide and at least 16 -feet high with 15 forts, 80 milecastles, and intermed turrets. Restored by Severus 200 - 205; Constantius c. 297, and again in 369.

N. Tyn

BROOMHOLM

BANNA
BEWCASTLE

BLATOBULGIUM
BIRRENS

BROCOL
CARRAWB

CASTRA EXPLORATORUM
NETHERBY

GT. CHESTERS
AESICA

CAMBOGLANNA
BIRDOSWALD

VERCOVIC
HOUSESTEADS

PETRIANA
STANWIX

Solway Firth

MAIA
BOWNESS

Carlisle

VXELLODUNUM
CASTLESTEADS

THROP
MAGNA
CARVORAN

VINDOLANDA
CHESTERHOLME

NETHER DENTON

CONGAVATA
DRUMBURGH

ABALLAVA
BURGH BY SANDS

LUGUVALIUM

OLD
CHURCH

WREAY

WHITLEY CASTLE

BIBRA
BECKFOOT

OLENACUM
OLD CARLISLE

Eden

KEY

Extent of the Wall

CAERMOTE

VOREDA
OLD PENRITH

Main fort.

Roman road.

2 Antonine Wall

Forth

Loch
Lomond

ROUGH CASTLE
CAMELON

Firth of Clyde

Leven

OLD KILPATRICK

DUNTOCHER

CASTLE HILL

BALMUILDY

AUCHENDAVY

BAR HILL

CASTLECARY

SEABEGS

FAL

WESTERWOOD

CROY HILL

WHITEMOSS

NEW KILPATRICK

CADDER

KIRKINTILLOCH

Clyde

© Arthur Banks

TANCUM
GHAM

ONNUM
HALTON

VINDOVALA
RUDCHESTER

CONDERCUM
BENWELL

PONS AELIUS
NEWCASTLE

SEGEDUNUM
WALLSEND

ARBEIA
SOUTH SHIELDS

CORSTOPITUM
CORBRIDGE

Tyne

VINDOMORA
EBCHESTER

CONCANGIUM
CHESTER-LE-STREET

LONGOVICIUM
LANCHESTER

Devils Water

0   5
Miles

TYPICAL SECTION OF WALL (PLAN VIEW)

Not to scale

MILECASTLE

Parapet walk [8ft. wide]

ENEMY COUNTRY

1 mile

PATROL TURRETS

Ditch [9ft. deep X 30ft. wide]

FORT

F C   E   B C
A
F C   D   C

Parapet & battlements

Forts were built to take either 1,000 or 500 men. Some had stables for cavalry. The fort shown above contains Headquarter Block **(A)**, Hospital **(B)**, Stables **(C)**, Workshops and grain stores **(D)**, Commander's House **(E)**, and Barracks **(F)**.

Milecastles accommodated patrols of less than 50 men.

Turrets (two between each pair of milecastles) were mainly for signalling purposes.

PICAL CROSS-SECTION OF WALL (ELEVATION VIEW)

ENEMY COUNTRY

WALL

DITCH

0   30
Feet

...l consisted of a ditch and rampart of turf, about 37 miles
..., 14-feet broad and about 10-feet high, with a grass-
...ered cobbled parapet, and a ditch 40-feet wide and 12-
... deep. There were forts at about half-mile intervals.
...t under Antoninus Pius by Lollius Urbicus in 142;
...ndoned soon after 185.

Forth

Firth of

CREDIGONE
CARRIDEN

KINNEIL
...RAVON

CRAMOND

INVERESK

Almond

0   5
Miles

KEY

▬▬▬ Extent of the Wall.

⬛ Main fort.

═══ Roman road.

73

ROMAN DEFENCE SYSTEMS - continued

❸ The 'Limes' of Germany

KEY
- Frontier of Vespasian.
- Frontier of Domitian.
- Frontier of Hadrian.
- Frontier of Antoninus Pius.
- Roman roads.
- ✪ Fortified town.
- ★ Fort.

GERMANIA SUPERIOR

The Limes was a frontier road with forts and earthworks, and watchtowers. The frontier was withdrawn to the Rhine and Danube after Frankish attacks c.260.

RAETIA

❹ The 'Limes' of Syria

The Limes was a frontier road with forts, built along a natural defensive line. Begun by Trajan, and later reconstructed by Diocletian.

KEY
- ✪ Fortified town.
- ★ Fort.
- Frontier roads.
- Other roads.

ⓒ Arthur Banks

❺ A Typical Roman Camp

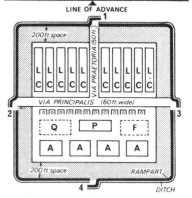

L Legionaries' lines, in 8-men leather tents.
C Centurions' tents, at end of men's lines.
P Praetorium: Commander's tent and HQ area.
Q Quaestorium: Quartermaster's area.
F Forum: Market-place or parade-ground.
A Lines of allied troops.
▣ Tents of officers (legionary tribunes & praefecti).
Area required for one legion's camp: about 20 acres.
1 *PORTA PRAETORIA.*
2 *PORTA PRINCIPALIS SINISTRA.*
3 *PORTA PRINCIPALIS DEXTRA.*
4 *PORTA DECUMANA.*

6 Camp Entrances

To prevent direct enemy assaults on the gates of camps, the following methods of construction were used:

(A) DITCH / BANK — CAMP / INTERIOR

(B) DITCH / BANK — CAMP / INTERIOR

(C) DITCH / BANK — CAMP / INTERIOR

(D) DITCH / BANK — CAMP / INTERIOR

KEY

(A) External clavicular.   (B) Internal clavicular.   (C) Tutulus.   (D) Agricolan.

7 The 'Limes' of Africa

KEY
- ✪ Fortified town.
- ★ Fort.
- ═ Roads.
- Sand 'seas' (chotts).

Caesarea — Cirta — Carthage — Sitifis — Hadrumetum — Lambaesis

LIMES OF MAURETANIA

LIMES OF NUMIDIA

LIMES TRIPOLITANUS

The Limes was a series of fortresses linked by road. In the late Third Century, a rampart, ditch, and earthworks were added.

0   100
Miles

8 The 'Limes' of Dacia and the Danube

In 80, Domitian constructed fortifications north of the Danube, and in 106, Trajan established a Limes in Dacia. In 271, Aurelian abandoned Dacia to the barbarians, and the frontier fell back to the river Danube.

0   100
Miles

Castra Regina (Regensburg)
Lauriacum (Lorch)
DANUBE
Vindobona (Vienna)
Carnuntum (Altenburg) (Petronell)
Brigetio (Oszöny)
Aquincum (Obuda)
Lake Balaton
Drava
Aquileia
Tisza
Sava
Drina
POROLISSENSIS
Apulum
APULENSIS
Mures
D A C I A
Olt
Troesmis (Igliţa)
The Earth Wall of Dobrudja
Singidunum (Belgrade)
Viminacium (Koštolac)
MALVENSIS
DANUBE
Durostorum (Silistra)
Ratiaria (Arčar)
Novae (Swisjtow)

KEY
- ✪ Fortified town.
- ★ Fort.

© Arthur Banks

BASIC ORGANIZATION OF THE ROMAN LEGION

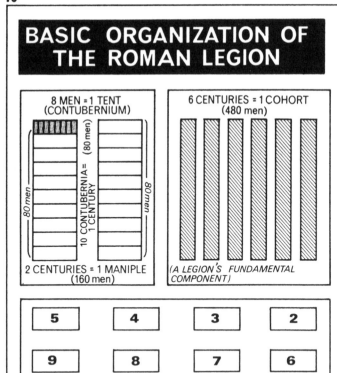

8 MEN = 1 TENT (CONTUBERNIUM)

80 men

10 CONTUBERNIA = 1 CENTURY

80 men

(80 men)

2 CENTURIES = 1 MANIPLE (160 men)

6 CENTURIES = 1 COHORT (480 men)

(A LEGION'S FUNDAMENTAL COMPONENT)

5	4	3	2
9	8	7	6

COHORT 1 HAD 5 DOUBLE CENTURIES

10

10 COHORTS = 1 LEGION (about 5,120 men)

ROMAN LEGION IN BATTLE ORDER

↑ DIRECTION OF ADVANCE

COHORTS

5	4	3	2	1

10	9	8	7	6

COHORTS

(Note: strongest cohorts shown [▨])

Allies (auxilia) stationed where required.

Cavalry often positioned on the wings.

Least experienced soldiers in cohorts **7** and **9**. Cohort **1** could be a useful independent sub-unit.

(above arrangement according to Vegetius)

OFFICERS

1 Commander (legatus);   1 senior tribune;
1 Praefectus castrorum;   5 junior tribunes.

60 Centurions (senior one is _primipilus_).
120 horsemen per legion (scouts and despatch riders).

IMPORTANT ROMAN NAVAL BASES

KEY
● Main base for western Mediterranean operations.
◉ Main base for eastern Mediterranean operations.
• Other bases.

First permanent base. Later superseded by Misenum.

Gesoriacum

Colonia Agrippinensis

Rhine

Danube

Aquileia

Noviodunum

Chersonesus

MOVED c. A.D. 135

CLASSIS (Ravenna)

Forum Iulii

Taurunum

Salonae

Centumcellae

Trapezus

Aleria

Ostia

MISENUM

Cyzicus

Seleucia

Carales

Caesarea

Alexandria

0   50
Miles

© Arthur Banks

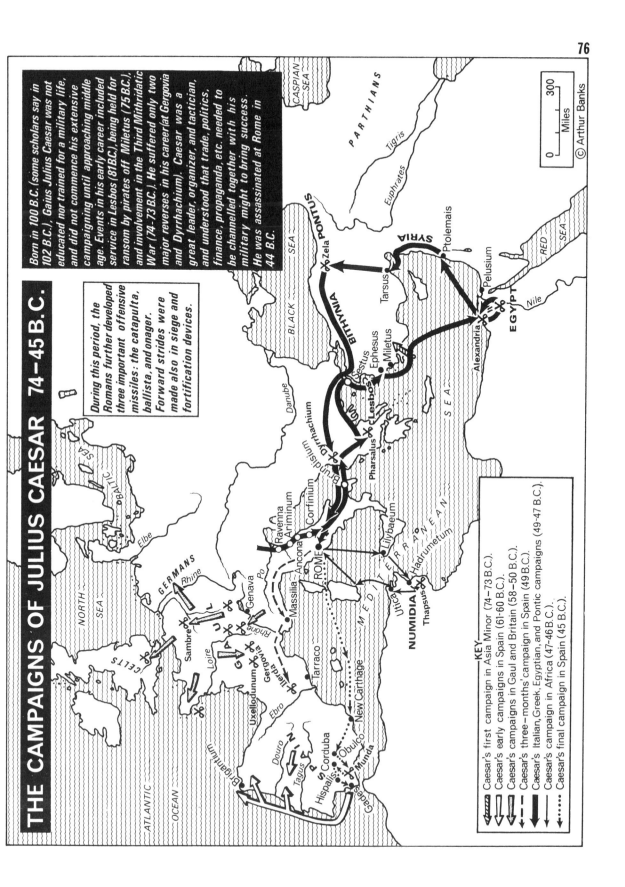

THE CAMPAIGNS OF JULIUS CAESAR 74–45 B.C.

Born in 100 B.C. (some scholars say in 102 B.C.), Gaius Julius Caesar was not educated nor trained for a military life, and did not commence his extensive campaigning until approaching middle age. Events in his early career included service in Lesbos (81B.C.), being held for ransom by pirates off Miletus (75B.C.), and involvement in the Third Mithridatic War (74–73 B.C.). He suffered only two major reverses in his career(at Gergovia and Dyrrhachium). Caesar was a great leader, organizer, and tactician, and understood that trade, politics, finance, propaganda, etc. needed to be channelled together with his military might to bring success. He was assassinated at Rome in 44 B.C.

During this period, the Romans further developed three important offensive missiles: the catapulta, ballista, and onager. Forward strides were made also in siege and fortification devices.

© Arthur Banks

0   300
Miles

KEY

Caesar's first campaign in Asia Minor (74–73 B.C.).
Caesar's early campaigns in Spain (61-60 B.C.).
Caesar's campaigns in Gaul and Britain (58–50 B.C.).
Caesar's three–months' campaign in Spain (49 B.C.).
Caesar's Italian, Greek, Egyptian, and Pontic campaigns (49-47 B.C.).
Caesar's campaign in Africa (47–46B.C.).
Caesar's final campaign in Spain (45 B.C.).

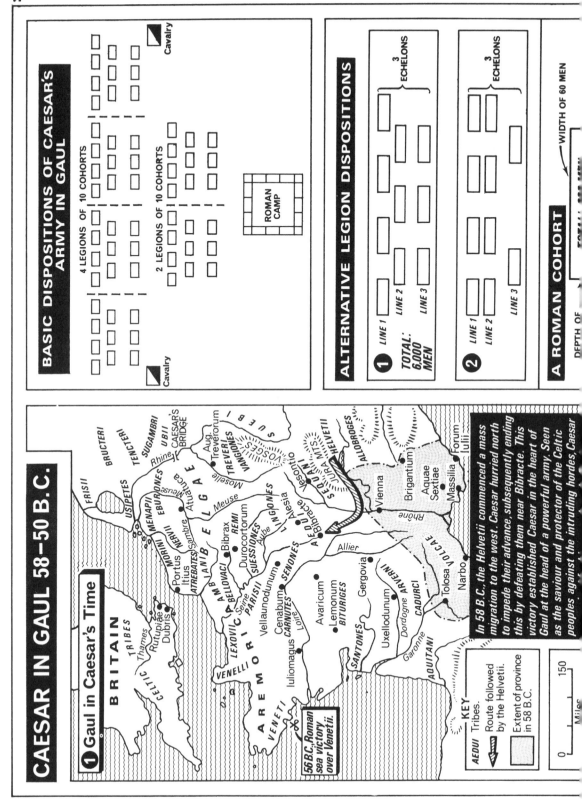

CAESAR IN GAUL 58–50 B.C.

1 Gaul in Caesar's Time

BRITAIN

TRIBES

CELTIC

FRISII
BRUCTERI
USIPETES
TENCTERI
SUGAMBRI
UBII
CAESAR'S BRIDGE
MENAPII
EBURONES
Rhine
Aug. Treverorum
TREVERI
VANGIONES
SUEBI
Moselle
MORINI
NERVII
Atuatuca
Meuse
Portus Itius
ATREBATES Sambre
Dubris
Rutupiae
Thames
BELGAE
BELLOVACI Bibrax
REMI
Durocortorum
SUESSIONES
LINGONES
VOSGES
Yesontio
SEQUANI
JURA MTS.
HELVETII
AMBIANI
LEXOVII
PARISII
Seine
Vellaunodunum
Cenabum
CARNUTES
SENONES
Albe
Alesia
AEDUI
Bibracte
Allier
Vienna
Rhône
ALLOBROGES
Brigantium
Aquae Sextiae
Massilia
Forum Iulii
Iuliomagus
Loire
VENELLI
AREMORICI
VENETI
Avaricum
Lemonum
BITURIGES
Gergovia
Uxellodunum
ARVERNI
CADURCI
Dordogne
Garonne
AQUITANI
SANTONES
VOLCAE
Tolosa
Narbo

56 B.C. Roman sea victory over Veneti.

KEY
AEDUI Tribes.
→ Route followed by the Helvetii.
▨ Extent of province in 58 B.C.

0 — 150 Miles

In 58 B.C. the Helvetii commenced a mass migration to the west. Caesar hurried north to impede their advance, subsequently ending this by defeating them near Bibracte. This victory established Caesar in the heart of Gaul at the head of a powerful army. Seen as the saviour and protector of the Celtic peoples against the intruding hordes, Caesar

BASIC DISPOSITIONS OF CAESAR'S ARMY IN GAUL

Cavalry

4 LEGIONS OF 10 COHORTS

2 LEGIONS OF 10 COHORTS

Cavalry

ROMAN CAMP

ALTERNATIVE LEGION DISPOSITIONS

1 LINE 1 / LINE 2 / LINE 3 — 3 ECHELONS

TOTAL: 6,000 MEN

2 LINE 1 / LINE 2 / LINE 3 — 3 ECHELONS

A ROMAN COHORT

DEPTH OF

WIDTH OF 60 MEN

③ Victory over the Belgae 57 B.C.

PHASE 1

ROMAN RIGHT IS HEAVILY ATTACKED

ROMAN CAMP

NERVII
VIROMANDUI
ATREBATES
BELGIC CAMP

Sambre

KEY
- Roman legions (numbered).
- Roman cavalry.
- Movements, in sequence.
- Belgic dispositions.
- Belgic retreats.
- Woods.

PHASE 2

Sambre
Captured by Romans

B

NERVII

R

arriving

KEY
- Roman legions (numbered).
- R Roman camp.
- B Belgic camp.
- Movements, in sequence.
- Woods.

0 ___ Mile

② Victory over the Helvetii 58 B.C.

↑ to Augustodunum
↑ to Bibracte

Arroux
Montmort
Armecy
Auzon Brook

R

Toulon-
sur-Arroux

H

The loss of their camp compelled the Helvetii to surrender. Caesar ordered them to return home.

KEY
- R Roman camp.
- H Helvetian 'laager' (camp encircled by wagons).
- Roman first positions.
- Helvetian first position.
- Roman second position.
- Helvetian flank attack from 'laager.'
- Helvetian second position.
- Helvetian advance from high ground.
- Helvetian retreat into 'laager.'
- Final Roman attack.

0 ___ 1 ___ 2 Miles

⑤ Successful Siege of Alesia 51 B.C.

CAESAR DEFEATED TWO ARMIES, THE FIRST IN ALESIA, THE SECOND A RELIEVING FORCE.

Ose
ALESIA
MT. DE FLAVIGNY
MT. RÉA
Brenne
Brenne
PLAINE DES LAUMES

Relief army attacks are repulsed.

GALLIC RELIEF ARMY
(Commius, Eporedorix, Vercassivellaunus, Viridomarus)

KEY
- Roman infantry camps.
- Roman cavalry camps.
- Wall built by Gauls prior to siege.
- Trenches dug by Romans.
- Roman wall of contravallation.
- Roman wall of circumvallation.

STRENGTHS
- Caesar's army: 70,000
- Army of Vercingetorix (besieged): 80,000
- Gallic relief army: 258,000

0 ___ ½ Mile

④ Unsuccessful Siege of Gergovia 52 B.C.

↑ to Clermont–Ferrand

ROMAN MAIN CAMP
1

Two Communication Trenches dug by Romans

Roman small camp
2

GERGOVIA
SMALL GALLIC FORCE
G

Auzon River

Hill taken by Caesar prior to siege.

KEY
- Gallic camps south of town.
- Gallic wall screening camps.
- 1 Caesar's first position.
- 2 Caesar's second position, captured from Gauls.
- Trenches for secret movement of Romans between camps.
- G Gallic foraging force.
- Roman feint attacks.
- Roman main attacks.

0 ___ 1 Mile

© Arthur Banks

CAESAR VERSUS POMPEY

① Rival Strengths

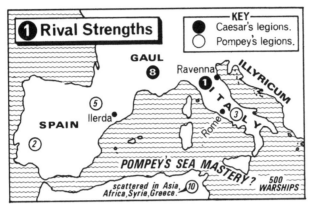

KEY
- ● Caesar's legions.
- ○ Pompey's legions.

GAUL ⑧
Ravenna ❶
ILLYRICUM
SPAIN ⑤
Ilerda ③
② ROME
ITALY
POMPEY'S SEA MASTERY?
scattered in Asia, Africa, Syria, Greece. ⑩
500 WARSHIPS

② Ilerda Operations 49 B.C. [not to scale]

CAESAR'S FIRST TASK WAS TO CONQUER POMPEY'S LEGIONS IN SPAIN.

Ilerda
C
A
new ford
Segre (Sicoris)
AFRANIUS AND PETREIUS SURRENDER

KEY
- ← Caesar's first and unsuccessful raid.
- ← Afranius' retreat.
- ← Caesar's pursuit.
- C Caesar's camp.
- A Afranius' camp.
- Town bridge.
- ✕ Defile.

③ Operations in Greece 48 B.C.

Nymphaeum
February, Antony lands with 12,800 troops.
Lissus
Pompey's base, besieged by Caesar. Pompey breaks siege.
Dyrrhachium
Heraclea
Egnatian Way
Apollonia
POMPEY
POMPEY
ADRIATIC SEA
CAESAR
CAESAR
Palaeste
THESSALY
January, Caesar lands with 25,000 troops.
Aeginium
Larissa
Gomphi
Ambracia
Corcyra
Pharsalus
Both Caesar and Antony pierce Pompey's sea screen.

After Caesar crossed the Rubicon and moved to the south, Pompey gradually retired, eventually crossing the Adriatic to Dyrrhachium. Caesar saw that pursuit was unwise until Pompey's legions in Spain were immobilized. He accomplished this between May - July 49 B.C. near Ilerda. Returning to Italy, Caesar evaded Pompey's naval patrols and crossing to Greece, invested Dyrrhachium. Pompey broke the siege but his army was defeated at Pharsalus, 15,000 being killed and 24,000 being captured. He escaped to Egypt, only to be murdered.

④ Pharsalus: the decisive battle 48 B.C.

PHASE 1

<u>Note</u>: Caesar's infantry lines equalled Pompey's in <u>length</u> but not in <u>density</u>.

Enipeus
CAESAR C 6 P POMPEY
Pharsalus

PHASE 2

Enipeus
6
right flank
D
①
②
③

PHASE 3

Enipeus
④
6 ①
② ②
③
⑤ ⑤ ⑤

CAESAR'S DISPOSITIONS
- C Encampment.
- ◪ Cavalry (1,000).
- ▬ Infantry, in three lines (18,000).
- 6 Line of six cohorts in reserve (3,000).

POMPEY'S DISPOSITIONS
- P Encampment.
- ◻ Cavalry (6,700).
- ▭ Infantry, in three lines (38,000).

OPENING MOVES

<u>Opening gesture</u>: a champion from each side advances to fight a duel →D← (object, to inspire their respective front lines).
① Caesar's infantry moves forward, hurling 'pila' (javelins) at enemy.
② Pompey's cavalry charges Caesar's cavalry (numerically inferior).
③ Caesar's cavalry moves back, thus (apparently) exposing his right flank. Caesar's reserves ▬ alerted.

CAESAR'S ATTACKS

① Caesar's reserve line of six cohorts engages Pompey's cavalry who panic and flee ②.
③ Cohorts advance to attack left wing of Pompey's infantry, while Caesar's three lines close up to form one concerted unit ▬.
④ Caesar orders general advance.
⑤ Attacked from two directions at same time, Pompey's army flees.

© Arthur Banks

CAESAR'S LATER CAMPAIGNS 48-45 B.C.

0   1
Mile

❶ Siege of Alexandria

Mediterranean   Sea

Pharos Island

GREAT HARBOUR

Harbour of Eunostus

Canal

Canal

LAKE MAREOTIS

KEY
1 Lighthouse.
2 Redoubts.
3 Archways.
4 Mole.
5 King's Harbour.
6 Royal Palace.
7 Theatre.
8 Library.

Caesar pursued Pompey to Egypt where he was informed of the latter's death. At Alexandria, he was besieged by Ptolemy XII and former Pompey supporters. Mithridates of Pergamum marched to Caesar's aid and together they defeated Ptolemy at the Battle of the Nile (47 B.C.). Later, Caesar went on to fight successful campaigns against Pharnaces in Pontus, and against other units of Pompey's forces in Africa (main battle was at Thapsus). His final campaign was in Spain where he defeated the sons of Pompey, Gnaeus and Sextus, plus Labienus.

❷ Battle of Thapsus 46 B.C.

Ships sent to watch Scipio from sea.

Djezira I.

CAESAR'S BLOCKADE

SCIPIO (40,000)

CAESAR (40,000)

Thapsus

LAKE

Line of five cohorts in reserve.

Mediterranean Sea

Fort constructed by Caesar to block approach route to Thapsus from the south.

AFRANIUS (10,000)   *JUBA (10,000)*

KEY
CAESAR'S FORCE
■ Infantry.
◪ Cavalry.
▲ Siege lines.
SCIPIO'S FORCE
▢ Infantry.
◻ Cavalry.
ᵒᵒᵒ Elephants (64).

OPERATIONS
①Caesar's right-wing attacks line of elephants. Wheeling round, elephants panic Scipio's left-wing cavalry. Whole army flees ②. Part of Caesar's force moves south ③, whereupon Juba and Afranius flee ④.

❸ Caesar's Final Campaign in Spain 45 B.C.

0   10   20
Miles

Sextus with two legions.

Corduba   *Guadalquivir*   Obulco

Ategua   Soricaria

Ulia ✳   Ucubi   *Guadajoz*

Carmo

Hispalis   *Peinado*   Ventipo   *Genil*

Munda

In minor battle, Gnaeus loses 500.

Gnaeus loses 30,000, Caesar loses 1,000.

to Gades

Ⓒ Arthur Banks

RIVAL FORCES   Caesar's strength: 40,000. / Gnaeus' strength: 50,000.

OPERATIONS
⬅ Caesar's movements.
◄--- Gnaeus' movements.
① Caesar arrives at Obulco to learn that Ulia ✳ is besieged by Gnaeus. ② Caesar advances to Corduba to entice Gnaeus to aid brother Sextus. Ruse succeeds ③ but Gnaeus refuses a direct clash. Caesar moves to capture fresh grain at Ategua, following which Gnaeus advances ④ to Ucubi, and then to Soricaria. ⑤ Caesar pursues Gnaeus to Munda ⑥ & ⑦, wins victory, deals with Sextus ⑧, and ends tour ⑨ & ⑩. *(Gnaeus and Labienus are killed; Sextus escapes).*

THE ROMAN MILITARY OCCUPATION OF BRITAIN c.A.D. 43 – 446

CELTIC TRIBES

CORNAVII
LUGI
SMERTAE
DECANTAE
CARNONACAE
CREONES
CALEDONII
VACOMAGI
TAEZALI
BORESTI
VENICONES
DAMNONII
VOTADINI
SELGOVAE
NOVANTAE
EPIDII
BRIGANTES
PARISI
CORNOVII
DEGEANGLI
CORITANI
ORDOVICES
DEMETAE
SILURES
ICENI
TRINOVANTES
CATUVELLAUNI
CANTII
ATREBATES
REGNI
DOBUNI
BELGAE
DUROTRIGES
DUMNONII

0   50   Miles

KEY
★ Legionary fortresses.
★ Forts.
▲ Signal stations.
═ Roman roads.
⌐⌐⌐ Frontier works.
⊛ Roman colony.

ANTONINE WALL
For more detailed coverage see "Roman Defence Systems"

HADRIAN'S WALL
For more detailed coverage see "Roman Defence Systems"

Pinnata Castra
Inchtuthil

Most northerly Roman legionary fortress in the world.

Horrea Classis
Credigone – *Bodotria aestuarium*

DEVIL'S CAUSEWAY
Trimontium
Alauna
Bremenium
Ormium
DERE STREET
Vindovala
Condercum
Segedunum
Arbeia
Concangium
Longovicium
Vinovia
Vercovicium
Banna
STANEGATE
Vindolanda
Voreda
MAIDEN WAY
Lavatrae
Maglona
Verterae
Virosidum
Galauna
Alauna
Galacum
Derventio
Eburacum
York
ERMINE ST.
Lagentium
Danum
Doncaster
ROMAN RDG.
Olicana
Ilkley
DERE ST.
Ardotalia
LONG CSWY.
HIGH ST.
Maia
Bibra
Alauna
Blatobulgium
WELL PATH
Gabrosentum
Tunnocelum
Mediobogdum
Glannaventa
Coccium
Wigan
Mamucium

MONAVIA INS.
Isle of Man

MONA INS.
Anglesey

82

Gariannonum

Venta
Caister

PYE ROAD

PEDDARS WAY

FEN ROAD

Durobrivae

GARTREE RD.

Durovigutum
Godmanchester

Camulodunum
Colchester

Othona

Tamesis flumen

Regulbium

Rutupiae
Richborough

Dubris Dover

Durobrivae
Canterbury

Lemanis
Lympne

STONE ST.

Durovernum

WATLING ST.

STANE ST.

Sacked by Boadicea
(Boudicca) in A.D.61.

Verulamium
St. Albans

ERMINE ST.

Ratae
Leicester

WATLING STREET

LONDINIUM
London

STREET

Ad Pontes
Staines

Calleva
Silchester

Venta
Winchester

STANE STREET

Anderita
Pevensey

Noviomagus
Chichester

VECTIS
INS.
Isle of Wight

Glevum
Gloucester

AKEMAN ST.

Corinium
Cirencester

ERMIN ST.

PORTWAY

Cunetio

Portus Adurni

Aquae
Sulis
Bath

FOSSE WAY

Durnovaria
Dorchester

ACKLING DYKE

Pennocrucium

Letocetum

Salinae

RYKNILD ST.

WATLING ST.

Viroconium
Wroxeter

Lavobrinta

STREET (WEST)

Gobannium
Burrium

Isca
Caerleon

Cicutio

Alabum

Nidum
Neath

Moridunum
Carmarthen

Lindinis
Ilchester

FOSSE WAY

Isca
Exeter

Sabrina flumen

Mediomanum

Bremia

Durobrivae

FOSS

Note: contrary to popular belief, the Romans
did not formally name their roads. Watling
Street, Ermine Street, etc. are Saxon in origin.

BASIC CHRONOLOGY

1 55 - 54 B.C., Julius Caesar makes two expeditions to Britain from Gaul.

2 A. D. 43, Claudian invasion under Aulus Plautius. Campaigns in west, midlands, and east undertaken by four legions.

3 51, Caratacus is defeated in northern Wales.

4 61, Anglesey attacked. Revolt of Iceni (under Boudicca) suppressed.

5 71 - 74, Petillius Cerealis moves frontier north from Lincoln to York.

6 78, conquest of Anglesey and north Wales completed.

7 83 - 84, Agricola defeats Caledonians. Roman fleet circumnavigates Britain.

8 122, construction of Hadrian's Wall commenced.

9 139 - 142, construction of Antonine Wall; broken 180 - 184.

10 196 - 197, Hadrian's Wall destroyed by Maeatae.

11 205 - 208, Hadrian's Wall rebuilt by order of Septimius Severus.

12 211, Britain divided into two provinces.

13 288 - 296, Britain breaks away from Empire, under Carausius.

14 360 - 370, Picts, Scots, Attacotti, and Saxons raid Britain.

15 410, civitates instructed by Emperor Honorius to protect themselves.

16 446, final appeal of civitates to Aetius.

THE CAMPAIGN OF ACTIUM 31 B.C.

MAIN CAUSES OF THE WAR BETWEEN OCTAVIAN AND ANTONY

1. Antony's marriage to Cleopatra VII of Egypt following his divorce from Octavia, sister of Octavian. Antony's will, formally publicized by Octavian, left some Roman possessions to his children by Cleopatra. This was seen as a future threat to Rome.

2 Antony's naval and army concentrations in Greece. These were regarded in Rome as preliminaries to an invasion of Italy.

① Strengths, Dispositions, and Early Moves

Note: Agrippa was Octavian's naval commander.

RIVAL STRENGTHS

	OCTAVIAN	ANTONY
Troops:	92,000	Troops: 145,000
Ships:	400	Ships: 500

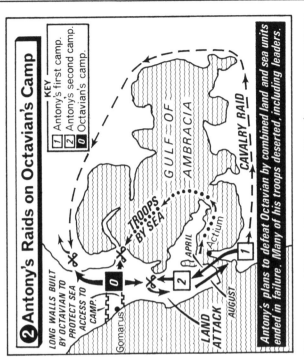

KEY
- ⩗⩗⩗ Antony's winter defence line.
- ⊙ Antony's bases and signal stations.
- --→ Route of Antony's Egyptian supply-ships.
- ⇧ Agrippa's attacks on Antony's bases.
- → Octavian's sea crossing to Epirus.

② Antony's Raids on Octavian's Camp

KEY
- 1 Antony's first camp.
- 2 Antony's second camp.
- 0 Octavian's camp.

Antony's plans to defeat Octavian by combined land and sea units ended in failure. Many of his troops deserted, including leaders.

③ The Decisive Sea Fight: 2 September

KEY
- ■ Agrippa's naval divisions.
- □ Antony's naval divisions.

SHIP STRENGTHS
OCTAVIAN: 400
ANTONY: 230

Main battle area. Antony loses 10-15 ships sunk in fierce fight.

Leaving Canidius in command on shore, Antony sailed out to meet Agrippa but was defeated. His 2 and 3 divisions surrendered. 4, 5, and 6 raced back to harbour. Cleopatra fled south. Octavian went on to capture 4,5, and 6, plus most of Antony's land army.

© Arthur Banks

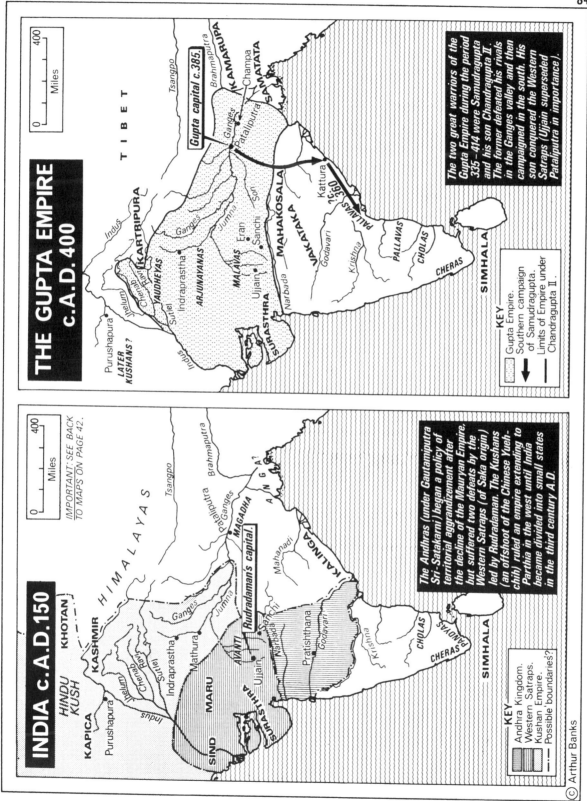

THE GUPTA EMPIRE c.A.D. 400

400

0   Miles

Gupta capital c.385.

TIBET

Indus

Jhelum
Chenab
Ravi
Sutlej

KARTRIPURA

Ganges

YAUDHEYAS

Indraprastha

ARJUNAYANAS

MALAVAS
Eran
Sanchi
Ujjain

SURASTHRA

Narbada

Jumna
Son

Ganges
Pataliputra

MAHAKOSALA

Brahmaputra

KAMARUPA
Champa
SAMATATA

Kattura
?c.360
PALLAVAS

VAKATAKA

Godavari

Krishna

PALLAVAS

CHOLAS

CHERAS

SIMHALA

Purushapura

LATER KUSHANS?

The two great warriors of the Gupta Empire during the period 335–414 were Samudragupta and his son Chandragupta I. The former defeated his rivals in the Ganges valley and then campaigned in the south. His son conquered the Western Satraps (Ujjain superseded Pataliputra in importance).

KEY
Gupta Empire.
Southern campaign of Samudragupta.
Limits of Empire under Chandragupta II.

INDIA c.A.D.150

400

0   Miles

IMPORTANT: SEE BACK TO MAPS ON PAGE 42.

HINDU KUSH
KHOTAN
KAPICA
KASHMIR

HIMALAYAS

Tsangpo

Purushapura
Indus

Jhelum
Chenab
Ravi
Sutlej

Indraprastha

Mathura

Ganges

Jumna

Brahmaputra

Pataliputra
Ganges

MAGADHA

ANGA?

Rudradaman's capital.

AVANTI
Ujjain
SURASTHRA
MARU
SIND

Narbada
Sanchi

Mahanadi

KALINGA

Pratishthana
Godavari

Krishna

CHOLAS

CHERAS
PANDYAS

SIMHALA

The Andhras (under Gautamiputra Sri-Satakarni) began a policy of territorial aggrandizement after the decline of the Mauryan Empire, but suffered two defeats by the Western Satraps (of Saka origin) led by Rudradaman. The Kushans (an offshoot of the Chinese Yueh-chih) ruled an empire extending to Parthia in the west until India became divided into small states in the third century A.D.

KEY
Andhra Kingdom.
Western Satraps.
Kushan Empire.
Possible 'boundaries'?

© Arthur Banks

84

85

THE "MARCH" OR "MARK" SYSTEM (BORDER LANDS OF THE HOLY ROMAN EMPIRE).
In Britain, the border areas of Wales and Scotland were known as the "Marches".

⊙ Marchlands
1 Slesvik.
2 Billungs.
3 North March.
4 Lausitz.
5 Meissen.
6 Sorbian.
7 Bohemia.
8 Moravia.
9 Austria.
10 Carmithia.
11 Pannonian.
12 Friuli.
13 Carniola.
14 Istria.
15 Verona.
16 Ancona.
17 Barcelona.
18 Spoleto.
19 Benevento.
20 Spanish.
21 Aragon.
22 Navarre.
23 Brittany.
24 Isle of France.

The object of this map is to present a generalised indication of the vast and important events that occurred in and around Europe preceding the Norman invasion of Britain in A.D. 1066.
In 476, the nominal reign of the last Western Roman emperor, Romulus Augustulus, came to an end when he was deposed by the Herulian, Odoacer.

© Arthur Banks

409, withdrawal of Roman troops leads to invasion by Jutes, Angles, and Saxons, who drive Celtic Britons westward.

Note: following maps do not include 'A.D.' in titles, but this still applies.

439, Vandals capture Carthage. It becomes their chief naval base.

CONQUESTS, MIGRATIONS, AND SETTLEMENTS IN EUROPE AND NEARBY AREAS   A.D. 150 - 1066

KEY

Goths.
Vandals.
Huns.
Norse, Danes, Swedes.
Arabs.

RUS

Novgorod

Volga

Huns migrating from Asia force other tribes to increase pressure on Roman frontiers.

from Asia

RUS
c.830
c.850
RUS
c.860

Dnieper
Volga

HUNS

GOTHS

INDIANS

LOMBARDS

c.150-200
Pripet
Kiev

MAGYARS

HUNS

EAST GOTHS

KHAZARS

MAGYARS

ALANS

Caspian Sea

HUNS

c.372

HUNS

8
9

MAGYARS (HUNGARIANS)

PATZINAKS

c.390

WEST GOTHS

VARANGIANS

c.860-914

Black   Sea

Constantinople

c.380

ARABS

Baghdad

Tigris

AVARS
402

11

WEST GOTHS

Danube
376
Adrianople

395

397

Viking fleets attack Constantinople in the ninth century.

Antioch

Euphrates

640

636

ARABS

639

ARABS

NORMANS
c.1050

Mediterranean   Sea

ARABS   642

Nile

0   300

Miles

THE PERIOD OF THE THREE KINGDOMS (SAN KUO) IN CHINA 221-279

Strife among the three kingdoms led to a period of anarchy in China and made possible barbarian raids on the outskirts of Chinese civilization. Wei (Tsin after 265) became the dominant power.

0   200
Miles

H S I E N - P I

T Z U L U
L I A N G

Hsi-hai

HSIUNG-NU
(HUNS)

Pei Ho

Ruins

WU-HUAN

Y U

Liao-tung

Chi

Yen

Ruins

Wu-wei

CH'IANG

P I N G

S S U - L I

C H I

T'ai yuan

Wei

Y E N

Chi

C H I N G

Han-yang

T S I N

Y U N G

Tung

HO-NAN
(Lo-yang)

Ch'iao

P'eng

H S U

Han-chung

Ch'ang-
an

C H' I N G

Hsiang-yang

Y U

Huai

Huai-nan

Y A N G

CHIEN-YEH

c.263, SHU ARMY FLEES WEST FOLLOWING MAJOR DEFEAT BY WEI

L I A N G

Nan

Chiang

c.263

CH'ENG-TU

Chiang

Pa

Y A

c.279

C H I N G

N G

I (-CHOU)

c.263

Tsang-k'e

Chien-ning

I
CHIAO

K U A N G

Nan-hai

c.250, WU EXPEDITION TO INDIAN OCEAN

C H I A O

Chiao-chih

MILITARY KEY
➤ Conquests by Tsin (Chin).
⇨ Raids by barbarians.

© Arthur Banks

GENERAL KEY
▨ Wei kingdom.
▦ Wu kingdom.
▥ Shu (or Minor Han) kingdom.
⋯ Regional boundaries.

THE WESTERN TSIN (CHIN) DYNASTY IN CHINA 265 – 317

Inter-tribal wars aided by nomads.

Huns invade north China and begin a Hun dynasty.

The Chinese princes invite nomad tribes to aid them in their struggles for power. The nomads seize this opportunity to obtain power for themselves and by 317 most of northern China is ruled by Huns or other nomads. The Tsin (Chin) dynasty moves to eastern China.

KEY

→ Invasions by Huns (c.310).

⇨ Retreat of Western Tsin. They form Eastern Tsin, 317.

Ssu Ma Yen (later, Wu Ti) established himself as Emperor in 280. Upon his death, there followed a period of civil war. In the north, the barbarians raided without opposition, killing two Chinese emperors in 313 and 316.

© Arthur Banks

Miles
0   200

Kao-ch'ang
Damna

Ku-mo

Yu-t'ien

Hsi-hai
Wu-wei
T'ien-shui
Shu
Ching-chao (Chang-an)
Han-chung
Nan-p'ing
Chien-ning
Chiao-chih

Ch'ang-sha
Nan-hai (P'an-yü)
Yu-chang

T'ai-yuan
Chao
Ping-yang
Yen
Ho-nan (Loyang)
Yen
Chi
Tan-yang
P'eng
Wu

Liao-tung

Yü-ping

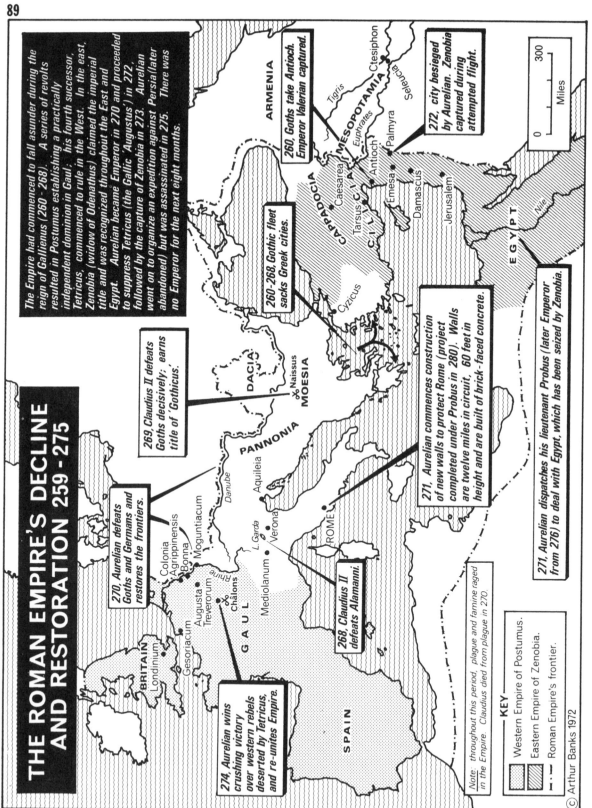

THE ROMAN EMPIRE'S DECLINE AND RESTORATION 259 - 275

The Empire had commenced to fall asunder during the reign of Gallienus (260 - 268). A series of revolts resulted in Postumus establishing a practically independent dominion in Gaul: his fourth successor, Tetricus, commenced to rule in the West. In the east, Zenobia, (widow of Odenathus) claimed the imperial title and was recognized throughout the East and Egypt. Aurelian became Emperor in 270 and proceeded to suppress Tetricus (the Gallic Augustus') in 272, followed by the capture of Zenobia in 273. Aurelian went on to organize an expedition against Persia (later abandoned) but was assassinated in 275. There was no Emperor for the next eight months.

260, Goths take Antioch. Emperor Valerian captured.

272, city besieged by Aurelian. Zenobia captured during attempted flight.

260-268, Gothic fleet sacks Greek cities.

269, Claudius II defeats Goths decisively: earns title of 'Gothicus'.

270, Aurelian defeats Goths and Germans and restores the frontiers.

271, Aurelian commences construction of new walls to protect Rome (project completed under Probus in 280). Walls are twelve miles in circuit, 60 feet in height and are built of brick-faced concrete.

271, Aurelian dispatches his lieutenant Probus (later Emperor from 276) to deal with Egypt, which has been seized by Zenobia.

268, Claudius II defeats Alamanni.

274, Aurelian wins crushing victory over western rebels deserted by Tetricus, and re-unites Empire.

Note: throughout this period, plague and famine raged in the Empire. Claudius died from plague in 270.

KEY
- Western Empire of Postumus.
- Eastern Empire of Zenobia.
- Roman Empire's frontier.

© Arthur Banks 1972

ARMENIA
MESOPOTAMIA
Ctesiphon
Seleucia
Tigris
Euphrates
CAPPADOCIA
Caesarea
Tarsus
CILICIA
Antioch
Emesa
Palmyra
Damascus
Jerusalem
EGYPT
Nile
DACIA
MOESIA
Naissus
PANNONIA
Cyzicus
Aquileia
Danube
L. Garda
Verona
Mediolanum
ROME
GAUL
Colonia Agrippinensis
Bonna
Moguntiacum
Augusta Treverorum
Châlons
Rhine
Gesoriacum
BRITAIN
Londinium
SPAIN

0   300
Miles

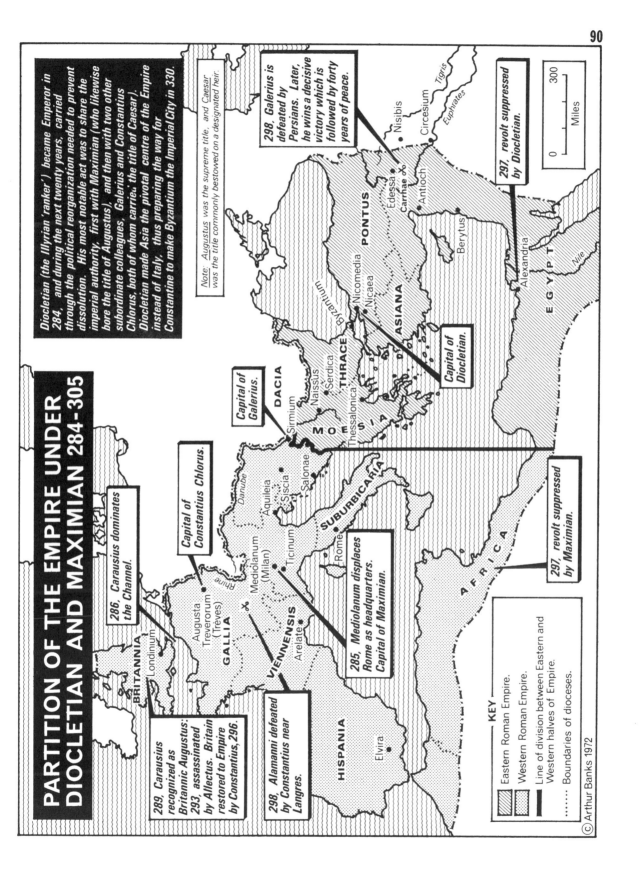

PARTITION OF THE EMPIRE UNDER DIOCLETIAN AND MAXIMIAN 284-305

Diocletian (the Illyrian 'ranker') became Emperor in 284, and during the next twenty years, carried through the political reorganization needed to prevent dissolution. His most notable act was to share the imperial authority, first with Maximian (who likewise bore the title of Augustus), and then with two other subordinate colleagues, Galerius and Constantius Chlorus, both of whom carried the title of Caesar). Diocletian made Asia the pivotal centre of the Empire instead of Italy, thus preparing the way for Constantine to make Byzantium the Imperial City in 330.

Note: Augustus was the supreme title, and Caesar was the title commonly bestowed on a designated heir.

298, Galerius is defeated by Persians. Later, he wins a decisive victory which is followed by forty years of peace.

297, revolt suppressed by Diocletian.

Capital of Diocletian.

Capital of Galerius.

286, Carausius dominates the Channel.

Capital of Constantius Chlorus.

289, Carausius recognized as Britannic Augustus; 293, assassinated by Allectus. Britain restored to Empire by Constantius, 296.

298, Alamanni defeated by Constantius near Langres.

285, Mediolanum displaces Rome as headquarters. Capital of Maximian.

297, revolt suppressed by Maximian.

KEY

- Eastern Roman Empire.
- Western Roman Empire.
- Line of division between Eastern and Western halves of Empire.
- Boundaries of dioceses.

© Arthur Banks 1972

NORTHERN CHINA IN CONFLICT 317-534

❶ 317-352

KEY
- ⊞ Han or Former Chao 304 - 329.
- ▨ Ch'eng Han 304 - 347.
- ▬ Boundary of Later Chao.
- ▨ Former Liang 314 - 376.
- ← Yu invasion to form Later Chao 319 - 352.

Kao-ch'ang

H S I E N - P I

CHIH-PO

Liao-tung

TOBA

YU WEN

MU YUNG

FORMER

Hsi-hai

SHUO

Tai

Yen

YU

Chiu-ch'uan

HSIUNG-NU

c.329

Ku-tsang

Ho

Ho

Chi

T'U-YU-HUN

LIANG

Wei

LIANG

LATER CHAO

Ching-ch'eng

c.329

YEN

Ho-nan

YU

Huai

Ching-chao

c.329

Chien-k'ang

YANG -TI

Han

E. TSIN

CH'ENG HAN

Ch'eng-tu

Shih Lo, an escaped slave, led an army of Huns and annexed most of Former Chao, and founded Later Chao.

0 ———— 200
Miles

---

❷ 352-384

KEY
- ◀ Former Ts'in invasions.
- ▬ Boundary of Former Ts'in.
- ▨ Former Yen 349 - 370.
- ▨ Former Ts'in 351 - 394.

Kao-ch'ang

H S I E N - P I

Liao-tung

TOBA

YU

YEN

FORMER

Tai

Yen

Hsi-hai

376

HSIUNG-NU

376

Chiu-ch'uan

370

Chao

Chi

T'U-YU-HUN

Ho

FORMER

Ho

FORMER

T S'I N

HO

Ching-ch'eng

Ho-nan

YU

YUNG

Following the collapse of Later Chao in 352, Fu Chien, supported by his Tibetan kinsmen, conquered the whole of north China by 376. His invasion of Eastern Ts'in in 383 failed.

Ching-chao

YANG

383

LIANG

CHING

Huai

Chien-k'ang

0 ———— 200
Miles

Ch'eng-tu

E. TSIN

③ 384 - 397

KEY

- Later Yen 384 - 407.
- Western Yen 384 - 394.
- Later Ts'in 384 - 417.
- Western Ts'in 385 - 400,
- (expanded) 409 - 431.
- Later Liang 386 - 403.
- Toba (T'o-pa) position before southern invasion.
- Toba invasion 397.

In 384 the Former Ts'in broke up into tribal states. The Toba nomads (later called Wei) invaded northern China.

0 ___ 200 Miles

④ 397 - 534

KEY

- Southern Liang 397 - 404,
- (expanded) 408 - 414.
- Northern Liang 397 - 439.
- Southern Yen 398 - 410.
- Western Liang 400 - 421.
- (Ta) Hsai 407 - 431.
- Northern Yen 407 - 436.
- Toba expansion.
- Boundary of Northern Wei.

In 417, Later Ts'in fell, and was absorbed into Eastern Ts'in, Wei, and Hsia. The Wei (Toba) then united the whole of north China, and adopted Chinese culture and language.

c. 507, invasion of south China fails, leading to break-up of Northern Wei.

0 ___ 200 Miles

93

THE GOTHS

KEY

➡ Routes of Gothic expansion.

✕ Important battles.

▓ Roman Empire c. 300.

Note: **Ostrogoths** (East Goths) from Dnieper - Don steppes were mainly horsemen. **Visigoths** (West Goths) from the Carpathian region, were mixed horsemen and infantry.

The Goths, emanating from the Baltic, drove out the Sarmatians and dominated eastern Europe as far as the Black Sea. Later, they extended their penetration into Italy and western Europe. Their military tactics were based on forays from their 'laagers' (wagon - forts). An important weakness in attack was their inability to storm walled fortresses.

251, Goths defeat and kill Roman Emperor Decius.

253 - 267, Goths attack coast towns.

378, Goths destroy army of Roman emperor Valens. The result of this battle rocks Roman Empire to its foundations. It marks first victory of heavy cavalry over infantry.

379 - 386, Theodosius makes peace with Goths on Danube and allows them to settle within Empire.

238 - 268, Goths conduct terror-raids.

250, Goths under Cniva defeat Decius at Beroe, and take Philippopolis.

270, Aurelian defeats Goths.

269, Claudius defeats Goths.

451, Goths and Romans under Aetius defeat Attila and Huns.

402, Stilicho the Vandal, general of Emperor Honorius, defeats Alaric.

498, Ostrogoth kingdom established in Italy by Theodoric.

408, Visigoths under Alaric besiege Rome but are bought off. 410, Alaric returns and sacks the "eternal city."

419, Visigoth kingdom founded in south-west Gaul, with consent of Honorius.

© Arthur Banks

THE HUNNISH ASSAULT ON EUROPE c. 400 – 455

KEY

THE ROMAN EMPIRE c. 400

Prefecture of Italy.
Prefecture of Illyricum.
Prefecture of Gaul.
Prefecture of the East.

→ Main advance of the Huns, with dates.

⦿ Cities attacked by the Huns.

1 Arras.
2 Tournai.
3 Amiens.
4 Cambrai.
5 Cologne.
6 Trèves.
7 Mainz.
8 Strasbourg.
9 Rheims.
10 Châlons.
11 Metz.
12 Paris.
13 Orléans.
14 Bergamo.
15 Brescia.
16 Milan.
17 Pavia.
18 Verona.
19 Vicenza.
20 Patavium.
21 Altinum.
22 Aquileia.
23 Sirmium.
24 Singidunum.
25 Viminacium.
26 Ratiaria.
27 Naissus.
28 Sardica.
29 Philippopolis.
30 Constantinople.

BATTLE OF CHÂLONS JUNE 451

Châlons
Marne
AETIUS
ROMANS & FRANKS
GERMANS
① ②
ALANS
HUNS
③
THEODORIC & VISIGOTHS
OSTROGOTHS
ATTILA
◌ Wagon 'laager' (camp)

Strengths and casualties are unknown but are generally accepted as enormous. Had Attila triumphed, Europe would have been ruled by peoples of Asian stock.

454, Huns defeated and dispersed by German coalition at Battle of Nedao.

451, important Hunnish defeat, by Romans and Goths.

451, Huns fail to overrun this important city.

The most important warrior-leader of the Huns was Attila (died, 453).

Roman naval base.

© Arthur Banks

Caspian Sea
Tigris
Euphrates
0 200 Miles
EGYPT
ASIA
PONTUS
Black Sea
Heraclea
Adrianople
Danube
ROME
ITALY
AFRICA
SPAIN
Ebro
Rhine
GAUL
BRITAIN

312
376
c. 376-400
436-450
c. 452
453

THE AGE OF ODOACER, THEODORIC, CLOVIS, AND JUSTINIAN 476 – 568

This map depicts the changing boundaries of the Roman and Teuton powers. During this period, important events included the establishment of the Ostrogothic kingdom of Theodoric, the destruction of the Vandal kingdom by Belisarius, the eviction of the Ostrogoths from Italy by Belisarius and Narses, the expansion of the Eastern Roman Empire, and the Frank advance under Clovis, breaking up the Visigothic kingdom.

Justinian's capital.

538-553, Belisarius and Narses regain Italy for Eastern Emperor, Justinian I.

534, Byzantine general Belisarius destroys Vandal Empire.

554, Restored to Empire under Justinian.

AVARS 559-61

LOMBARDS 568

KEY

■	Original Kingdom of the Franks.
·—··—·	Boundary of Kingdom of the Franks 526.
▨	Extension of Kingdom of the Franks 568.
▦	Kingdom of Syagrius.
▢	Visigothic Kingdom.
▨	Lost part of Visigothic Kingdom.
	Kingdom of Odoacer.
	Boundary of Ostrogothic Kingdom.
	Vandal Kingdom.
□	Boundary of Roman Empire.
	Roman Empire at the death of Justinian 565.
▨	Lombard Kingdom.

0   250
Miles

© Arthur Banks

Tigris
Euphrates
ARABIA
Red Sea
Nile
EGYPT
Alexandria
Damascus
Antioch
ASIA MINOR
Smyrna
Athens
Constantinople
Black Sea
Mediterranean Sea
THRACE
Philippopolis
Sirmium
Danube
Oder
Danube
Elbe
Weser
Vienna
Ravenna
Po
Rome
Carthage
AFRICA
Cologne
Châlons
Seine
Paris
London
Bordeaux
Arles
Barcelona
Ebro
Douro
Cordova
Atlantic Ocean

TRIBAL CONFLICT IN EASTERN EUROPE c.455 – 750

The strife was centred on three main tribes, the Slavs, the Avars, the Khazars. To a lesser extent, the Bulgars (an off-shoot of the Huns) were involved. By 455, the Hunnish invasion of Europe had ebbed, and the Slavs spread rapidly. However, a Mongol tribe known as the Avars penetrated into central Germany by c.550, and this brought them into conflict with the Slavs who eventually gained supremacy (c.650). Meanwhile, the Khazars from Asia had penetrated into the Ukraine, and by 750 had established a kingdom north of the Black and Caspian Seas. The main bulwark against further expansion of all these tribes was the Eastern Roman (or Byzantine) Empire, while, south of the Caspian and expanding westwards, Islam was rapidly becoming a major threat to the whole of southern Europe.

KEY

	Slav expansion 450 - 550.
	The Avar Khanate in 600.
	The Khazar Kingdom in 650.
	Eastern Roman (Byzantine) Empire.

611-619, Syria, Palestine and Egypt taken by Persians. Regained by Heraclius in 628 after brilliant campaign.

c.650, Khazars defeat Alans and Bulgars.

689, Bulgars defeat Justinian II.

c.605, Slavs throw off Avar domination.

c.617-626, Avar attacks supported by Slavs and Persians. 712, Bulgar attack.

597, Slav invasion of Thessaly and settlements in Macedonia and Greece.

582, captured by Avars.

689

ISLAM

Aral Sea

Oxus

Caspian Sea

Volga

ALANS

Don

Dnieper

Black Sea

Constantinople

BULGARS

Dniester

Danube

Sirmium

Vistula

Oder

Dvina

Baltic Sea

Elbe

Rhine

FRANKS

North Sea

Mediterranean Sea

0   200
Miles

97

CHINA 535 – 580

① 535 – 554

KEY
• Capitals of chou (provinces).

The north was locked in conflict whilst the south changed dynasties.

JOU-JAN OR JUAN-JUAN (AJWAR AND KHUNNI)

300 Miles
0

KITAI

EASTERN WEI

WESTERN WEI

LIANG

Chen-La

T'U YU HUN

CHIANG

LIAO

NOTE: THE LIANG DYNASTY WAS FOUNDED BY HSIAO YEN IN 502.

② 555 – 580

KEY
→ Invasions by Northern Chou.
⇨ Invasion by Chen.
━ Boundary of Northern Chou.

T'U - CHUEH (TURKS)

556. Wall renewed.

By 555, the Turks had destroyed the Juan-juan.

Northern Chou gained additional territory by intrigue and invasion.

557. Chen Pa-hsien seizes throne. He founds Ch'en dynasty.

NORTHERN CH'I

NORTHERN CHOU

LATER LIANG

CH'EN

KITAI

T'U YU HUN

CHIANG

LIAO

Chen-La

300 Miles
0

© Arthur Banks

THE SUI SUPREMACY IN CHINA

0 — 200 Miles

Yang Chien rose to power, seized the throne of Northern Chou and founded the Sui dynasty in 581 which endured until 618. The Sui invasion of southern China (589) was successful, and China was re-united after four centuries of chaos.

615, Eastern Turks make a surprise attack against emperor Yang Ti and surround him at Yen-men. He is extricated by the young Li Shih-min whose father, Li Yuan, later seizes the throne and founds T'ang dynasty (618).

Assault against Korea has small success.

NORTHERN (EASTERN) T'U-CHUEH (TURKS)

General Pei Chu defeats the T'u-yu-hun and reaches Sinkiang in 609.

KITAN
TATABI
HSI
611-614
KO-KU-RYE

607-609

T'U - YU - HUN

Tun-huang
Wu-wei
Pei Ho
BUILT 585
BUILT 607
RENEWED 607
Yü-lin
Yen-men Che
Ma-i
Po-ling
Yu-yang
T'ai-yuan
Hsin-tu
Chao Kuo
Hsiang Wu-an
Wei
Chi
Pei-hai
Yen-ch'uan
Yen-an
Shang-tang
Chi
Lu
Ho-tung
Ho-nei
P'eng
Tung-hai
P'ing-i
Ho-nan (Lo-yang)
Shui
Fu-feng
Ching-chao (Ch'ang-an)
Yu-yang
Shun-cheng
An-lu
P'u-an
LIANG
Tan-yang
Wu
Lin-chi'ung
Shu (Ch'eng-tu)
Pa
Chiang
Nan
Chiang
Yin-shan
T'sang-k'e
CHING
Ch'ang-sha
Yu-chang
589
KUN - CHOU
Ch'eng chiang
607-610
Chih-an
I-an
610
(NAN - CHAO)
602-605
Sui forces conquer Yunnan.
General Liu Fang reconquers Tongking and Annam.
Chiu-chen

KEY
← Sui campaigns.
═ Major routes.
⊙ Important administrative centres or local capitals.

© Arthur Banks

ISLAM'S CENTURY OF CONQUEST 632 – 732

1 In the Mediterranean Area

From Egypt the Saracens advanced westwards across northern Africa and secured control of the Mediterranean. In 711 a Saracen force under Tarik crossed the Strait of Gibraltar to Spain and fought a seven-days' battle against Roderic, whose army was annihilated. The Saracens went on to overrun the whole of the Iberian peninsula. Their further penetration into Europe was stayed by Charles Martel who drove them back across the Pyrenees in 732.

716 - 717, Emperor Leo III repels Saracen army besieging Constantinople.

670 - 677, Saracen fleets attack Constantinople.

655, Saracen fleet defeats Byzantine navy in heaviest sea-action since Actium.

642, Byzantines surrender Alexandria.

While Tarik defeats Ostrogoths in Spain, Saracen fleet annexes Sardinia to provide an extra naval base.

711, Gothic king Roderic defeated and killed by Saracens.

732, Charles Martel defeats Saracens under Abdur Rahman.

KEY

- Kingdom of the Franks.
- Eastern Roman Empire.
- The Caliphate.
- Date of conquest.
- ⚔ Important battle.

250

0 Miles

SYRIA 638
Damascus
Antioch
Cyprus 649
Jerusalem
EGYPT 640
SARACEN ARMY 716
CAPPADOCIA
Sinope
Halys
Black Sea
Constantinople
Nicaea
Phoenix ⚔
BARCA (CYRENAICA) 643
Alexandria
TRIPOLIS 644
Tripoli
MAGYARS
BULGARS
Adrianople
Athens
SLAVS
Syracuse
Mediterranean Sea
AVARS
Danube
Sava
Vienna
Vistula
SLAVS
Elbe
SAXONS
Rhine
AUSTRASIA
Danube
NEUSTRIA
Paris
London
Strasbourg
Poitiers ⚔
Loire
AQUITAINE
Lyon
Rhône
Pyrenees
Ebro
Barcelona
Sardinia
682 - 699
Naples
Rome
Venice
Po
Ravenna
LOMBARD KINGD.
Sicily
Carthage
BERBERS
MAURETANIA
SPAIN
Toledo
Tagus
Cordova
Guadalete ⚔
Jebel Tarik 711
Strait of Gibraltar
Atlantic Ocean

© Arthur Banks

100

2 In Asia

Islam absorbed Syria, Egypt, and Armenia. Following their victory at Nehavend in 642, the Saracens went on to gain the whole of Persia, afterwards extending their dominions to the river Indus.

711

652

711

644

632

712, King of Sind defeated and killed by Mohammed bin Kasim.

c.570, birth of Mohammed.

642, Omar defeats Yezdigird. Omar's force of 30,000 troops shatters Persian army of 150,000.

693, Justinian II defeated by Saracens, who seize Armenia.

693

637, Saracens defeat Persian army under Rustom.

638

659, indecisive 2-day battle in civil war between Ali and Muawiya.

Saracen victories over Byzantines (634) and Persians (636).

SARACEN ARMY 716

640

Kashgar

Samarkand

Bokhara

Balkh

Kabul

Multan

PUNJAB

Herat

Aral Sea

Oxus

Jaxartes

Merv

KHORASAN

PERSIA

(SASSANID EMPIRE)

MEDIA

Isfahan

Nehavend

Basra

Caspian Sea

FARS

KERMAN

MEKRAN

Persian Gulf

Arabian Sea

ARABIA

Mecca

Medina

Red Sea

Nile

EGYPT

Alexandria

Jerusalem

Damascus

Yermak

Siffin

Antioch

Edessa

MESOPOTAMIA

Tigris

Euphrates

Baghdad

Kadesia

ARMENIA

Tiflis

Sebastopolis

CAPPADOCIA

Halys

Sinope

Nicaea

Constantinople

Black Sea

INDUS

KEY

Eastern Roman Empire.

The Caliphate.

Date of conquest.

Important battle.

0   250

Miles

© Arthur Banks

THE T'ANG DYNASTY IN CHINA 618 – 907

EARLY GUNPOWDER
c.850, SOME ELEMENTARY FORM OF FLASH POWDER WAS USED BY THE CHINESE FOR SPECTACULAR EFFECTS (EARLY FIREWORKS?).

The T'ang dynasty was commenced by Li Yuan (later, Kao Tsu), and under it, China became large, prosperous, and powerful. The dominant military figure was T'ai Tsung (Li Shih-min) who built up a large cavalry arm, and fought campaigns against the Eastern and Western Turks. Hsuan Tsung repelled Arab penetration in Central Asia, and strengthened Chinese influence in the world.

The T'ang attacks on Turkestan keep open trade routes and separate Tibetan and Turkish nomads from uniting as one army.

The T'ang win the support of the Uigur cavalry in their fight against the common foe – the Eastern and Western Turks.

U I G U R S

NORTHERN (EASTERN) T'U-CHUEH (TURKS)

HUNS?

AVARS?

c.630

c.751

KITAN

PO-HAI

HSI

c.630

c.645-647, 660-668

Jao

Liao-tung

c.640

c.648, c.659

c.737, c.751

T'U-YU-HUN

L U N G

Su

Feng

So

Shan-yu

Wei

Yu

T'sang

Ying

Chi

Te

Lai

HO-PEI

Tai-yuan

Hsi

Pei

Ming

Wei

Yun

Ha

Shan

Yu

KUAN-NEI

Hsiang

Huang Ho

Yen

Chiang

Tsao

c.641

763

Ching-chao

Pien

Sung

HO-NAN

Po

Huai

Sung

Li

Chin

Mao

Kuo

SHAN-NAN

Ch'eng-tu

CHIEN-NAN

Li

829

874

Chiang

Chiang-ling

An

Lu

HUAI-NAN

Jun

Ch'ang

Sheng

Su

Hsuan

Hang

Yueh

Wu

751

754

Yao

T'U-FAN

(TIBET)

CHIANG-NAN

Fu

Fu

PIRATE ATTACKS ON COAST c.765-800

Tao

Lien

NAN-NING, LIU-CHAO (NAN-CHAO)

863

Wu

LING-NAN

Hsun

Kuang

Chiao

Ai

─ MILITARY KEY ─
◀━ T'ang campaigns.
◁━ Invasions by others.

0   200
Miles

© Arthur Banks

─ GENERAL KEY ─
⊙ Important administrative centres with local capitals underlined.
─·─ Western and eastern T'ang frontiers.

TRIPARTITE WAR

Pratiharas fail in attempts to drive Kashmiris from this region.

Pratiharas capital.

Cholas, allied with Eastern Chalukyas, annex Kanchi.

The ninth century was marked by a long three-cornered struggle between the Pratihara (Gurjara) dynasty of Rajputana, the Pala of Bengal, and the Rashtrakuta kings of the Deccan. The two greatest Pratihara rulers were Bhoja I (836-885) and Mahendrapala I (885-910). They drove their two main enemies back from the Ganges valley, and by the early tenth century Pratihara held most of northern India.

ASSAM · TIBET · KASHMIR · SHAHIS · ARABS · PALAS · UTKALA · KALINGA · EASTERN CHALUKYAS · GURJARA–PRATIHARAS · ANARTA · RASHTRAKUTAS · CHOLAS · CHERAS · Kanchi

Indus · Brahmaputra · Tsangpo · Ganges · Jumna · Kanauj · Mahanadi · Narbada · Godavari · Krishna · Jhelum · Chenab · Ravi · Sutlej · Indraprastha · Ujjain

0 — 400 Miles

KEY
— · — Probable boundaries.
▨ Areas of border strife.
⇄ The three-cornered struggle.

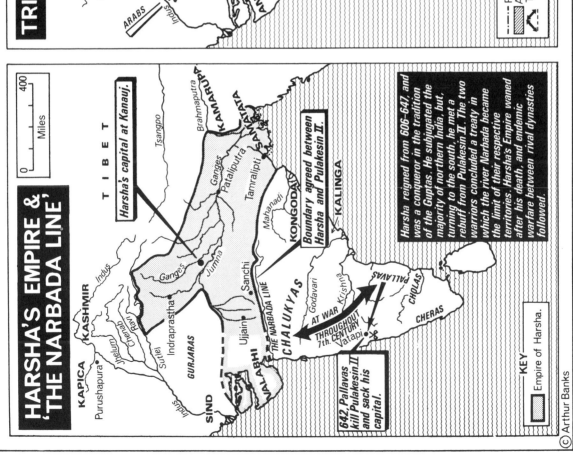

HARSHA'S EMPIRE & 'THE NARBADA LINE'

Harsha's capital at Kanauj.

Boundary agreed between Harsha and Pulakesin II.

642, Pallavas kill Pulakesin II and sack his capital.

Harsha reigned from 606-647, and was a conqueror in the tradition of the Guptas. He subjugated the majority of northern India, but, turning to the south, he met a rebuff from Pulakesin II. The two warriors concluded a treaty in which the river Narbada became the limit of their respective territories. Harsha's Empire waned after his death, and endemic warfare between rival dynasties followed.

KAPICA · Purushapura · KASHMIR · TIBET · KAMARUPA · SAVATA · ASSAM · SIND · GURJARAS · VALABHI · CHALUKYAS · KONGODA · KALINGA · PALLAVAS · CHOLAS · CHERAS · THE NARBADA LINE · Vatapi

AT WAR THROUGHOUT 7th. CENTURY

Indus · Brahmaputra · Tsangpo · Ganges · Jumna · Pataliputra · Tamralipti · Mahanadi · Godavari · Krishna · Jhelum · Chenab · Ravi · Sutlej · Indraprastha · Ujjain · Sanchi

0 — 400 Miles

KEY
▨ Empire of Harsha.

© Arthur Banks

STAGES IN THE MAKING OF ENGLAND AND WALES 600 - 886

In Britain, the Britons were restricted to an ever more limited area in the west, and Northumbrian supremacy passed, first to Mercia, and thence to Wessex. Egbert's "peace" (in 800) was marred by Danish incursions culminating in the Danelaw becoming an independent region. The "Peace of Guthrum" (886), altered its boundaries in favour of Alfred the Great.

© Arthur Banks

The Vikings can be regarded generally as Norse, Danes, and Swedes. The attacks on the British Isles were undertaken by the Norse and Danes, c. 793-900. The Swedes (and Danes) attacked Russia.

THE VIKING ASSAULT ON THE BRITISH ISLES

KEY
- ← Main Viking attacks.
- ▢ Districts settled by Norse or Danes in England, Wales, and Scotland, c.865-900.
- ■ Viking foundations in Ireland.
- ▨ Important Viking base.
- ✂ Important battles.
- Fens or marshes.

Orkney Islands

NORSE

HEBRIDES

SUTHERLAND

CAITHNESS

ROSS

KINGDOM OF PICTS & SCOTS

Iona

NORSE

Edinburgh

Melrose

Lindisfarne Is.

NORSE 793

NORSE c.789

NORSE 794

ENGLISH NORTHUMBRIA

Luel

Durham

STRATHCLYDE

NORSE c.794

Jarrow

Whitby

DANISH NORTHUMBRIA

GALLOWAY

DANES c.836-842

DANES

ULSTER

Armagh

c. 840, taken by Turgeis of Norway.

I. of Man

LANCS

D A N E L A W

Lincoln

NORSE c.800-840

CONNAUGHT

Kells

Tara

795

Chester

DANISH MERCIA

Derby

Nottingham

Stamford

Peterborough

EAST ANGLIA

Dublin

LEINSTER

Limerick

Shannon

Leicester

Cambridge

Cashel

Offa's

Severn

ENGLISH

London

Thames

MUNSTER

Wexford

SOUTH WALES

MERCIA

Ashdown

Waterford

Dyke

Ellandune

Salisbury

Basing

Cork

Wedmore

Winchester

E S S E X

c.800

795

Glastonbury

W

DEVON

Swanage

836-840

DANES

0   60
Miles

WELSH CORNWALL

838 DANES

© Arthur Banks

ALFRED THE GREAT 849–899

1

Territorial key for all maps
- ■ Territory of Wessex at Alfred's accession, April 871.
- ▥ Kingdom of Guthrum.
- ▦ English Mercia.
- ▤ Danish Mercia.

Alfred, fourth of King Æthelwulf's sons to be king, succeeded his brother Æthelred I in April 871. The Danes captured and murdered King Edmund of East Anglia in 869, and next year entered Wessex in force.

11 Winter 877, Gloucester held in force by Danes. They move out in mid-winter (unusual for them), and advance to Chippenham where they defeat Alfred. He seeks refuge west of Selwood.

12 878, Large Danish raiding force from Wales defeated at Countisbury Hill. They lose 800 men.

13 878, Battle of Edington, after seven weeks of hit and run raids by Alfred. Danes decisively defeated. At the Peace of Wedmore Guthrum agrees to leave Wessex and to be baptized into the Christian faith.

9 877, Alfred besieges Danish forces. Later that year they pull back to Gloucester.

Athelney, Alfred's base camp.

8 877, Danes break solemn vow to leave Wessex and night-march to Exeter pursued by Alfred.

Countisbury Hill

Wedmore

Athelney

Exeter

Wareham

Line of R. Avon

CORNWALL

0   15
Miles

NOTE: THE COASTLINE OF SOUTHERN ENGLAND IN ALFRED'S TIME WAS DIFFERENT FROM TODAY. TO AVOID ANY POSSIBLE CONFUSION, MODERN COASTLINES HAVE BEEN SHOWN ON THESE MAPS.

2

0   10
Miles

KEY
- ⬅ Alfred's movements.
- ⬅ Viking movements.

1 Autumn 878, Vikings enter Thames and winter at Fulham. November 879 they return to the Low Countries.

3 885, Alfred captures sixteen Viking ships, but on way home is intercepted and defeated by the Danish fleet.

R. Stour

Benfleet

Fulham

London

Rochester

879

884

878

4 886, Alfred advances into London where his lordship is recognized.

2 Late 884, Vikings return and besiege Rochester. Alfred relieves siege; some Danes flee; others pledge to keep the peace but break promise. Subsequently they leave from Benfleet.

ALFRED THE GREAT – continued

5 *Summer 893, Danes take Chester after day and night marching. English starve them out by burning local corn and seizing local cattle. Danes head into Wales, staying until summer 894.*

1 *893, Hæsten raids Mercia. English force from London attacks his Benfleet camp. Danes remuster at Shoebury.*

4 *893, Danes return to Shoebury.*

3 *Spring 893, fight at Buttington.*

2 *893, Danes from Shoebury ravage up the rivers Thames and Severn.*

Alfred organized his men so that half were being trained to fight while the other half were working on the land. At intervals these halves were changed over, to ensure that a fresh army was always at hand.

0   40
Miles

(Map labels: Chester, Buttington, London, Benfleet, Shoebury)

2 *894-895, Danes move along the River Lea to twenty miles above London.*

3 *895, Alfred dams River Lea forcing Danes to abandon camp.*

4 *895, Danes leave their River Lea camp for Bridgnorth where they stay until 896. In 897 they disperse finally.*

1 *894, Danes from Wales regroup, and establish new camp on Mersea Island.*

5 *896, Danish fleet defeated off Isle of Wight. Danes lose twenty ships.*

0   40
Miles

(Map labels: Bridgnorth, Mersea I., London, Isle of Wight)

ALFRED'S SYSTEM OF FORTIFIED TOWNS

This map shows the most important fortresses.

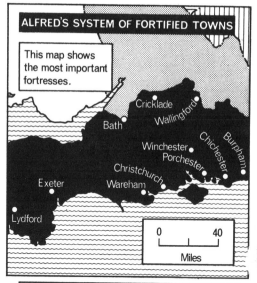

(Map labels: Cricklade, Wallingford, Bath, Winchester, Porchester, Chichester, Burpham, Christchurch, Exeter, Wareham, Lydford)

0   40
Miles

The story of Alfred "burning the cakes", is based on an interpolation from the annals of St. Neot in Asser's "Life of Alfred".

THE ANGLO-SAXON CHRONICLE

The Anglo-Saxon Chronicle consists collectively of 7 annalistic compilations written in Old English. (There are, too, at least 3 Latin versions.) Each begins with an outline of history from Julius Caesar until the ⑤. Until the entry for 891 the compilations are remarkably similar and until 915 much common material is used. Then the details recorded in each manuscript diverge considerably. The latest entry of all the manuscripts is for 1154 in that written at Peterborough Abbey.

The story of Alfred wandering in the Danish camp dressed as a minstrel is based on an account told in William of Malmesbury's "De Gestis Regum".

Alfred, born 849 at Wantage. Before the age of 7 he had undertaken two journeys to Rome. He was taught Latin later in life by Asser, and between 892 and 899 when he died, he produced five Latin works. (Translations of Gregory's Cura Pastoralis, Orosius's history of the ancient world, Bede's Historia Ecclesiastica, Boethius's De Consolatione Philosophiae, and St. Augustine's Soliloquies).

EUROPE c. 800

The principal historical event in Europe at this period was the creation of the Holy Roman Empire as the main power in Western Europe. As established by Charlemagne it comprised Gallo-Latin Neustria, Lombard Italy, and Teutonic Austrasia. In Spain, the Ummayad emirate was established by Abd-er-Rahman. Islam was in control of Africa and western Asia (but not Asia Minor). Finally, Bulgarian and Serbian kingdoms were coming into being.

781, Alcuin of York appointed by Charlemagne to lead revival of learning.

Charlemagne subdues Saxons (772-804), Bavarians (788), and Avars (791-796).

773-4, Charlemagne helps Pope against Lombard invasion.

800, Charlemagne crowned Holy Roman Emperor.

810, Charlemagne makes peace with Emir of Cordova.

Charlemagne's capital.

778, Charlemagne's rearguard ambushed by Wascones.

798, allied with Charlemagne.

KEY
- Charlemagne's Empire.
- Lands tributary to Charlemagne.
- The Eastern Roman Empire.
- The Caliphate of the Abbasids.

© Arthur Banks

THE SHORT-LIVED KITAN ASCENDANCY IN CHINA

❶ Later Liang 907-923

KITAN (reindeer-using people)

UIGURS · Kan
Liang
SHA-T'O
c. 923
TSIN
Yu
YEN
· T'ai yuan
T'U-FAN
CH'I
W. Capital
LATER LIANG
TERRITORY OF SHENG-SHIH
CHU
CHING-NAN
E. Capital
Yang
Hang
Ch'eng-tu
Ching
FORMER SHU
WU
WU-YUEH
MIN
Fu
Kuang

Struggles for power dominated the period 907-960 (the main moves are shown by arrows on maps). The Kitan were granted land in northern China for aid extended to the Later Tsin in their fight for supremacy. Thus, the Kitan gained a strategic foothold for their invasion.

0 ——— 300
Miles

❷ Later T'ang 923-936

KITAN 936

UIGURS · Kan
Ling
SHA-T'O
Yu
N. Residency
LATER T'ANG
W. Capital
E. Capital
Chiang-tu
T'U-FAN
S. P'ING
LATER SHU
Ching
Hang
T'an
Hung
WU YUEH
Ta-li
TA-TIEN-HSING
TA-I-NING
C'HU
MIN
Ch'ang-lo
ANNAM
S. HAN
Kuang
Ta-lo

0 ——— 300
Miles

❸ Later Tsin 936-946 and Later Han 947-950

KITAN

UIGURS · Kan
Yun
S. Residency
Ling
SHA-T'O
947
N. Residency
LATER TSIN (KITAN)
W. Capital & E. Capital
T'U FAN
LATER HAN
S. P'ING
Chiang-tu
LATER SHU
Ching
Hang
T'an
S. T'ANG
WU YUEH
LO-TIEN
CH'U
YIN
Fu
Ta-li
TA-LI
S. HAN
MIN
ANNAM
Kuang
Ta-lo

0 ——— 300
Miles

❹ Later Chou 951-960

KITAN E. Residency

UIGURS · Kan
S. Residency
SHA-T'O
N. HAN
Ping
TANGUT
LATER CHOU
W. Residency
E. Residency
LATER SHU
S. P'ING
Chiang-ning
Hang
Ching
T'an
CH'U
S. T'ANG
WU YUEH
Ta-li
LO TIEN
TA-LI
S. HAN
ANNAM
Kuang
Ta-lo

0 ——— 300
Miles

© Arthur Banks

NOMADIC ASCENDANCY IN CHINA 960-1281

Chao K'uang-yin (Sung dynasty) united southern China but the north remained under the Kitan (Liao dynasty). The Jurchen nomads invaded Liao and founded the Chin dynasty. The Mongols invaded China conquering the Chin (1234) and the Southern Sung (1279).

Mongols besiege and capture K'ai-feng-tu.

EARLY GUNNERY?
The refining of organic saltpetre by distillation is usually attributed to Francis Bacon (an English Franciscan friar) in 1249. However, during the siege of K'ai-feng-tu by the Mongols in 1233, the defenders employed an iron tube filled with a drug which produced 'heaven-quaking thunder'. Whether or not it was a propellant is undetermined.

KEY

↓ Mongol (Yuan) invasions.

⊙ Important administrative centres.

CHIN ⎯⎯ Boundary between Southern Sung
S.SUNG ▬▬ (1127-1279) and Chin (after 1234, Yuan).

© Arthur Banks

111

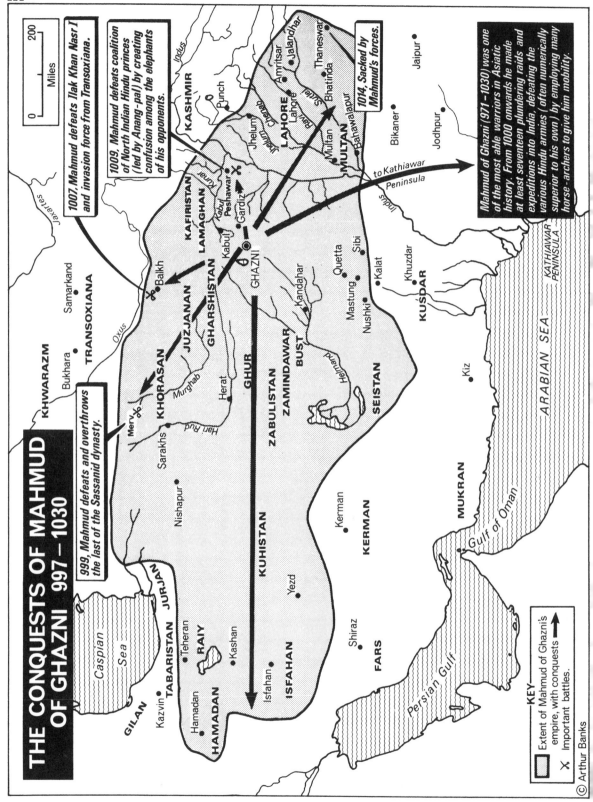

THE CONQUESTS OF MAHMUD OF GHAZNI 997–1030

999, Mahmud defeats and overthrows the last of the Sassanid dynasty.

1007, Mahmud defeats Ilak Khan Nasr I and invasion force from Transoxiana.

1009, Mahmud defeats coalition of North Indian Hindu princes (led by Anang-pal) by creating confusion among the elephants of his opponents.

1014, Sacked by Mahmud's forces.

Mahmud of Ghazni (971–1030) was one of the most able warriors in Asiatic history. From 1000 onwards he made at least seventeen plundering raids and expeditions into India, defeating the various Hindu armies (often numerically superior to his own) by employing many horse-archers to give him mobility.

KEY
Extent of Mahmud of Ghazni's empire, with conquests
Important battles.

© Arthur Banks

112

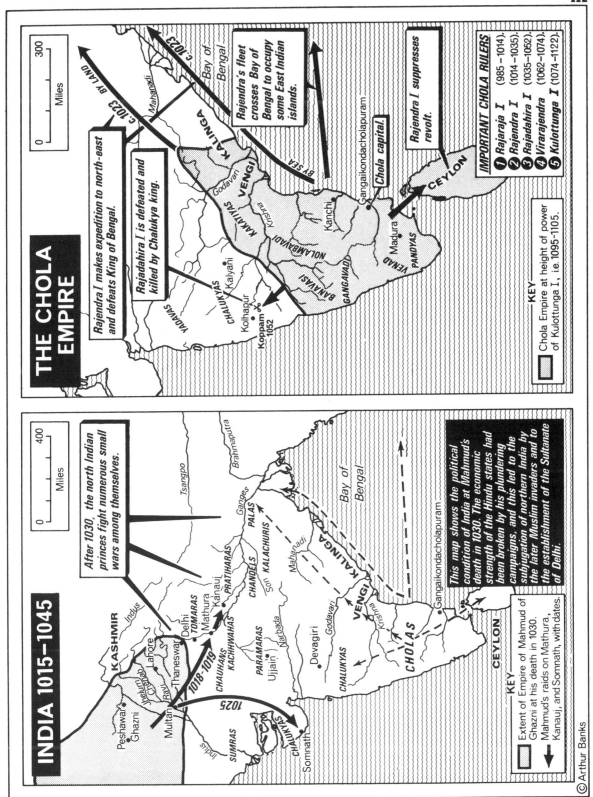

THE CHOLA EMPIRE

300
0
Miles

Rajendra I makes expedition to north-east and defeats King of Bengal.

c. 1023

BY LAND
c. 1022

Mahanadi

Bay of Bengal

KALINGA

VENGI

Godavari

Rajadahira I is defeated and killed by Chalukya king.

KAKATIYADS

Krishna

CHALUKYAS
Kalyani

Kolhapur
Koppam
1052

YADAVAS

NOLAMBAVADI

GANGAVADI

BANAVASI

Kanchi

VENAD

Madura

PANDYAS

Gangaikondacholapuram

Chola capital.

BY SEA

Rajendra's fleet crosses Bay of Bengal to occupy some East Indian islands.

Rajendra I suppresses revolt.

CEYLON

IMPORTANT CHOLA RULERS

❶ Rajaraja I (985–1014).
❷ Rajendra I (1014–1035).
❸ Rajadahira I (1035–1052).
❹ Virarajendra (1062–1074).
❺ Kulottunga I (1074–1122).

KEY

Chola Empire at height of power of Kulottunga I, i.e. 1095–1105.

INDIA 1015–1045

400
0
Miles

After 1030, the north Indian princes fight numerous small wars among themselves.

Tsangpo

Brahmaputra

KASHMIR

Indus

Jhelum
Chenab
Ravi

Peshawar
Ghazni
Lahore
Multan

Thaneswar
Delhi
TOMARAS
Mathura
Kanauj
PRATIHARAS

Ganges

PALAS

CHANDELS

KALACHURIS
Son

CHAUHANS
1018–1019
KACHHWAHAS

1025

SUMRAS

Indus

Somnath

CHALUKYAS

PARAMARAS
Ujjain

Narbada
Narbada

Devagiri

Mahanadi

Godavari

Krishna

VENGI

CHALUKYAS

KALINGA

Bay of Bengal

Gangaikondacholapuram

CHOLAS

CEYLON

This map shows the political condition of India at Mahmud's death in 1030. The economic strength of the Hindu states had been broken by his plundering campaigns, and this led to the subjugation of northern India by the later Muslim invaders and to the establishment of the Sultanate of Delhi.

KEY

Extent of Empire of Mahmud of Ghazni at his death in 1030.

Mahmud's raids on Mathura, Kanauj, and Somnath, with dates.

© Arthur Banks

② Normandy in 1066

Wind direction
mid August - 26 September → EAST

0 ———— 30
Miles

700 SHIPS

St. Valéry

Somme

12 September, William moves his fleet from Dives to St. Valéry to reduce time and distance when crossing Channel.

① ROUEN

Lillebonne

Seine

Dives

⑥

BAYEUX

CAEN

LISIEUX

ÉVREUX

⑤

③

②

COUTANCES

④

SÉES

AVRANCHES

⑦

Early summer, William calls conference of barons to discuss plans for the invasion of England.

———— NORMAN BISHOPRICS ————

❶ Rouen ❷ Évreux ❸ Lisieux ❹ Sées ❺ Bayeux ❻ Coutances ❼ Avranches

③ The Battle of Hastings

0 ———— 400
Yards

PHASE ONE

Harold's rendezvous.

to London

CALDBEC HILL

to Lewes

KEY

⚑ Harold's Command Post.

▬ Saxon phalanx (formed into a 'shield wall').

⚐ William's Command Post.

▲▲▲ William's forces (in 3 divisions).

HOUSECARLS IN FRONT. MILITIA IN CENTRE AND REAR RANKS.

HAROLD (8,000)

ARRANGED IN 10 RANKS

FRANCO-FLEMISH (1,600)

BRETONS (2,400)

NORMANS (4,000)

WILLIAM ⚐

to Hastings →

▲▲▲ ARCHERS.
▭ INFANTRY.
▱ CAVALRY.

PHASE TWO

HIGH GROUND

HAROLD
SAXON SHIELD WALL

① William's infantry opens attack uphill. Saxon house-carls stand firm and fight off assaults. William notes lack of progress and begins a mock retreat hoping to lure Saxons from their high ground. Ruse succeeds ②.

WILLIAM
LOW GROUND

PHASE THREE

Harold slain.

As Saxons reach the lower ground, William commits his cavalry (manoeuvrable on this terrain) and archers (effective now that Saxon shield wall no longer exists). Despite fierce resistance, the Saxons are defeated.

THE IMPORTANCE OF THE ENGLISH CHANNEL IN WAR

❶ In 1066

North Sea

LONDON

8 September, Harold disbands his fleet.

WESSEX — Hastings

STRAIT OF DOVER

Pevensey Bay

FLANDERS

NIGHT 27-28 SEPTEMBER

ENGLISH CHANNEL

PONTHIEU

St. Valéry

Somme

12 SEPTEMBER

NORMANDY

Dives

0 20 40
Miles

Without any Saxon opposition in the English Channel, William of Normandy was able to move his invasion force across the water barrier.

❷ In 1588

NORTH SEA

ENGLAND

Plymouth

LONDON

Dunkirk

ENGLISH CHANNEL

August, Duke of Parma cannot cross to England until the Armada gains sea control.

KEY
English naval screen.

BAY OF BISCAY

The main Spanish ships were ponderous floating forts – no match against the English ships (fast and small; ideal in the Channel).

❸ In 1805

NORTH SEA

E N G L A N D

LONDON

BRITISH
Boulogne

ENGLISH CHANNEL

BRITISH
Brest

Napoleon cannot invade England until his Fleet can ensure unhindered passage across Strait of Dover.

BAY OF BISCAY

Rochefort

BRITISH

F R A N C E

The British sea blockade of French ports, coupled with Nelson's victory at Trafalgar, ended French plans to cross Channel.

0 50 100
Miles

❹ In 1940

North Sea

LONDON

ENGLAND

R.A.F. FIGHTER COMMAND

Dunkirk

Calais
Boulogne

ENGLISH CHANNEL

Summer, Hitler is unable to invade Britain without air-mastery.

GERMAN-OCCUPIED FRANCE

'Operation Sealion' (German plan for invading Britain) was abandoned following defeat of Luftwaffe (German Air Force) in Battle of Britain.

0 20 40
Miles

© Arthur Banks

WILLIAM THE CONQUEROR 1066

0 10 20 30
Miles

Archbishop of Canterbury comes to do homage.

Berkhamsted

MIDDLE DECEMBER

Unopposed advance

Chief men of England meet William and submit London. He is crowned King William I of England on 25 December.

Wallingford

LONDON • Barking

NOVEMBER

Ravaging

Thames

Southwark Set ablaze

Ravaging

EARLY DECEMBER

Canterbury 29 OCT.

OCTOBER

21 OCT.

Normans racked by sickness.

William realized the strategical importance of London but could not attack it with his small disease-stricken force. He decided to isolate it by an outflanking march to the west.

Dover

Folkestone

Cities submit after William devastates Romney.

Normans regroup.

Winchester

OLD WEST SAXON CAPITAL

Edith (widow of Edward the Confessor) offers submission of city to William. News received with dismay in London.

Northiam 20 OCTOBER

Romney

14 OCTOBER ⚔ Hastings

KEY
William's campaign following the Battle of Hastings (Senlac).

LATER NORMAN CAMPAIGNS IN ENGLAND

0 50 Miles

1068, William negotiates truce with Scottish king Malcolm III. January 1069, William relieves siege of York by rebels. During 1069 Danes capture York but are expelled by William and in 1070 they sail home. In 1072, William invades Scotland by land and sea. Malcolm submits.

to Scotland

NORTH-UMBRIA

1070, laid waste.

NORTHERN CAPITAL

York

Humber

KEY
Norman campaigns (main stages) 1067.
Norman campaigns (main stages) 1068.
Norman campaigns (main stages) 1070.
Sweyn Estrithson's first attack 1069.
Area of Danish activity in 1069.
Sweyn Estrithson's second attack 1070.

Chester

Lincoln

NORTH SEA

Nottingham

Peterborough

FENS

EAST ANGLIA

1070, Hereward the Wake supports Danes in raid.

Stafford

MERCIA

Ely

1071, Earl Morcar joins rebels who surrender. Hereward escapes.

1068-1069, Harold's sons raid Somerset with Viking fleet from Ireland.

Rebels defeated.

Huntingdon

Cambridge

1069, Osbearn (Sweyn Estrithson's brother) leads attack on Kent, later moving north.

WALES WAS NOT ATTACKED IN FORCE UNTIL circa 1100

Hereford

Warwick

240 SHIPS

Bristol

E S S E X

LONDON

1067, revolt of Edric, Bleddyn, and Riwallon comes to naught.

1067, city submits following siege.

W E S S E X

Winchester

Dover

FLANDERS

to Cornwall

Exeter

Boulogne

ENGLISH CHANNEL

1067, attack by Eustace on Dover repelled.

© Arthur Banks

117

NORMAN RULE IN ENGLAND

There were no surnames in England before William's invasion. The Norman barons brought names with them which often still remain, sometimes with adaptations. For examples, **Robert de Mortain** (Morton); **William de Warenne** (Warren), etc. (Note: "fitz" means 'son of').

Two features of the Norman conquest were castles and feudalism. Before the conquest, defence was in the form of 'burghs' (fortified towns) and was communal. The Norman barons (who were rewarded with land for their services) built private forts of their own to protect their properties. The early castles were primitive, but later versions were of stone, and the 'keep' became an important feature. Land tenure was a vital part of feudal society as the barons were required to supply knights for the King's service. The Royal forests caused great hardship to the peasants who were forbidden to fell trees or kill deer.

ROYAL FORESTS

0 20 40
Miles

Bamburgh
Morpeth
Tynemouth
Carlisle
Newcastle on Tyne
Durham
Robert de Mortain
Richmond
Alan of Brittany
Clitheroe
William de Percy
Gilbert de Gand
Archbishop of York
York
Hugh d'Avranches
Bishop of Durham
Roger de Poitou
Pontefract
Ilbert de Lacy
Gilbert de Gand
William de Warenne
Tickhill
William Peverel
Blyth
Alan of Brittany
Chester
Peak
Roger de Busli
Lincoln
William de Percy
Hugh d'Avranches
Henry de Ferrers
Nottingham
Ivo Taillebois
Binham
Tutbury
Alan of Brittany
Castle Acre
Norwich
Oswestry
Stafford
Derby
Belvoir
Shrewsbury
Robert de Tosny
William de Warenne
Roger Bigod
Montgomery
Thorkill of Arden
Count of Meulan
Peterborough
Ely
Thetford
Roger de Montgomery
Ralph de Mortimer
Rockingham
Robert Malet
Eye
Wigmore
Dudley
William Peverel
Huntingdon
Richard's Castle
Roger de Lacy
Warwick
Cambridge
Bury St Edmunds
William fitz Osbern
Worcester
Alan of Brittany
Richard of Clare
Clifford
Hereford
Countess Judith
Clare
Ewyas Harold
Henry de Gifford
Aubrey de Vere
Colchester
Carmarthen
Tewkesbury
Robert d'Oilly
Roger d'Ivry
Hertford
Pleshey
Monmouth
Gloucester
Oxford
Ralph de Tosny
Geoffrey de Mandeville
Chepstow
Berkeley
St Albans
Pembroke
Caerleon
Bristol
Henry de Ferrers
Wallingford
Eustace de Boulogne
LONDON
Rochester
Geoffrey de Mowbray
Malmesbury
Windsor
Odo Bishop of Bayeux
Canterbury
Edward of Salisbury
Hugh de Port
Tonbridge
Richard of Clare
Dover
Dunster
Old Sarum
Winchester
William de Braose
Battle
Barnstaple
Bishop of Winchester
Romsey
Bramber
Lewes
Hastings
Baldwin the Sheriff
Robert de Mortain
Christchurch
Arundel
Pevensey
Okehampton
Exeter
Chichester
Corfe
Carisbrooke
William de Warenne
Launceston
William fitz Osbern
Robert Count of Eu
Judhael of Totnes
Robert de Mortain
Robert de Mortain
Totnes

KEY

★ Important castles.   ⊕ Churches, abbeys, monasteries, etc.   ▮ Principal lords.

© Arthur Banks

THE EARLY NORMAN KINGDOMS 1067 – 1199

1072, Malcolm III of Scotland submits to William I.

1069, rebels trap and kill Robert de Comines.

1069, Anglo-Danish rising in North. Rebels take York, but William I suppresses revolt.

1138, Northern barons defeat David I of Scotland at the Battle of the Standard.

1069-1070, 'harrying' of the North by William.

1075, William I suppresses revolt of Earls of Hereford and Norfolk.

1136, Griffith ap Rhys routs Norman and Flemish colonists.

1170, Norman knights kill Thomas-à-Becket.

1167-1171, invasions by Henry II or vassals.

1197, Richard I defeats Philip II.

1081-1171, Norman attacks.

1119, Henry I defeats Louis VI.

1106, Henry I defeats Robert of Normandy.

1087, William and Philip I at war. 1087-1100, William II and his brother Robert continually at war.

1199, Richard I dies of wound incurred during siege.

IRELAND

Durham

Northallerton

York

ENGLAND

WALES

Norfolk

Hereford

London

Canterbury

Calais

Rouen

Château Gaillard

Gizors
Brémule
Paris

Caen

NORMANDY

Marne

Tinchebrai

Seine

BRITTANY

MAINE

Le Mans

Orléans

Angers

ANJOU

Loire

POITOU

Poitiers

AQUITAINE

Châlus

Dordogne

Bordeaux

Rhône

GASCONY

Garonne

Nîmes

Toulouse

TOULOUSE

0   100
Miles

KEY

- Areas ruled by William the Conqueror (1071-1087).
- French province (revolted 1069) retaken by William 1073.
- Invaded by William 1076, but campaign abandoned.
- Possessions of King of France by 1189.
- Dependencies of King of France by 1189.
- Possessions of Henry II in 1189.
- Dependencies of Henry II in 1189.
- ✗ Important battles.

© Arthur Banks

NORMAN CONQUESTS IN SICILY AND SOUTHERN ITALY

0   100
Miles

1 1053, Normans defeat and capture Pope Leo IX.

7 1081, Robert Guiscard is defeated in naval battle. The Venetian fleet is present at this engagement. October 1081, he gains land victory over Byzantine Emperor Alexius Commenus, in which Anglo-Saxons are involved on the Byzantine side.

4 1071, Robert Guiscard captures last Byzantine stronghold in Italy.

6 1081, Robert Guiscard defeats George Paleologus.

8 1084, Robert Guiscard raises Henry IV's siege, but the Normans sack city.

2 1059, at Melfi, Pope Nicolas II grants Normans Capua, Apulia, Calabria, and Sicily (when captured from the Saracens).

3 1061, Robert and Roger Guiscard take Messina.

5 1071, Robert and Roger Guiscard capture Saracen capital.

9 1084, indecisive sea battle between Normans and Byzantines/Venetians.

11 1061-1090, Roger Guiscard takes Sicily from Saracens and becomes Count of Sicily (1072). His son Roger is crowned King of Sicily 1130. In 1146, his capture of Tripoli initiates a Norman colony in Africa.

10 1086, surrender of Syracuse to Roger Guiscard.

12 1090, Malta is taken by Roger Guiscard.

ADRIATIC SEA

TYRRHENIAN SEA

IONIAN SEA

PRINCIPALITY OF CAPUA

PRINCIPALITY OF BENEVENTO

COUNTY OF APULIA

COUNTY OF AVERSA

PRINCIPALITY OF SALERNO

PULIA

CALABRIA

SICILY

Rome — Tiber

Civitate — S. Michele — Siponto — Troia — Cannae — Bari — Durazzo

Alifa — Capua — Beneventum — Melfi — Spinazzola

Gaeta — Naples — Salerno — Amalfi

Tarentum — Otranto — Corfu

Rossano — Croton

Palermo — Messina — Rhegium — Castrogiovanni — Catania — Girgenti — Syracuse

1058 — 1063 — 1077 — 1042 — 1137 — 1030 — 1077 — 1077 — 1080 — 1057 — 1090

KEY

- First Norman territories, with dates.
- Territory captured from Lombards, with dates.
- Territory captured from Eastern Roman Empire, with dates.
- Territory captured from Saracens, with dates.
- ✂ Important battles, with dates.

© Arthur Banks

The first Norman stronghold was established at Aversa in 1027, and in later years, Norman influence spread across Southern Italy and Sicily. Robert and Roger Guiscard were the most prominent Norman leaders at this period, and were engaged in wars and battles with the Moslems and Byzantines. Robert's son Bohemund and other Normans took part in the Crusades.

THE GROWTH OF THE FRENCH MONARCHY 987–1328

0   100
Miles

London

Winchester   Canterbury

Hastings

Nijmegen

Antwerp

Bruges   Ghent   Brussels   Cologne

Ypres   Bouvines   Maastricht

Maas

PICARDY

PONTHIEU

COUNTY OF ARTOIS

Rheims

Trier

Luxemburg

HOLY ROMAN EMPIRE

Verdun   Metz

DUCHY OF NORMANDY

Saint–Denis

Paris

COUNTY OF CHAMPAGNE

DUCHY OF LORRAINE

DUCHY OF BRITTANY

MAINE

Seine

Orléans

DUCHY OF ANJOU

BLOIS

DUCHY OF BURGUNDY

TOURAINE

Loire

Bourges

DUCHY OF BERRY

COUNTY OF BURGUNDY

POITOU

Poitiers

DUCHY OF BOURBON

Saône

COUNTY OF SAVOY

ANGOULEME

BRESSE

Lyon

GUYENNE

AUVERGNE

DUCHY

COUNTY OF PÉRIGORD

DAUPHINÉ

Valence

Bordeaux

DUCHY OF OF AQUITAINE

Garonne

Rhone

Avignon

GASCONY   COUNTY OF TOULOUSE

COUNTY OF PROVENCE

Arles

Albi

LANGUEDOC

ARMAGNAC

Toulouse

KINGDOM OF ARAGON

KEY

▦ Crown domains on accession of Philip II Augustus in 1180.

▦ Acquisitions under Philip II (1180–1223).

☐ Acquisitions under Louis VIII, Louis IX, and Philip III (1223–1285).

▤ Acquisitions under Philip IV (1285–1314).

⋯ English territory in 1328.

■ The County of Flanders.

▥ Other areas under French suzerainty.

– – – Domain of French Monarchy in 987.

••••• English "fiefs" (land held by feudal tenure) in 1180.

–·–·– County of Toulouse in 1208.

▬▬ Boundary between France and Holy Roman Empire in 1208.

© Arthur Banks

In 987, the French nobles elected Hugh Capet, Count of Paris, as King. By the time he died in 996, he had created the basis for a future strong monarchy. The Capet dynasty reigned without a break in the male line of succession until the Revolution.

THE EARLY CRUSADES 1096 - 1192

0   300
Miles

IRELAND

KINGDOM
OF
ENGLAND

London

Paris

Metz

Rhine

Regensburg

KINGDOM

Orléans

Vézelay

HOLY

OF

Lyon

ROMAN

FRANCE

EMPIRE

Toulouse

Turin

Genoa

Venice

Za

Marseilles

KDM. OF LEON

Burgos

KINGDM.
OF
CASTILE

PORTUGAL

Ebro

Barcelona

Rome

Tagus

Lisbon

DMNS.

Cordova

THE

Naples

OF

Br

ALMORAVIDES

Almeria

M e d i t e

Palermo

Tunis

Sicily

r
a
n
e
a
n

The Crusades were military expedi
undertaken by West Europeans ost
for religious motives, and their av
object was the liberation of the Ho
(particularly Jerusalem). Howeve
political motives were also involve
1071, the defeat of the Byzantines
Moslem Seljuk Turks at Manzikert
followed by the Seljuk conquest o
Jerusalem, focused Western atten
the Holy Land. The persecution of
Christians and the Seljuk conquest
Anatolia inflamed Christendom, a
Urban II's appeal for material actio
1095 ignited the smouldering rage
West. (Note: the term 'crusade' wa
applied to any expedition against a
Christian foe).

Note: military orders of monks made their debût: the Teutonic Knights; the Knights
Templars; the Knights Hospitallers (St. John). Also growing friction between the Greek Orthodox
Church of Constantinople and the Roman Catholic Church had ominous signs for the future, and
was reflected in the worsening relations between the Crusaders and the Byzantine Emperor,
culminating in the shameful sack of Constantinople in 1204.

The First Crusade proper was preceded by a "People's
Crusade" of French and German peasants, led by the
fanatical Peter the Hermit. In 1096, they marched
through Europe murdering Jews, looting, and fighting
the Balkan peasantry. About one-third eventually
crossed the Bosporus and were annihilated by the
Seljuks near Nicaea.

KEY

⟹ First Crusade.

⟹ Second Crusade.

➤ Third Crusade.

ERS

nar de Monteil (Papal Legate).
mund of Taranto.
ed (Bohemund's nephew).
ond of Toulouse.
ey de Bouillon of Lorraine.
vin (Godfrey's brother).
of Vermandois.(Louis VI's brother)
t of Normandy.(William I's son).
en of Blois.(William I's son-in-law).
t of Flanders.

Leaders of later Crusades are
n on map entitled:
Later Crusades 1202-1270"

SECOND CRUSADE 1147-1149

LEADERS
Conrad III of Germany.
Louis VII of France.
Baldwin III of Jerusalem.

THIRD CRUSADE 1189-1192

LEADERS
Frederick I (Barbarossa) of Germany.
Philip II (Augustus) of France.
Richard I (Cœur de Lion) of England.
Leopold of Austria.

MILITARY LESSONS OF THE CRUSADES

TACTICS
The value of manœuvrability; the use of light cavalry
for reconnaissance; the significance of horse-archery;
the importance of combining cavalry and infantry.

FORTIFICATIONS
Castle and city defence systems were completely
revised in the West. The turreted walls (with double
or triple concentric defence lines) of Byzantine
strongpoints were noted in particular.

LOGISTICS
The importance of sea-power; the need for supply
bases; the improvement of organization techniques.

1109, Norman, Lombard, and
German Crusaders under Raymond
and Stephen of Blois, severely
defeated in attempt to rescue
Bohemund.

1100-1103, Bohemund
imprisoned here.

Caspian Sea

NGDOM OF UNGARY

Belgrade
Danube
KDM. OF BULGARIA
Black Sea
Adrianople
Constantinople
Sinope
Trebizond
BIA
hessalonica
Nicaea 1101
Kastamuni
Mersivan
SELJUK KINGDOM OF ICONIUM
Sivas
Dorylaeum
Angora
Athens
Iconium (Konya)
Edessa
COUNTY OF EDESSA
Tigris
Smyrna
Aleppo
Antioch
PRIN. OF ANTIOCH
Euphrates
Cyprus
Tripoli
KINGDOM OF JERUSALEM
Crete
Tyre
Acre
Sea
Jaffa
Jerusalem
Damietta
Ascalon
Cairo

123

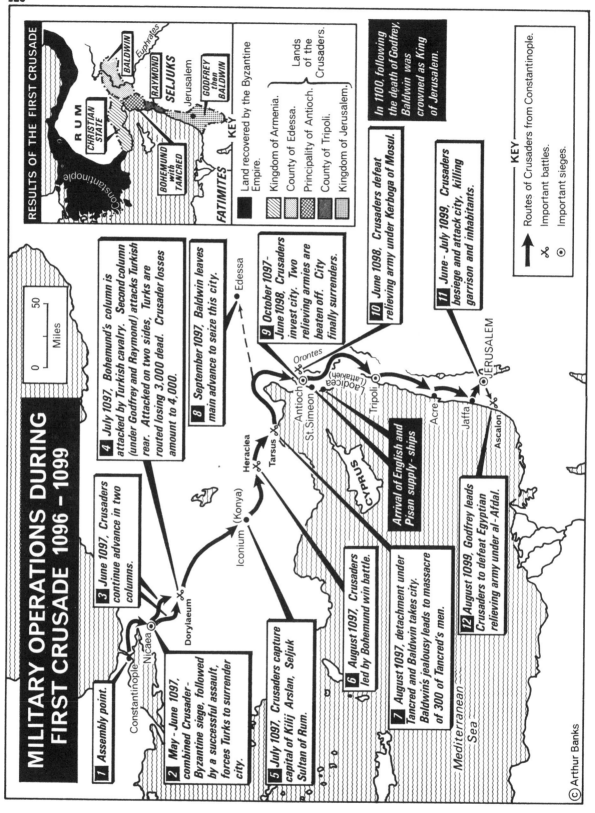

MILITARY OPERATIONS DURING FIRST CRUSADE 1096 – 1099

RESULTS OF THE FIRST CRUSADE

0 50 Miles

KEY

- Land recovered by the Byzantine Empire.
- Kingdom of Armenia.
- County of Edessa.
- Principality of Antioch.
- County of Tripoli.
- Kingdom of Jerusalem.

KEY
- → Routes of Crusaders from Constantinople.
- ✗ Important battles.
- ⊙ Important sieges.

CHRISTIAN STATE
RUM
SELJUKS
FATIMITES
Constantinople
Euphrates
BALDWIN
RAYMOND
GODFREY then BALDWIN
BOHEMUND with TANCRED
Jerusalem

Lands of the Crusaders.

In 1100, following the death of Godfrey, Baldwin was crowned as King of Jerusalem.

1 Assembly point.

2 May - June 1097, combined Crusader-Byzantine siege, followed by a successful assault, forces Turks to surrender city.

3 June 1097, Crusaders continue advance in two columns.

4 July 1097, Bohemund's column is attacked by Turkish cavalry. Second column (under Godfrey and Raymond) attacks Turkish rear. Attacked on two sides, Turks are routed losing 3,000 dead. Crusader losses amount to 4,000.

5 July 1097, Crusaders capture capital of Kilij Arslan, Seljuk Sultan of Rum.

6 August 1097, Crusaders led by Bohemund win battle.

7 August 1097, detachment under Tancred and Baldwin takes city. Baldwin's jealousy leads to massacre of 300 of Tancred's men.

8 September 1097, Baldwin leaves main advance to seize this city.

9 October 1097 - June 1098, Crusaders invest city. Two relieving armies are beaten off. City finally surrenders.

10 June 1098, Crusaders defeat relieving army under Kerboga of Mosul.

11 June - July 1099, Crusaders besiege and attack city, killing garrison and inhabitants.

12 August 1099, Godfrey leads Crusaders to defeat Egyptian relieving army under al-Afdal.

Arrival of English and Pisan supply - ships

Nicaea
Constantinople
Dorylaeum
Iconium (Konya)
Heraclea
Tarsus
St. Simeon
Antioch
Orontes
Laodicea (Lattakieh)
Tripoli
Acre
Jaffa
JERUSALEM
Ascalon
Edessa
CYPRUS
Mediterranean Sea

© Arthur Banks

THE CRUSADERS IN THE MIDDLE EAST 1100 – 1146

This map depicts the Middle East in turmoil after most of the First Crusaders had returned home. The four leaders remaining in the area were Godfrey (who died in 1100), Baldwin, Bohemund, and Raymond. Godfrey was succeeded by his brother Baldwin who became King of Jerusalem. The Crusaders' objective was to consolidate their positions, and reinforcements were sent from Europe to assist them. Their main asset was not their strength, but disunity among their enemies.

17 1144, city falls to Imad-al-Din Zengi, Papal call for a Second Crusade.

9 1104, Bohemund, released from imprisonment, is defeated.

1 1100, Bohemund is captured by Turks and is imprisoned for three years at Sivas. Tancred rules in Antioch.

16 1125, Baldwin II wins major victory over Moslems.

4 1101, Baldwin defeats Egyptian Saad-el-Dawleh.

6 1102, Baldwin is defeated by Egyptian army, but he escapes and regroups. Stephen of Blois is killed.

11 1105, in third battle of Ramleh, Baldwin defeats Egyptians.

2 August 1101, William of Nevers' expedition smashed by Turks.

15 1119, Roger of Antioch is defeated and killed by Ilghazi of Aleppo.

12 1109, surrenders to Baldwin.

14 1111 - 1112, Crusaders unsuccessful in attempt to capture this city. It falls to Venetians and Crusaders in 1124.

Fortress built by Baldwin.

3 September 1101, armies of Bavaria and Aquitaine annihilated by Turks. Hugh of Vermandois dies of wounds.

8 1103, besieged and taken by Tancred from Byzantines.

5 1102, Raymond destroys Moslem army.

13 1110, captured by Baldwin, assisted by Sigurd I of Norway.

10 1104, taken by Baldwin.

7 27 May 1102, Baldwin defeats Egyptians.

Tigris

Euphrates

Melitene

Edessa

Harran

Azaz

Antioch

Lattakieh (Laodicea)

Tripoli

Sidon

Tyre

Acre

Jaffa

Ramleh

Jerusalem

Ascalon

Bosra

Jordan

Le Krak de Montreal

Eilat

SINAI

Heraclea

Mediterranean Sea

Nile

EGYPT

0   100
Miles

KEY

→ Baldwin's expedition 1116 - 1117.

⇒ Baldwin's unsuccessful expedition to Egypt 1118.

⇒ Crusaders' successful raid 1146.

© Arthur Banks

THE MIDDLE EAST IN TURMOIL 1147 - 1189

This map includes the period of the Second Crusade (1147 - 1149), but the main feature was the temporary alliance between Arabs, Turkish Moslems, and Egyptians, to fight their common enemy – the Crusaders. The two military figures of stature were Nur - ed - Din (who conquered Syria and Egypt) and Saladin (whose Holy War provoked the Third Crusade).

1149, Nur - ed - Din attacks Principality of Antioch. Raymond of Antioch killed.

1148, Crusaders invest city but three leaders quarrel, which leads to end of Second Crusade.

1179, Saladin routs Crusaders.

1156, Moslems defeat Crusader forces during passage across the River Jordan.

1187, Saladin routs Crusaders.

1187, Saladin captures city.

1177, Baldwin IV defeats Saladin.

1183, Saladin enters Aleppo.

1187, Saladin attempts to seize city; repulsed by Conrad of Montferrat.

1153, Baldwin III captures city and goes on to conquer entire coastal strip.

1167, Crusaders take Cairo and instal Shawar as Vizier. He is killed in 1169 by Shirkuh and Saladin for Nur - ed - Din.

1147, Turks devastate Crusading force under Conrad III of Germany.

1176, Emperor Manuel Comnenus crushed by Turks under Kilij Arslan.

Louis VII by sea from here.

LOUIS VII's ARMY

1156, Reynald de Châtillon with Armenian support raids and loots Cyprus.

1189 - 1191, Crusaders under Guy of Lusignan invest city, and repel relieving forces.

GENOESE AND PISAN FLEETS CONTROL SEA, THUS ENSURING CRUSADERS' SUPPLIES TO ACRE.

1187, captured by Saladin.

1168, Crusaders take towns and massacre inhabitants.

1148, indecisive battle between Turks and Louis VII of France.

1169, Saladin holds Damietta against Crusaders and Byzantine fleet.

1169, Saladin becomes Vizier of Egypt.

1163, Almaric I of Jerusalem campaigns against Nur - ed - Din without success.

LOUIS VII's ARMY

50 Miles
0

Tigris

Euphrates

Aleppo
Antioch
Inab
Krak des Chevaliers
Damascus
Jacob's Ford
Tiberias
Jerusalem
Horns of Hattin
Montgisard
Tripoli
Tyre
Acre
Ascalon
Tarsus
Iconium (Konya)
Myriocephalum
Attalia
Laodicea
Antiocheia
CYPRUS
Constantinople
Nicaea
Dorylaeum
Damietta
Tanis
Bilbeis
Cairo
EGYPT

© Arthur Banks

RICHARD VERSUS SALADIN 1191-1192

RESULTS OF THE THIRD CRUSADE

Concerning the three leaders of the Third Crusade, only Richard I of England achieved any concrete results. Frederick I of Germany captured Iconium in 1190, but was drowned in Cilicia. His son Frederick of Swabia continued to Acre, but without a powerful army. Philip II of France returned to Europe after the capitulation of Acre. This was basically because of quarrels between Richard and himself.

1187 - 1192. Turkish general Saladin conquers these areas during his Jihad (Holy War). His capture of Jerusalem following the battle of Hattin, sparks off the Third Crusade.

Richard pauses to conquer Cyprus, thus establishing his supply base.

1 *July 1191. Richard repels Saladin's army of relief and garrison surrender. Philip II returns to France.*

2 *August - September 1191. Richard resists Saladin's harassing tactics by employing horse cross- bowmen to keep enemy at bay.*

3 *September 1191. Richard attacks Turks who suffer 7,000 dead; rest are scattered. Crusaders lose 700 men. Saladin never again opposes Richard in direct confrontation.*

4 *Winter 1191 - 1192. Crusaders winter here. Conrad of Montferrat is murdered by Assassins.*

5 *1192. Saladin precedes Richard, destroying crops and poisoning water. Dissension among Richard's ranks compels him to abandon proposed siege of Jerusalem.*

6 *1192. Richard and Saladin conclude treaty which gives special concessions for the Christian pilgrims to Jerusalem. Saladin dies in 1193.*

KURDISTAN

MESOPOTAMIA

Tigris

Euphrates

SYRIA

Antioch

Tripoli

Acre

Hattin

Jerusalem

Arsouf

Ascalon

CILICIA

CYPRUS

Nile

SELJUK TURKS

Constantinople

Antioch

Euphrates

Tripoli

Jerusalem

Acre

EGYPT

KEY

Empire of Saladin.

Remnants of Crusader States.

KEY

Richard's advance 1191 - 1192.

Important battle.

Miles

0   75

© Arthur Banks

THE LATER CRUSADES 1202 – 1270

0 200 Miles

KINGDOM OF TREBIZOND

Kinsmen of Byzantine Emperors establish new dominions here and in Epirus after 1204.

1206, Mongols crushed by Mamelukes.

1228 - 1229, Frederick II secures these cities. Proclaims himself King of Jerusalem.

1244, captured by Khwarezmians in alliance with Egyptians.

1244, Crusaders are defeated by Egyptians and Khwarezmians.

ARABIA

Nazareth • Ain Jalut
Acre • Bethlehem
• Jerusalem
Gaza • Ascalon

ARMENIA

CYPRUS

Damietta •
Fariskur • • Mansura

1218 - 1219, city is besieged and falls to Fifth Crusaders. Later it is relinquished.

1204, Crusaders sack Constantinople. It is recaptured in 1261 by Michael Palaeologus, but most of its European territory remains in Latin and Venetian hands, and Christendom's Eastern bastion never truly recovers.

Black Sea

Constantinople •

EMPIRE OF NICAEA

Smyrna •

Crete

1250, Moslems capture Louis IX who is later ransomed.

1250, fight between Louis IX and Moslems. Robert of Artois and William of Salisbury killed. Crusaders turn back.

1247, Mamelukes capture city.

BULGARIA

SERBIA

EPIRUS

Athens •

CROATIA

Zara •

Venice •

Rome •

Brindisi •

Sicily

← From Marseille

1202, assembly point for Fourth Crusade. Venetians promise to transport Crusaders in return for assistance in recapturing Zara (now occupied by Hungary).

1202, city is taken and sacked.

KEY

Fourth Crusade (1202 - 1204).
Sixth Crusade (1228 - 1229).
Seventh Crusade (1248 - 1254).
(*Note: routes of Fifth and Eighth Crusades are omitted from map.*)

Islam.
Roman Catholic states.
Greek Orthodox states.
Latin Empire.

FOURTH CRUSADE 1202-1204

LEADERS
Boniface of Montferrat.
Louis of Blois.
Baldwin of Flanders.
Henry (brother of Baldwin).
Henry Dandolo, Doge of Venice.
Simon de Montfort.

FIFTH CRUSADE 1218-1221

LEADERS (*who never participated*)
Frederick II of Germany.
John of Brienne, King of Jerusalem.
Hugh of Cyprus.
Cardinal Pelagius.
Hermann von Salza.
Louis of Bavaria.
Andrew of Hungary.
Leopold of Austria.

CHILDREN'S CRUSADES 1212

There were two crusades by children. The first was led by a French shepherd boy named Stephen; the second by a German boy named Nicholas. Both crusades were marked by intense suffering.

SIXTH CRUSADE 1228 - 1229

LEADERS
Frederick II of Germany.
Hermann von Salza.

SEVENTH CRUSADE 1248 - 1254

LEADERS
Louis IX of France.
Robert of Artois ⎫ brothers of Louis IX
Charles of Anjou ⎭
William, Earl of Salisbury.

EIGHTH CRUSADE 1270

LEADERS
Louis IX of France, (died at Tunis).
Charles of Anjou.

Note: Prince Edward of England arrived in the Holy Land (1271) to find that the Crusade had ended. After a year in Acre he made a truce and returned to England.

© Arthur Banks

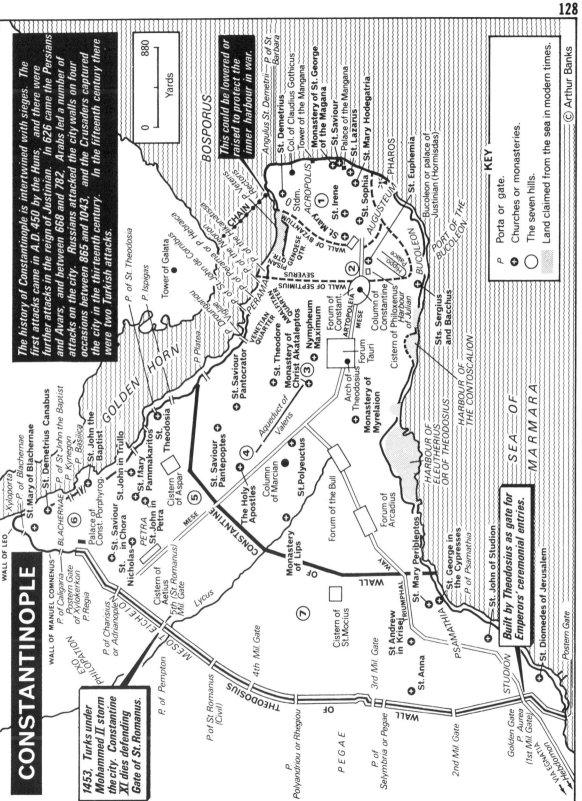

CONSTANTINOPLE

1453, Turks under Mohammed II storm the city. Constantine XI dies defending Gate of St. Romanus.

The history of Constantinople is intertwined with sieges. The first attacks came in A.D. 450 by the Huns, and there were further attacks in the reign of Justinian. In 626 came the Persians and Avars, and between 668 and 782, Arabs led a number of attacks on the city. Russians attacked the city walls on four occasions between 865 and 1043, and the Crusaders captured the city in the thirteenth century. In the fifteenth century there were two Turkish attacks.

This could be lowered or raised to protect the inner harbour in war.

Built by Theodosius as gate for Emperors' ceremonial entries.

0 880
Yards

KEY

P   Porta or gate.
✠   Churches or monasteries.
○   The seven hills.
░   Land claimed from the sea in modern times.

© Arthur Banks

BOSPORUS

GOLDEN HORN

SEA OF MARMARA

Tower of Galata

WALL OF LEO

WALL OF MANUEL COMNENUS

BLACHERNAE

St. Demetrius of Blachernae

St. Mary of Blachernae

St. Demetrius Canabus

P. of St John the Baptist

P. Basilica

P. Kynegon

St. John the Baptist

P. Regia

P. of Caligaria

Postern Gate of Xylokerkon

P. Charisius or Adrianople

Palace of Const. Porphyrog.

St. Saviour in Chora

St. Nicholas

St. John in Trullo

St. Mary Pammakaritos

St. Theodosia

St. John in Petra

PETRA

Cistern of Aetius

Cistern of Aspar

5th (St Romanus) Mil. Gate

St. Mary Pantepoptes

St. Saviour Pantocrator

St. Theodore

VENETIAN QUARTER

PERAMA

P. Platea

P. Ispigas

P. of St. Theodosia

Drougarion

P. of St. John

of the Ikanatissa

P. Neorion

P. or Perama

of the Hebraica

P. of Vigleie

CHAIN

John de Cornibus

PISAN

AMALFITAN

GENOESE QTR.

OTR.

WALL OF SEPTIMIUS SEVERUS

Nympheum Maximum

Monastery of Christ Akataleptos

Aqueduct of Valens

Column of Marcian

St. Polyeuctus

The Holy Apostles

St. Saviour in Chora

Forum of Constant.

Forum Tauri

Column of Constantine

MESE

ARTOPOLEIA

Arch of Theodosius

Monastery of Myrelaion

Forum of Arcadius

Forum of the Bull

Cistern of Philoxenus

Cistern of Aetius

Monastery of Lips

MESE OF CONSTANTINE

Lycus

Cistern of St.Mocius

PHILOXATION

MESOLI

EICHELION

EXOPATION

P. of Pempton

P. of St Romanus (Civil)

P. Polyandriou or Rhegiou

P. of Selymbria or Pegae

WALL OF THEODOSIUS

4th Mil. Gate

3rd Mil. Gate

2nd Mil. Gate

PEGAE

TRIUMPHAL WAY

St Andrew in Krise

St. Mary Peribleptos

St. George in the Cypresses

St. Anna

P. of Psamathia

PSAMATHIA

St. John of Studion

STUDION

VIA EGNATIA

Hebdomon

Golden Gate P. Aurea (1st Mil. Gate)

St. Diomedes of Jerusalem

Postern Gate

WALL OF

Angulus St. Demetrii— P. of St. Barbara

St. Demetrius

Col. of Claudius Gothicus

Tower of the Mangana

Monastery of St. George of the Magana

St. Saviour

Palace of the Mangana

St. Lazarus

St. Mary Hodegatria

St. Irene

St. Sophia

St. Euphemia

PHAROS

AUGUSTEUM

Bucoleon or palace of Justinian (Hormisdas)

PORT OF THE BUCOLEON

BUCOLEON

Hippo.

Hippo. Palace

Sts. Sergius and Bacchus

HARBOUR OF ELEUTHERIUS OR OF THEODOSIUS

HARBOUR OF THE CONTOSCALION

ACROPOLIS

WALL OF BYZANTIUM

St. Mary

Stdm.

1 St. Irene
2
3 Monastery of Christ Akataleptos
4
5
6 Palace of Const. Porphyrog.
7 Cistern of St.Mocius

GENGHIS KHAN AND THE MONGOLS

...nghis Khan (1162 - 1227), one of the greatest captains in military history, was the son of a Mongol chieftain whose ...mily lived in the area south-east of Lake Baikal. As a boy he was known as Temujin, and succeeded his father ...s chief at the age of thirteen. After a number of early struggles to maintain his position, he proclaimed himself ...nghis Khan in 1206. He went on to conquer a huge area of Asia and Europe, and by the time of his death, an ...mpire had been established from China to the River Dnieper in Russia. Its making, however, cost 18,000,000 lives, ...s the Mongols were savage horse-warriors who massacred and destroyed wherever they rode. The Mongols settled ...ventually in the area to the north of the Caspian and Black Seas, their domain being the Empire of the Golden Horde.

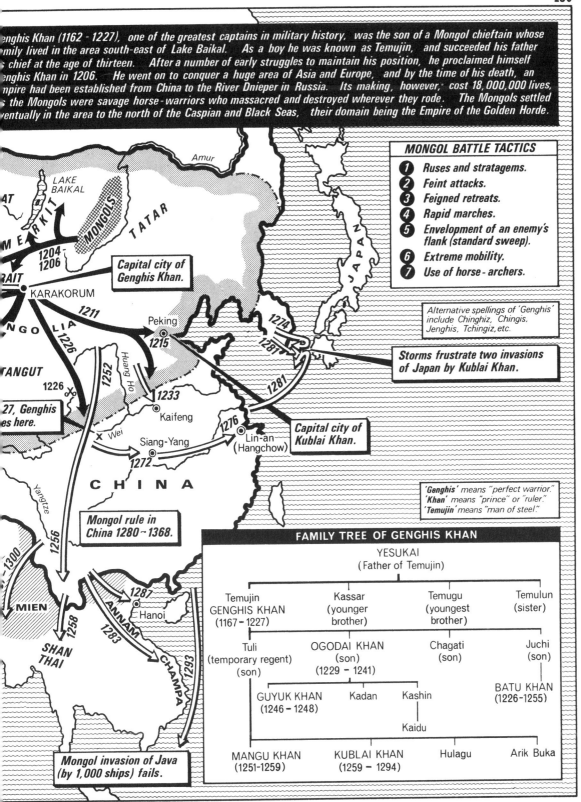

Amur

LAKE BAIKAL

MONGOLS

TATAR

MERKIT

MONGOLS

1204-1206

RAIT

KARAKORUM

Capital city of Genghis Khan.

1211

Peking

NGOLIA

1226

TANGUT

Huang Ho

1252

1215

1233

1226

27, Genghis ...es here.

Kaifeng

X Wei

Siang-Yang

1272

1276

Lin-an (Hangchow)

Capital city of Kublai Khan.

1274

1281

1281

JAPAN

MONGOL BATTLE TACTICS

1. Ruses and stratagems.
2. Feint attacks.
3. Feigned retreats.
4. Rapid marches.
5. Envelopment of an enemy's flank (standard sweep).
6. Extreme mobility.
7. Use of horse-archers.

Alternative spellings of 'Genghis' include Chinghiz, Chingis, Jenghis, Tchingiz, etc.

Storms frustrate two invasions of Japan by Kublai Khan.

'Genghis' means "perfect warrior." 'Khan' means "prince" or "ruler." 'Temujin' means "man of steel."

C H I N A

Yangtze

Mongol rule in China 1280~1368.

1256

1300

MIEN

1258

ANNAM

1283

1287

Hanoi

CHAMPA

1293

SHAN THAI

Mongol invasion of Java (by 1,000 ships) fails.

FAMILY TREE OF GENGHIS KHAN

YESUKAI
(Father of Temujin)

| Temujin GENGHIS KHAN (1167 - 1227) | Kassar (younger brother) | Temugu (youngest brother) | Temulun (sister) |

| Tuli (temporary regent) (son) | OGODAI KHAN (son) (1229 - 1241) | Chagati (son) | Juchi (son) |

GUYUK KHAN (1246 - 1248)   Kadan   Kashin

BATU KHAN (1226-1255)

Kaidu

| MANGU KHAN (1251-1259) | KUBLAI KHAN (1259 - 1294) | Hulagu | Arik Buka |

131

MOHAMMED BIN TUGHLUK 1325-1351

400

0

Miles

Note: in 1327 the capital moved from Delhi to Devagiri.

KAMERU

Brahmaputra

Tsango

HIMALAYAS

KASHMIR

Indus

LAHORE

MULTAN

UCH

SVASTAN

Thatta

1351, MOHAMMED DIES HERE

LAKHNAUT

BUDAUN

KALANJU

OUDH

Ganges

Delhi

KANAUJ

Kanauj

MALWA

Ujjain

GUJARAT

BAHMANI

BIHAR

Gandak

KARA

Son

KALANJU

MALWA

DEOGIR

Devagiri

Narbada

Godavari

Gulbarga

D

TELINGANA

Krishna

ORISSA

Mahanadi

C A

MALABAR

KEY

Empire of Mohammed in 1335.

Independent areas?

Mohammed defeated a Jagatai Mongol penetration under Tarmashirin, planned (but did not operate) an invasion of Persia, and fought a campaign against the mountain tribes of the Himalayas. In the middle of his reign the Sultanate of Delhi was at its largest extent, but towards the end (1347) the Bahmani kingdom in the Deccan became independent.

ILTUTMISH 1211-1236

400

0

Miles

1216, Iltutmish defeats Taj-ud-din.

1226, important Rajput fortress is taken by Iltutmish.

Mongol threat

Ghazni

Peshawar

KHOKHARS

KASHMIR

Indus

Jhelum

Chenab

Ravi

Lahore

Multan

Sutlej

PUNJAB

Tarain

Delhi

Muttra

SIND

RAJPUTANA

GUJARAT

Ujjain

Narbada

YADAVAS

Devagiri

HIMALAYAS

Tsango

Brahmaputra

Ganges

Kanauj

Jumna

Benares

Son

Ganges

Godavari

KAKATIYAS

Krishna

HOYSALAS

WARS AND UNREST

PANDYAS

CHOLAS

ORISSA

Mahanadi

1234, Rajput stronghold is taken by Iltutmish.

KEY

Sultanate of Delhi in 1236.

✕ Important battle.

Iltutmish, a Turkish general, crushed rebellions in the Punjab, conquered Sind, recovered areas in Rajputana, and commenced a campaign against the Khokhars. During this period, the Mongol warrior Genghis Khan reached the Indus, but did not penetrate into India proper.

© Arthur Banks

THE IMPORTANCE OF GEOGRAPHY IN THE MILITARY HISTORY OF NORTHERN INDIA

NOTE: modern coastlines and river courses shown on this map.

CONTOURS (in feet)

Over 18,000'
12,000'–18,000'
4,500'–12,000'
1,200'–4,500'
600'–1,200'
0'–600'

TIBETAN PLATEAUX

29,028' Mt. Everest

Nanda 'Devi 25,645'

H I M A L A Y A S

Tsangpo

Brahmaputra

PLAIN OF THE GANGES

Ganges

Ganges

Yamuna

MALWA FLAT

Narbada

Mahanadi

DECCAN PLATEAU

Godavari

Kistna

KHYBER PASS

GOMAL PASS

KHOJAK PASS

BOLAN PASS

Jhelum

Chenab

Ravi

Sutlej

INDUS

Indus

PLAIN OF THE INDUS

THAR OR INDIAN DESERT

THE RANN OF CUTCH

Arabian Sea

0 100 200
Miles

KEY

Over – 12,000'
1,200'–12,000'
0' – 1,200'

General direction of attacks on northern India.

INVASIONS

Indus

Ganges

0 300
Miles

Before the development of sea-power by the European nations, the invaders of India invariably attacked from the north-west direction. The Himalayas and Tibetan Plateaux proved to be an "impenetrable" barrier in the north-east, whereas the mountain passes in the north-west were fully exploited by generals such as Alexander, Timur, and Babur.

© Arthur Banks

133

THE CAMPAIGNS OF TIMUR (TAMERLANE) 1369 – 1405

1402, Timur invests city after Knights Hospitallers refuse to submit, (reinforcements by sea are in the offing). Timur fires heads of Christians at approaching warships and they withdraw. City falls.

1402, Timur defeats Sultan Bayazid of the Ottoman Turks. 200,000 troops on either side are involved; casualties are unknown, but Sultan is captured and city pillaged.

1380, Golden Horde defeated by Muscovite Prince Dmitri Donskoy.

1403, rulers submit to Timur.

1380, Tokhtamish defeats Mamay, and becomes Khan of re-united Golden Horde (Golden and White).

1395, captured by Timur.

1400, Timur destroys Mameluke army at Battle of Aleppo, captures city and slaughters many inhabitants.

1401, city is captured and gutted.

1401, Timur massacres citizens as punishment for uprising after previous submission in 1393.

1392, Timur kills Shah Mansur.

Constantinople · Brusa · Lesbos · Chios · Smyrna · Angora · Sivas · GEORGIA · Tiflis · ARMENIA · Aleppo · Mosul · Tabriz · Damascus · Gaza · Cairo · Baghdad · Basra · Yeletz · Kulikovo · Kalka · Tana · Saray

KEY
- Campaigns against Khwarazm and Moghulistan.
- Campaigns against Khorasan, Seistan, and Mazandaran (1381-1384).
- Three Years' Campaign in Azerbaijan and Persia (1386-1388).
- Campaign against the Golden Horde (1391-1392).
- Five-year campaign in West, and defeat of Tokhtamish (1392-1396).
- Campaign in northern India (1398-1399).
- Campaign in the West (1399-1404).

0 — 200 Miles

© Arthur Banks

1391, Timur defeats Tokhtamish in three-day battle.

Born in 1336, in 1369 Timur (Tamerlane) established himself as king of Samarkand. For twenty-five years he waged perpetual war, first with the eastern Khipchac Tartars, and then with the western Golden Horde. His conquests ranged across Persia and Georgia, and he massacred all those who resisted him. Whereas Genghis Khan "destroyed" his opposition, Timur "obliterated" it (e.g: in 1378 at Isfahan he raised a pyramid of 70,000 skulls). He conquered north-west India and Syria, and then fought a great battle at Angora (1402) where the Ottoman army was annihilated. He determined to attack China, but died "en route" at Otrar in 1405 at the age of seventy. His sole monument is the bloodbath he left in his wake; if his military genius had been equalled by statesmanship, he would have been regarded as one of the greatest captains in military history.

apital of Golden orde is ravaged.

Destroyed.

95, Timur destroys rces of Tokhtamish, eparably weakening lden Horde.

1405, Timur dies here.

1365, "Battle of the Mire"; Husayn and Timur lose 10,000 men in a battle characterized by a huge storm which turns the battlefield into a sea of mud.

1370, Timur defeats Husayn, who is subsequently murdered.

Timur's capital.

1386

1398, following victory over Mahmud Tughluk, Timur massacres 100,000 Indian prisoners and then storms Delhi. Five days of slaughter, rape, destruction, and plunder follow this event.

1383, captured by Timur. 2,000 captives cemented alive into towers.

1398, city falls following siege of six-months duration.

Volga

Kunduzcha (Kandurcha)

Ural

Hunger Steppe

Sari- Su

Aral Sea

Syr-Darya

KIZIL-KUM

Chu

SEMIRECHYE

Ili

Otrar

FARGHANA

KHWARAZM

Urganch

Khiya

Kat

Tashkent

Andijan

KARA KUM

MAWARANNAHR

Khokand

Bukhara

Kashgar

SAMARKAND

Yarkand

Amu-Darya (Oxus)

Tirmidh

Kara Korum Range

Khotan

Balkh

Kush

KHORASAN

1398

Hindu

Kabul

Herat

Isfizar

Indus

Jhelum

Chenab

Ravi

Zaranj

Kandahar

Multan

Sutlej

Bhatnair

Delhi

rmuz

135

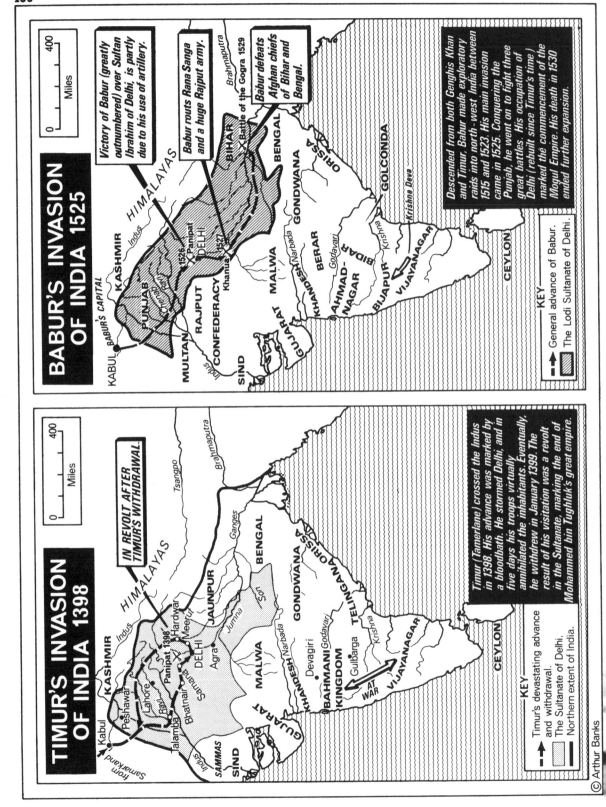

BABUR'S INVASION OF INDIA 1525

Victory of Babur (greatly outnumbered) over Sultan Ibrahim of Delhi, is partly due to his use of artillery.

Babur routs Rana Sanga and a huge Rajput army.

Babur defeats Afghan chiefs of Bihar and Bengal.

Descended from both Genghis Khan and Timur, Babur made exploratory raids into north-west India between 1515 and 1523. His main invasion came in 1525. Conquering the Punjab, he went on to fight three great battles. His occupation of Delhi (rebuilt since Timur's time) marked the commencement of the Mogul Empire. His death in 1530 ended further expansion.

HIMALAYAS

Brahmaputra

Battle of the Gogra 1529

BIHAR

BENGAL

ASSAM

ORISSA

GONDWANA

KASHMIR

Indus

1526 Panipat
1527
DELHI

Khanua

RAJPUT
CONFEDERACY

MALWA

BERAR

Narbada

KHANDESH

AHMAD-
NAGAR

Godavari

BIDAR

GOLCONDA

Krishna

Krishna Deva

VIJAYANAGAR

CEYLON

KABUL BABUR'S CAPITAL

PUNJAB

MULTAN

GUJARAT

SIND

Indus

BIJAPUR

KEY
→ General advance of Babur.

▨ The Lodi Sultanate of Delhi.

TIMUR'S INVASION OF INDIA 1398

IN REVOLT AFTER TIMUR'S WITHDRAWAL.

Timur (Tamerlane) crossed the Indus in 1398. His advance was marked by a bloodbath. He stormed Delhi, and in five days his troops virtually annihilated the inhabitants. Eventually, he withdrew in January 1399. The result of his visitation was a revolt in the Sultanate, marking the end of Mohammed bin Tughluk's great empire.

HIMALAYAS

Brahmaputra

Tsangpo

Ganges

BENGAL

GONDWANA

ORISSA

KASHMIR

Indus

Peshawar

Lahore

Ravi

Talamba

Bhatnair

Samana

Hardwar

Meerut

Panipat 1398

DELHI

Agra

Jumna

JAUNPUR

Son

MALWA

Narbada

KHANDESH

Devagiri

Godavari

BAHMANI
KINGDOM

Gulbarga

TELINGANA

Krishna

AT
WAR

VIJAYANAGAR

Kabul

from Samarkand

SAMMAS

SIND

Indus

GUJARAT

CEYLON

KEY
→ Timur's devastating advance and withdrawal.

▨ The Sultanate of Delhi.

— Northern extent of India.

© Arthur Banks

CHINA: INVASIONS AND EXPULSIONS 1260 – 1368

This period was marked by the conquest of China by the Mongols and the establishment of the Yuan Dynasty under Kublai Khan in 1279.

0 — 200 Miles

TATARS

KERAITS

LING - PEI

ONGGUTS

KONGIRATS

SHUKITAN

YANG

LIAO

KAN'SU

Kan-chou

Liao-yang

Ta-ning

Huang Ho

SHEN-HSI

CHUNG

1368

Ta-tu

Pao-ting

Ho-chien

Chi-ning

Chen-ting

Chi-nan

I-tu

Chin-ning

Ta-ming

Huai-ch'ing

Wei-hui

Feng-yuan

Pien-liang

Huang Ho

Huai-an

TIBET

HO - NAN

Chen-chiang

Ch'eng-tu

Chi-ch'ing

Ch'ang-chou

Chiang

Lu-chou

Ning-kuo

1356

CHE

Sung-chiang

Chia-hsing

SSU-CH'UAN

Chung-hsing

Wu-ch'ang

Hang-chou

Ch'ing yuan

Li-chou

Nan-k'ang

Chiang-chou

Hui-chou

Chien-te

Wu-chou

T'ai-chou

Ch'ang-te

Yo-chou

Shui-chou

Jao-chou

Ch'u-cho

T'ien-lin

Fu-chou

Shao-wu

Wen-chou

YÜN NAN

Yuan-chou

Chi-an

Lung-hsing

Chien-ning

Yen-p'ing

Heng-chou

Kuei-yang

CHIANG-HSI

Fu-chou

Chuan-chou

c.1368

Ch'ung-ch'ing

Nan-an

Shao-chou

Kan-chou

Ting-chou

Hsing-hua

Ching-chiang

Ch'uan-chou

Ta-lo

HU-KUANG

1368

Chang-chou

1287-1300

MIEN

ANNAM

1287

Kuang-chou

Chao-chou

CHANG-HSI

1283

KHMER

1293

© Arthur Banks

to Java

KEY

→ Mongol invasions (outside China).

⇨ Expulsion of Mongols by Mings c.1360 onwards.

◉ Important administrative centres with local capitals underlined.

TWO IMPORTANT SIEGES OF CONSTANTINOPLE

① The Unsuccessful Siege of 717 - 718

ARMED STRENGTHS

THE ATTACKERS (under Maslama)	THE DEFENDERS (under Leo III)
In 717. 80,000 troops, plus 80,000 troops aboard 1,800 ships under Suleiman **In 718.** 400 ships under Sofiam. 360 ships under Yezid. 40,000 troops under Merdasan.	Troop strengths unknown. Population of city: approx 600,000. Naval strength unknown, but much inferior to the Moslem force.

0 — 1 Mile

Defensive chain which can be raised or lowered.

Leo's safe anchorage.

Golden Horn — Galata — Bosporus

Moslem armies — WALL OF THEODOSIUS

CONSTANTINOPLE

Leo's two naval victories are fought in this area. 'Greek fire' contributes to Leo's successes.

Sea of Marmara

This siege was mainly a naval blockading action.

Note: 'Greek fire' was possibly a mixture of sulphur, naphtha, and quicklime, which ignited when wetted. It was probably sprayed by a hose operating from a siphon system.

MAIN EVENTS

August 717. Leo prepares for siege by stockpiling granaries and arsenals, repairing walls, and mounting defensive weapons.

September 717. Suleiman (Maslama's general) leads blockading squadron to sever sea communications between Constantinople and cities of Cherson and Trebizond. Leo's fleet advances from Golden Horn and destroys 20 Moslem ships.

Winter 717-718. Three months of bitterly cold weather decimates besiegers.

Spring 718. Reserve army and ships arrive to strengthen Moslems.

June 718. Leo's fleet sallies from Golden Horn and routs Moslem fleet, following which Leo attacks and defeats Merdasan on land.

August 718. Maslama raises siege.

② The Successful Siege of 1453

ARMED STRENGTHS

THE ATTACKERS (led by Mohammed II)	THE DEFENDERS (led by Constantine XI)
80,000 troops. 100 heavy cannon. 250 ships.	7,000 troops. 26 ships.

Turkish fleet.

Turkish bridge constructed over floating barrels.

TURKS HAUL 70 SHIPS OVERLAND

MAIN TURKISH ATTACKS — guns — WALL OF THEODOSIUS — Galata — Golden Horn — Bosporus

Boom defence.

Naval encounter.

CONSTANTINOPLE

ROUTE OF FOUR CHRISTIAN SHIPS

Sea of Marmara

This siege was mainly a military (land) action.

0 — 1 Mile

MAIN EVENTS

6 April. Mohammed's artillery opens fire.

12 April. First Turkish attack repulsed.

20 April. Four Christian vessels fight off Turkish fleet and enter Golden Horn.

22 April. Turks transport seventy ships overland to Golden Horn.

30 April. Turks construct bridge of barrels across Golden Horn to link two parts of besieging army.

7 May. Turkish attacks fail. Food short in city.

12 May. Further attacks fail.

18 May. 'Helepolis' (protected tower) attack fails.

20 May. Turkish mining attempts fail.

29 May. Colossal Turkish assaults eventually succeed in penetrating into city. Constantine is killed and city sacked.

© Arthur Banks

TWO IMPORTANT SIEGES OF RHODES

0 ——————— 300
Yards

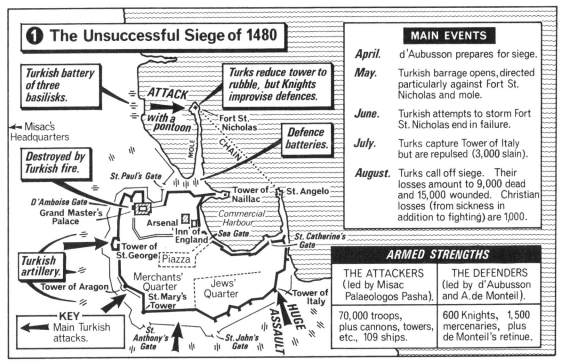

❶ The Unsuccessful Siege of 1480

Turkish battery of three basilisks.

ATTACK with a pontoon

Turks reduce tower to rubble, but Knights improvise defences.

Fort St. Nicholas

Defence batteries.

← Misac's Headquarters

Destroyed by Turkish fire.

MOLE

CHAIN

St. Paul's Gate

D'Amboise Gate
Grand Master's Palace

Arsenal

Tower of Naillac · St. Angelo

Commercial Harbour

Inn' of England · Sea Gate

St. Catherine's Gate

Tower of St. George

Piazza

Turkish artillery.

Tower of Aragon

Merchants' Quarter
St. Mary's Tower

Jews' Quarter

Tower of Italy

KEY
← Main Turkish attacks.

St. Anthony's Gate

St. John's Gate

HUGE ASSAULT

MAIN EVENTS

April.	d'Aubusson prepares for siege.
May.	Turkish barrage opens, directed particularly against Fort St. Nicholas and mole.
June.	Turkish attempts to storm Fort St. Nicholas end in failure.
July.	Turks capture Tower of Italy but are repulsed (3,000 slain).
August.	Turks call off siege. Their losses amount to 9,000 dead and 15,000 wounded. Christian losses (from sickness in addition to fighting) are 1,000.

ARMED STRENGTHS

THE ATTACKERS (led by Misac Palaeologos Pasha).	THE DEFENDERS (led by d'Aubusson and A. de Monteil).
70,000 troops, plus cannons, towers, etc., 109 ships.	600 Knights, 1,500 mercenaries, plus de Monteil's retinue.

❷ The Successful Siege of 1522

Sunken hulks.

Fort St Nicholas

CORTOGLU'S NAVAL BLOCKADE

BALI AGHA

CHAIN

St. Paul's Gate

Tower of Naillac

D'Amboise Gate
Grand Master's Palace

CHAIN
Commercial Harbour

St. Angelo

Arsenal

Inn' of England

Sea Gate

St. Catherine's Gate

AYAS PASHA

Tower of St. George

Piazza

Tower of Aragon

Merchants' Quarter
St. Mary's Tower

Jews' Quarter

Tower of Italy

PIR PASHA

AHMED PASHA

St. Anthony's Gate

St. John's Gate

QASIM PASHA

MUSTAPHA PASHA

MAIN EVENTS

July.	Artillery duel commences.
August.	Turks mount mining operations.
September–November.	Turkish assaults with garrison dwindling. Some Christian reinforcements arrive during November.
December.	Defences become untenable: city surrenders. Turks lose 50,000 men during siege. Christians lose all but 180 Knights and 1,000 auxiliaries.

ARMED STRENGTHS

THE ATTACKERS (led by Suleiman "the Magnificent").	THE DEFENDERS (led by Philip Villiers de L'Isle Adam)
200,000 troops, some siege artillery and engineer corps, plus 400 transports.	700 Knights, plus 3,000 auxiliaries, and some artillery. Also, mining expert, Tadini.

© Arthur Banks

139

THE HOLY ROMAN EMPIRE

0   200
Miles

1214, Philip II of France defeats Emperor Otto IV (of Germany).

1241, Kaidu (the Mongol) gains victory over Henry (the Pious) of Silesia.

In the Middle Ages, the Holy Roman Empire covered Germany, the Netherlands, Austria, Bohemia and Northern Italy. It was not a single state with one government, but a number of states each with its own ruler and government, and with the Holy Roman Emperor above them all. This emperor was chosen for a life term from among the great German princes.

1176, Frederick 'Barbarossa' is defeated by the Lombard League, whose victory is achieved by the skilled use of infantry and cavalry.

Haithabu, Oldenburg, Danzig, PRUSSIA, Hamburg, Lübeck, POMERANIA, POMERELIA, Luneburg, FRIESLAND, Egmont, Deventer, Bremen, Vistula, Bug, HOLLAND, SAXONY, Brunswick, BRANDENBURG, Hildesheim, Magdeburg, Bruges, Munster, Goslar, Quedlinburg, Liegnitz, POLAND, Ghent, LOWER, Liege, Cologne, Hersfeld, Merseburg, Meissen, Breslau, Bouvines, Aachen, Andernach, Salza, SILESIA, LORRAINE, Ingelheim, THURINGIA, Fulda, MEISSEN, Trier, Worms, FRANCONIA, Prague, UPPER, Mainz, Bamberg, BOHEMIA, Verdun, Metz, Speier, Ratisbon, MORAVIA, LORRAINE, Toul, Waiblingen, Passau, AUSTRIA, FRANCE, Staufen, SWABIA, Augsburg, Vienna, Clairvaux, Strasbourg, Reichenau, Benediktbeuern, Danube, Citaux, Constance, Salzburg, Cluny, St Gallen, BAVARIA, CARINTHIA, KINGDOM, HUNGARY, Lyon, OF, Legnano, MARCH OF VERONA, ARLES, Sava, La Grande, Milan, Belgrade, Chartreuse, LOMBARDY, Pavia, Verona, Lérins, Canossa, Venice, Arles, Genoa, Ravenna, CROATIA, St.Victor, KINGDOM, OF, ROMAGNA, ITALY, TUSCANY, Farfa, Rome, Subiaco, SARDINIA, Benevento, Monte Cassino, Lucera, Naples, APULIA, Castel del Monte, Amalfi, Salerno, CALABRIA, Croton, Palermo, SICILY

KEY
▥	The Holy Roman Empire under the Hohenstaufens.
▦	Guelf Lands.
▨	Hohenstaufen Lands.
▧	Ascanian Lands.
▤	Kingdom of Sicily.
▬	Papal States.
✕	Important battle.
★	Castle.
✛	Monastery.

© Arthur Banks

EXTENT OF THE EMPIRE
c.1000
c.1200
c.1550
c.1700

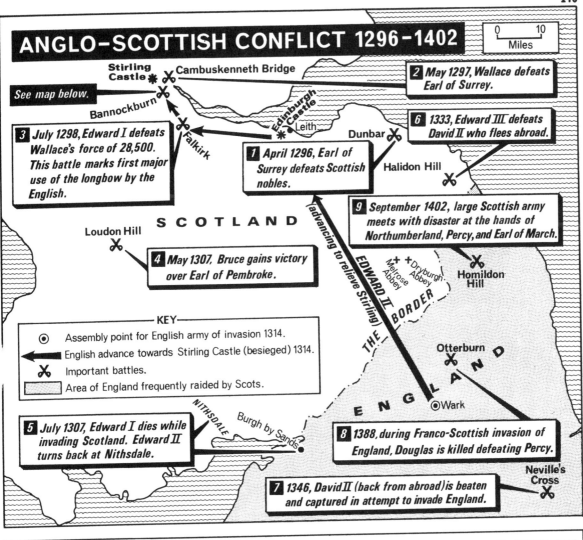

ANGLO-SCOTTISH CONFLICT 1296–1402

0 10
Miles

Stirling Castle ✳

Cambuskenneth Bridge ✂

See map below. ←

Bannockburn

Edinburgh Castle ✳
Leith

Dunbar ✂

2 May 1297, Wallace defeats Earl of Surrey.

6 1333, Edward III defeats David II who flees abroad.

Falkirk ✂

3 July 1298, Edward I defeats Wallace's force of 28,500. This battle marks first major use of the longbow by the English.

1 April 1296, Earl of Surrey defeats Scottish nobles.

Halidon Hill ✂

S C O T L A N D

9 September 1402, large Scottish army meets with disaster at the hands of Northumberland, Percy, and Earl of March.

(advancing to relieve Stirling)

Loudon Hill ✂

4 May 1307, Bruce gains victory over Earl of Pembroke.

Melrose Abbey ✛
✛ Dryburgh Abbey

Homildon Hill ✂

EDWARD II

THE BORDER

— KEY —

⊙ Assembly point for English army of invasion 1314.

← English advance towards Stirling Castle (besieged) 1314.

✂ Important battles.

▨ Area of England frequently raided by Scots.

Otterburn ✂

E N G L A N D

⊙ Wark

5 July 1307, Edward I dies while invading Scotland. Edward II turns back at Nithsdale.

NITHSDALE

Burgh by Sands

8 1388, during Franco-Scottish invasion of England, Douglas is killed defeating Percy.

Neville's Cross ✂

7 1346, David II (back from abroad) is beaten and captured in attempt to invade England.

THE SCOTTISH VICTORY AT BANNOCKBURN 24 JUNE 1314

0 500
Yards

PHASE ONE

↑ to Stirling Castle

St. Ninian's Kirk

Cavalry

CLIFFORD

Old Roman Road

FOREST

RANDOLPH

BRUCE

Bannock Burn

M A R S H

ford

Ⓔ

GLOUCESTER

Potholes dug by Scots to impede English cavalry.

RIVAL STRENGTHS

SCOTS	ENGLISH
10,000 foot plus small horse unit.	20,000 men (foot, horse, archers).

— KEY —

Ⓔ English camp during night 23/24 June.
■ Scottish positions.
⇐ First English cavalry attack, repelled by Bruce.
⇐ Second English attack.
➡ Scottish thrust.

PHASE TWO

BRUCE

'DRY FIELD'

KEITH

EDWARD II

Bannock Burn

CASUALTIES

English: 16,000
Scots: 4,000

The English were trapped in a position between a peat marsh and a thickly wooded hillside.

— KEY —

■◪ Scottish units.
➡ Main Scottish advance.
▢ English position.
△△ English archers.
Scottish cavalry attack on archers.
--→ Scottish camp followers (English assume they are reinforcements).

ⓒ Arthur Banks

THE HUNDRED YEARS' WAR 1337–1453

Note: the war actually spanned 120 years as French raids across the English Channel went on until 1457.

❶ The Sluys-Crécy Period 1337–1347

FRANCE IN 1337

ENGLAND — Sluys — Ponthieu — Crécy — PARIS — Brittany — Burgundy — FRANCE — Guyenne

0 50 Miles

KEY: French Holdings. English Holdings.

THE ENGLISH NAVAL VICTORY AT SLUYS 24 JUNE 1340

A French fleet of 190 ships, anchored in the Zwin river, is attacked by an English fleet of 150 ships. The English steer straight in to the French, and their archers lay down a hail of arrows. Blinded by the onslaught, the French are also cramped for movement because of their moorings. The English men-at-arms complete the carnage. 166 French ships are sunk or captured, and this victory gives England command of the English Channel.

MAIN CAUSES OF THE HUNDRED YEARS' WAR

1. English rage over French support for the Scots in their wars with England.
2. French suspicions concerning English commercial interests in Flanders.
3. The feudal relationship between French and English kings in France.

TEN BASIC STAGES OF THE HUNDRED YEARS' WAR

❶ 1337–1347, Sluys/Crécy period.
❷ 1347–1354, Period of truce.
❸ 1355–1360, Poitiers period.
❹ 1360–1367, Period of uneasy peace.
❺ 1368–1396, Du Guesclin and after.
❻ 1396–1413, Period of uneasy truce.
❼ 1413–1428, Period of Henry V.
❽ 1429–1444, Joan of Arc's influence.
❾ 1444–1449, Truce of Tours.
❿ 1449–1453, The French resurgence.

EDWARD III's CAMPAIGN IN NORTHERN FRANCE 1346–1347

E N G L A N D

Portsmouth — St. Helens — Calais

ENGLISH SEA MASTERY

11 July 1346, Edward's invasion force sets sail for France. It includes some 3,600 archers, 3,500 Welsh spearmen and archers, 2,740 hobelers, and 1,140 men-at-arms.

ENGLISH SEA MASTERY

4 September 1346, Edward besieges port. It surrenders on 4 August 1347. A truce is signed on 28 September 1347.

1–4 Sept. — Montreuil 28 August — Crécy 28 August — Abbeville — Somme — Amiens

26 August 1346, Edward defeats Philip VI.

ENGLISH FLEET

St. Vaast 12 July — Caen — Lisieux — Elboeuf 4 August — Rouen — Seine — RAVAGING — 24 August — 15–23 August — Poissy — PARIS

St. Lô 22 July — 2 August — 13 August

LOCATION OF FRENCH ARMY ON 2 AUGUST 1346

26 July 1346, English storm and sack city. Fleet lends support.

Note: the capture of the port of Calais, although it was England's only land gain, meant that England was immune from invasion.

KEY: → Route of Edward's advance to Calais.

0 50 Miles

© Arthur Banks

THE ENGLISH INFANTRY SUCCESS AT CRÉCY 26 AUGUST 1346

WEAPONS

The longbow (originally a Welsh weapon) had twice the range of the the crossbow, plus a much greater rapidity of fire.

Note: the valley in which the battle was fought is known as *VALLÉE AUX CLERCS* because Edward's clerks made a count of the corpses following the fight.

ARMOUR

French mail armour, though lighter than plate, was no shield against the English arrows.

Wadicourt

Estrées

DIRECTION OF BRIGHT, LOW, EVENING SUNLIGHT

EDWARD III *(TROOPS FIRM AND DISCIPLINED)*

3

HAIL OF ENGLISH ARROWS

1

Windmill

2

Edward's Command Post.

Crécy

CRÉCY GRANGE WOOD

P

PHILIP VI *(KNIGHTS RASH AND IMPETUOUS)*

1 2 3

Probable dispositions of Philip's forces at one early stage. For most of the battle, their lines were haphazard and their attitude was 'tournament-like'.

Fontaine

RESULTS OF CRÉCY

This battle marked the return of the superiority of infantry over cavalry. For the first time, England was regarded by the whole of Europe as a first rank military power.

Maye Stream

French advance becomes ragged.

FOREST OF CRÉCY

PHILIP VI'S ARMY (TOTAL 740,000) ADVANCING IN EIGHT DIVISIONS *(late afternoon 26 August).*

Changing the direction of their approach to a half-left wheel, the French cavalry charged to attack the English defensive positions. The English archers stood their ground and discharged a hail of arrows; simultaneously, the English fired three "cannon" at the enemy. Despite making fifteen suicidal assaults, the French could make no headway and suffered heavy losses in men and horses.

from Abbeville

KEY

▲▲▲▲▲ English archers (armed with longbows).

1 Edward's division (in reserve).

2 Division under nominal command of the 17-year old Black Prince.

3 Division under Earl of Northampton.

P Horse and baggage-wagon park.

△△△△△ Genoese crossbowmen.

🔲1 Division under king of Bohemia and Count of Alençon.

🔲2 Division under Count of Blois and Duke of Lorraine.

🔲3 Division under King Philip VI and Charles, king of the Romans.

SCORE SHEET

French strength: 40,000
English strength: 8,500
French losses: 11,500
English losses: 200

© Arthur Banks

143

THE HUNDRED YEARS' WAR – continued

❷ Spread of the Black Death to Europe

The Black Death, a form of bubonic plague, apparently commenced in China and was carried west by traders. In 1348 it devastated France and England alike, and one third of the population of each country died. During this period, the two states were in a state of truce, but no major campaigns could be undertaken while the pestilence raged. There were later visitations of the disease, but the first one was the most deadly in terms of numbers.

THE PLAGUE'S SPREAD IN FRANCE & BRITAIN

North Sea

York

Bristol
London
Calais
Melcombe Regis
Paris

Bay of Biscay

Marseilles

0   200
Miles

EUROPE
AFRICA
ASIA
CHINA
Constantinople
CARAVAN ROUTES
Mecca
SEA TRADE ROUTES
INDIAN OCEAN

KEY
Spread of the plague from China to Europe.

0   1000
Miles

❸ The Black Prince's Campaigns

0   50
Miles

KEY
- English holdings in 1368 (following the Treaty of Bretigny).
- ← Campaign of the Black Prince in 1355.
- ◄-- Campaign of the Black Prince in 1356.
- ◁◁ Campaign of the Black Prince in 1367.
- ✕ Important battles.

Paris
Bretigny
1356, DUKE OF LANCASTER (separate campaign)
KING JOHN II
8 Sept.
Amboise
Tours 8–11 Sept.
ANJOU
Vierzon 28 Aug.
Loire
18 Sept.
Poitiers ✕
POITOU
AQUITAINE
Bordeaux
GUYENNE
QUERCY ROUERGUE
Dax
Bayonne
GASCONY
Toulouse
Carcassonne
Narbonne
Vitoria
Pamplona
Nájera ✕
Burgos

19 September 1356, the Black Prince defeats King John II of France, who loses 2,500 men.

3 April 1367, the Black Prince defeats Don Enrico and du Guesclin.

© Arthur Banks

THE BATTLE OF POITIERS 19 SEPTEMBER 1356

PHASE ONE
to Poitiers
A
B
C

RIVAL STRENGTHS
French: 16,000
English & Gascons: 8,000

KEY
- A King John II. ⎫
- B Duke of Orléans. ⎬ French Units.
- C Dauphin. ⎭
- Cavalry.
- 1 Black Prince. ⎫
- 2 Salisbury. ⎬ English Units.
- 3 Warwick. ⎭
- Cavalry.
- ▲▲ Archers.

crossbowmen
HEDGE
MARSH
B Baggage wagons
HEDGE
0   500
Yards

PHASE TWO
KING JOHN II
fleeing
B
A
C
1 2
3
BLACK PRINCE
PICKED MOBILE FORCE

THE FRENCH ATTACKED IN WAVES, APART FROM ORLEANS DIVISION (WHICH FLED THE FIELD), AND THEY NEARLY SUCCEEDED IN OVERWHELMING THE ENGLISH. AT A CRITICAL MOMENT, THE BLACK PRINCE ORDERED A GENERAL ADVANCE AND HIS SPECIAL RESERVE CHARGED THE FRENCH REAR. BESET FROM FRONT AND BACK, THE FRENCH RAPIDLY COLLAPSED.

❹ The General Scene between 1381 and 1415

KEY
- Main areas of Peasants' Revolt in England 1381.
- → Henry Ⅴ's campaign in 1415.
- ✗ Important battles.
- o Towns raided by the French 1403–1404.

The French were eager to aid the Scottish and Welsh rebels so as to disperse England's military strength.

1 1402, French Orléanist troops assist Scots during invasion of England.

2 1403–1404, French raid English and Welsh coastal towns while Henry Ⅳ is preoccupied with internal rebellions.

4 1406, French attack English possessions in France.

3 1405, French land in Wales to assist Owen Glendower. Later, they withdraw.

5 1415, Henry Ⅴ besieges and takes Harfleur. He then marches towards Calais, winning the Battle of Agincourt en route.

SCOTLAND · Homildon Hill · IRELAND · WALES · Caernarvon · ENGLAND · LONDON · Plymouth · Dartmouth · Harfleur · Calais · Agincourt · to Vienne · NORTH SEA · PARIS · FRANCE · Orléans

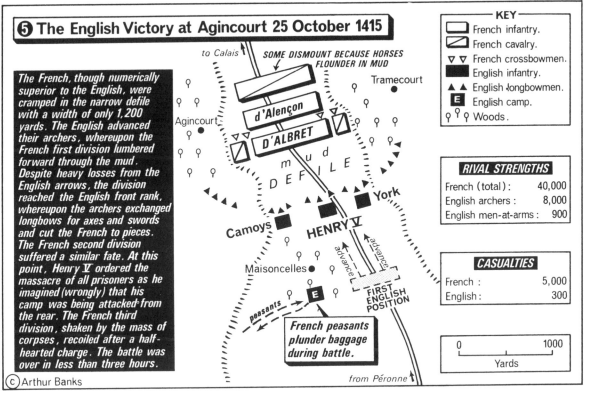

❺ The English Victory at Agincourt 25 October 1415

KEY
- French infantry.
- French cavalry.
- ▽ ▽ French crossbowmen.
- ■ English infantry.
- ▲ ▲ English longbowmen.
- E English camp.
- � Woods.

The French, though numerically superior to the English, were cramped in the narrow defile with a width of only 1,200 yards. The English advanced their archers, whereupon the French first division lumbered forward through the mud. Despite heavy losses from the English arrows, the division reached the English front rank, whereupon the archers exchanged longbows for axes and swords and cut the French to pieces. The French second division suffered a similar fate. At this point, Henry Ⅴ ordered the massacre of all prisoners as he imagined (wrongly) that his camp was being attacked from the rear. The French third division, shaken by the mass of corpses, recoiled after a half-hearted charge. The battle was over in less than three hours.

© Arthur Banks

to Calais · SOME DISMOUNT BECAUSE HORSES FLOUNDER IN MUD · Tramecourt · d'Alençon · D'ALBRET · Agincourt · mud DEFILE · York · Camoys · HENRY Ⅴ · Maisoncelles · advance · FIRST ENGLISH POSITION · E · peasants · French peasants plunder baggage during battle. · from Péronne

RIVAL STRENGTHS
French (total):	40,000
English archers:	8,000
English men-at-arms:	900

CASUALTIES
French:	5,000
English:	300

0 — 1000 Yards

145

THE HUNDRED YEARS' WAR – continued

❻ The French Resurgence 1429–1453

1453, this is the only remaining English possession in France, and the sole English land gain of the whole war.

Dec. 1431, Henry VI crowned. 1436, French recover Paris.

8 Sep. 1429, attack on Paris fails. Joan is wounded.

1435, treaty between Charles VII and Burgundy.

30 May 1431, Joan of Arc is burnt at the stake as a heretic.

23 May 1430, Joan of Arc is captured by Burgundians during sortie, and turned over to the English six months later.

15 April 1450, Clermont defeats Kyriel and Gough. English lose 4,000 men.

19 June 1429, Joan of Arc's forces defeat Talbot who is captured.

17 July 1429, Charles VII is crowned.

29 April 1429, Joan enters Orléans. Siege raised on 8 May.

8 March 1429, Joan is brought to the Dauphin.

Dec. 1429, Joan takes part in unsuccessful siege.

17 July 1453, Bureau defeats Shrewsbury (Talbot) who is killed.

19 October 1453, French capture Bordeaux. This is the virtual end of the Hundred Years' War.

Calais, Arras, Cherbourg, Caen, Formigny, Rouen, Rheims, Compiègne, Paris, Troyes, Domremy, Patay, Orléans, Chinon, La Charité, POITOU, MAINE, BOURBON, BURGUNDY, AUVERGNE, Castillon, Bordeaux, Dordogne, Garonne, Rhône, Saône, Loire, Seine, Rhine, SAVOY, PROVENCE, HOLY ROMAN EMPIRE, SPAIN

0 100 Miles

© Arthur Banks

The Siege of Orléans
12 OCTOBER 1428 – 8 MAY 1429

KEY
★ English 'bastilles'.
═ Roads.

Defended by seventy cannon plus culverins.

to Paris, ORLÉANS, moat, LOIRE, Pontereau

0 1 Mile

This map shows the fortress of Orléans with 'bastilles'(forts) built by the English besiegers. The siege was raised by Joan of Arc.

KEY
- English holdings in France 1429.
- French holdings in 1429.
- In alliance with England.
- Papal holdings.
- X Important battles.
- ⊙ Important sieges.
- ← Route of Joan of Arc in 1429.

The French resurgence began with Joan of Arc in 1429. She inspired the Dauphin (later Charles VII) to try to rid France of the English. However it was not until the French army was reorganized by the Bureau brothers (artillery experts) between 1445–1449 that France was able to reverse the English tide of success that had been emphasised at Sluys, Crécy, Poitiers, and Agincourt. Her most successful general was Dunois.

OWEN GLENDOWER AND WALES 1400 - 1412

Owen Glendower a Welsh figure of stature in a period of degenerate politics, revived Llewelyn's policy of independence for Wales. His ideas were appealing to the Welsh people who had grievances against the English, and he exploited rival factions amongst the common enemy. However, his guerilla warfare proved disastrous to the Welsh economy.

—KEY—

⇦ Welsh military operations.

⬅ English military operations.

★ Important strongholds where investments or attacks took place during this period of Welsh unrest.

◉ Other strongholds.

▨ Principality of Wales.

AUDLEY Important families.

Note: Owen Glendower is known in Wales as Owain Glyn Dŵr or Owain ab Gruffydd.

1401, William and Rhys ap Tudor seize castle temporarily for Glendower.

1400, Glendower quarrels with Grey of Ruthin and ravages his lands. 1402, he captures Grey.

Prince Henry's headquarters.

Percy (Hotspur) now supporting Glendower, is defeated and killed by Henry IV.

1403, French fleet attacks Caernarvon.

1404, Glendower takes Harlech. It is retaken in 1409, when Mortimer dies in the siege.

1404, taken by Glendower. 1408, recaptured by Prince Henry.

1402, Glendower defeats and captures Edmund Mortimer, who marries his daughter and joins him. They plot with Northumberland, who takes the field in 1405, but the revolt is crushed.

1401, Percy defeats rebels.

1403, Glendower's estates sacked by Prince Henry.

1400, border levies defeat Glendower.

1405, French land to aid Glendower, take Haverfordwest and Carmarthen, and move east. Force withdraws in 1406.

1405, English fleet foils attack on Tenby.

1403, French fleet causes panic, but cannot take Kidwelly Castle.

Glendower's base area.

Map labels: Anglesey, Beaumaris, Conway, Rhuddlan, Flint, Hawarden, Chester, Denbigh, MORTIMER, Ruthin, GREY, Holt, FITZALAN, Caernarvon, Snowdon, 1400 & 1402, 1403, 1400, 1401, CAERNARVON, Harlech, Glyndwvdvrdwy, MERIONETH, 1402, Dee, 1400, Oswestry, FITZALAN, Sycharth, Shrewsbury, 1402, Cader Idris, POWYS, Welshpool, 1403, CHARLTON, MORTIMER, Montgomery, FITZALAN, Pilleth, MORTIMER, Ludlow, TALBOT, Llanbadarn, BEAUCHAMP, 1401, Cardigan, AUDLEY, 1405, CARMARTHEN 1401, Towy, Builth, 1401 & 1403, MORTIMER, Wye, Hereford, 1402, Carmarthen, 1401 & 1403, Dynevor, Usk, Brecon, 1405, TALBOT, Haverfordwest, 1405, 1403, LANCASTER, 1403, Abergavenny, 1405, Milford Haven, PEMBROKE, Tenby, Kidwelly, GOWER, NORFOLK, DESPENSER, Coity, Usk, Caerleon, 1403, 1405, Newport, 1405, Cardiff, 1403, Bristol Channel

0 — 20
Miles

© Arthur Banks

THE WARS OF THE ROSES 1455 – 1485

❶ Lancastrian Strongholds and Areas of Support 1455

KEY
★ Lancastrian bastions.
Lancastrian areas of support in 1455.
PERCY Powerful families.

0 40 Miles

❷ Yorkist Strongholds and Areas of Support 1455

KEY
☆ Yorkist bastions.
Yorkist areas of support in 1455.
PERCY Powerful families.

0 50 Miles

No class interest was involved in the Wars and the mass of the people were generally onlookers. No principle was involved either, thus making 'changing of sides' frequent and easy. It was basically a quarrel between Marcher Lords for possession of more wealth, power, and the throne.

The actual contestants were brutal in their treatment of each other after battles had been decided, thus reducing the already small numbers of nobles in the land. Each switch of fortune meant more confiscations of great estates which further enriched the Crown.

© Arthur Banks

148

④ Yorkist Victories

6 1464. Montagu (Warwick's brother) defeats Somerset and Percy, who is killed.

7 1464. Montagu wins victory, following which many executions take place.

5 1461. Edward wins victory during blizzard. This success places him on throne as Edward IV.

3 1460. Warwick and Edward (Earl of March) defeat royal army marching on London and capture Henry VI.

8 1471. Warwick and Montagu (who have changed sides) are defeated and killed.

1 1455. Richard of York and Richard of Warwick defeat and kill Somerset. They seize Henry VI.

Hedgeley Moor ⚔

Hexham ⚔

Towton ⚔

Blore Heath ⚔

Mortimer's Cross ⚔

Northampton ⚔

Barnet ⚔

St. Albans ⚔

Tewkesbury ⚔

2 1459. Earl of Salisbury defeats Lancastrian force.

4 1461. Edward (now Duke of York) defeats Jasper Tudor, Earl of Pembroke, and executes Lancastrian noblemen.

9 1471. Edward wins victory, capturing Margaret and killing Prince of Wales and important Lancastrian nobles.

The longbow was the supreme weapon, although cannon and the new hand-gun were sometimes utilised for field work.

0 — 50 Miles

③ Lancastrian Victories

2 1460. Richard of York and Edmund are killed in an ambush and Salisbury executed.

3 1461. Margaret defeats Warwick and recaptures Henry VI.

Wakefield ⚔

Bosworth Field ⚔

Edgecote ⚔

St. Albans ⚔

Ludford Bridge ⚔

5 1485. Richard III dies during battle in which most of his army desert him. His death concludes the wars, and Henry Tudor becomes King Henry VII.

1 1459. Yorkists routed. York and Warwick flee abroad.

4 1469. Robin of Redesdale's rebels defeat William Herbert, Earl of Pembroke.

During the struggle, only the white rose of York was used as a badge. The red rose of Lancaster was not used as a badge until the final battle at Bosworth Field in 1485.

Cavalry fighting was an exception: most soldiers were really mounted infantrymen.

0 — 50 Miles

© Arthur Banks

149

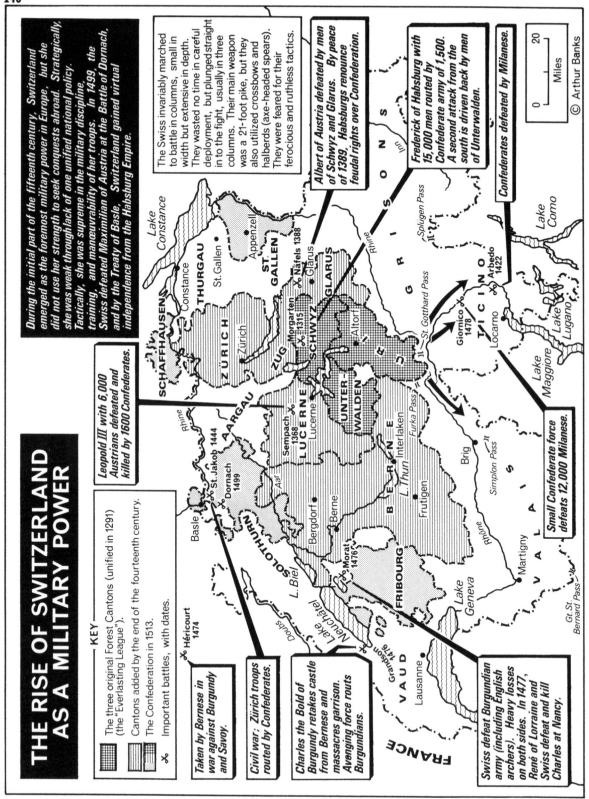

THE RISE OF SWITZERLAND AS A MILITARY POWER

KEY

The three original Forest Cantons (unified in 1291) (the "Everlasting League").

Cantons added by the end of the fourteenth century.

The Confederation in 1513.

Important battles, with dates.

During the initial part of the fifteenth century, Switzerland emerged as the foremost military power in Europe, but she did not use her strength to seek conquests abroad. Strategically, she was weak through lack of one unified national policy. Tactically, she was supreme in the military discipline, training, and manoeuvrability of her troops. In 1499, the Swiss defeated Maximilian of Austria at the Battle of Dornach, and by the Treaty of Basle, Switzerland gained virtual independence from the Habsburg Empire.

The Swiss invariably marched to battle in columns, small in width but extensive in depth. They wasted no time in careful deployment, but plunged straight in to the fight, usually in three columns. Their main weapon was a 21-foot pike, but they also utilized crossbows and halberds (axe-headed spears). They were feared for their ferocious and ruthless tactics.

Albert of Austria defeated by men of Schwyz and Glarus. By peace of 1389, Habsburgs renounce feudal rights over Confederation.

Frederick of Habsburg with 15,000 men routed by Confederate army of 1,500. A second attack from the south is driven back by men of Unterwalden.

Confederates defeated by Milanese.

Small Confederate force defeats 12,000 Milanese.

Leopold III with 6,000 Austrians defeated and killed by 1600 Confederates.

Taken by Bernese in war against Burgundy and Savoy.

Civil war: Zürich troops routed by Confederates.

Charles the Bold of Burgundy retakes castle from Bernese and massacres garrison. Avenging force routs Burgundians.

Swiss defeat Burgundian army (including English archers). Heavy losses on both sides. In 1477, René of Lorraine and Swiss defeat and kill Charles at Nancy.

© Arthur Banks

0   20
Miles

Lake Constance

THURGAU

Constance

St. Gallen

Appenzell

ST. GALLEN

SCHAFFHAUSEN

ZÜRICH

Zürich

ZUG

Näfels 1388

Glarus

GLARUS

Morgarten 1315

SCHWYZ

Altorf

UNTERWALDEN

Lucerne

LUCERNE

Sempach 1368

AARGAU

Rhine

St. Jakob 1444

Dornach 1499

Basle

SOLOTHURN

L. Biel

Bergdorf

Berne

BERNE

Interlaken

L. Thun

Frutigen

Furka Pass

Brig

Simplon Pass

FRIBOURG

Morat 1476

Lake Geneva

Martigny

VAUD

Lausanne

Grandson 1476

Héricourt 1474

Lake Neuchâtel

Doubs

Gt. St. Bernard Pass

VALAIS

Rhône

Rhine

GRISONS

Inn

Splügen Pass

Arbedo 1422

TICINO

Giornico 1478

Locarno

St. Gotthard Pass

Lake Maggiore

Lake Lugano

Lake Como

FRANCE

EXPANSION OF THE OTTOMAN EMPIRE TO 1566

The Osmanli (Ottoman) branch of the Turkish peoples was responsible for creating an empire which grew from a small area in north-west Asia Minor (in the thirteenth and fourteenth centuries) to cover a huge area of south-west Europe and the Middle East by the time of Suleiman the Magnificent. In 1453, Sultan Mohammed the Conqueror captured Constantinople and this became the capital of the Ottoman Empire until its final collapse after the First World War.

200

0   Miles

PERSIA

Caspian Sea

DAGHISTAN

Tabriz

Baghdad

Persian Gulf

RUSSIA

ARMENIA

Chaldiran 1515

Erzinjan 1473

MESOPOTAMIA

Tigris

Euphrates

Azov

Trebizond

Aleppo

SYRIA

Angora 1402

Jerusalem

Yaunis Khan 1516

Black Sea

POLAND 1497-1498

Dnieper

Dniester

MOLDAVIA

Constantinople 1453

Coilepe 1329

ANATOLIA

Capital 1453 - 1918.

Capital until 1365.

WALLACHIA

Nicopolis

Danube 1396

Varna 1444

Bursa 1326

Gallipoli 1416

Rhodes 1480 1522

AUSTRIA

Vienna 1529

Buda 1529

HUNGARY

Mohacs 1526

Sabac 1521

Sava

Belgrade 1456 1521

Kossovo 1389 1448

Adrianople 1361

BULGARIA

Athens

ALBANIA

Lepanto 1499 1500

Preveza 1538

Sapienza 1499

Capital 1365 - 1453.

Otranto

ITALY

Mediterranean Sea

Adriatic Sea

Danube

KEY

■	Ottoman territory in 1307.
▨	Ottoman territory in 1359.
▨	Ottoman territory in 1451.
▨	Territory gained by Sultan Mohammed the Conqueror, 1451 - 1481.
▨	Territory gained by Selim I, 1512 - 1520
▨	Territory gained by Suleiman the Magnificent, 1520 - 1566.
⚔	Important battles, with dates.
⊙	Important sieges, with dates.

CHINA UNDER THE MINGS 1368-1644

The Mings drove the Mongols from China, and their warships dominated the South China Sea. Their influence extended to the Indian Ocean and the Red Sea.

0   200
Miles

Ho-lin (Karakorum)
1409 ✗

Kerulen

✗ 1388

KHORCHIN

c.1610, early Manchu activity.

H A L H A - M O N G O L S

S   H   A   M   O

KHANATE OF CHAHAR

c.1391

KHANATE OF ORDOS TUMET

Ta-t'ung

Liao-tung

Shan-hsi

GREAT WALL

Peking

CHING-SHIH

Chen-ting

MONGOLS

SHEN-

T'ai-yuan-fu

Lai-chou

Yen-an

Chi-nan-fu

S H A N T U N G

P'ing-liang

HSI

1356, rise of the Ming in this area.

Wei Ho

K'ai-feng-fu

Hsi-an-fu

H O - N A N

Huang Ho

TIBET

Lung-an

Ying-t'ien-fu

NAN-CHING

Ch'eng-tu-fu

Chang-chou

SSU-CH'UAN

Wu-ch'ang

Chiang

Hang-chou

1360?

CHE-CHIANG

Nan-ch'ang-fu

Chiang

H U - K U A N G

Wu-wei

Tsun-i

Shao-wu

Kuei-yang-fu

CHIANG-HSI

FU-CHIEN

Yung-chou

Fu-chou

Yun-nan-fu

KUEI-CHOU

Kuei-lin-fu

MONGOLS

Y U - N A N

Ch'uan-chou

c.1382

Chen-an

Tai-wan

MIEN

KUANG-HSI

Kuang-chou-fu

Hui-chou

KUANG-TUNG

Admiral Cheng Ho leads a series of naval expeditions to invade Sumatra (1405-1407), and Ceylon (1408-1411). Later, he leads expeditions to Hormuz (1412-1415) and Mecca (1431-1433). A notable feature of Chinese naval design is the introduction of watertight compartments in the hulls of junks.

Hai-nan

KEY
Expulsion of Mongols.
Ming invasions.
✗ Important battles.

© Arthur Banks

JAPAN AND KOREA BEFORE THE PORTUGUESE ARRIVAL IN 1542

KEY
- Chinese attacks 611-647 (all repulsed).
- War between Paekche and Silla (allied with China) 660-663. Silla victorious.
- War between Koguryo and Silla (allied with China) 663-668. Silla victorious.
- Internal wars in Japan (main areas shown).
- Important battles, with dates.

Capital of Koryo kingdom.

Japanese foothold in Korea until 668.

Capital 794.

Area of intermittent wars between Ainu and Nara.

Area of Onin War.

Area of Gempei War.

INTERNAL WARS IN JAPAN
1. *1180–1185, GEMPEI WAR.* This was between the Taira and the Minamoto factions.
2. *1467–1477, ONIN WAR.* This was between Yamana Mochitoyo and Hosokawa Katsumoto. Both were killed.

Not known as Tokyo until 1868. Tōkyō means 'eastern capital.'

1185, military headquarters established by Yoritomo (Minamoto leader).

Capital 710-794.

1542, Portuguese introduce Western firearms, mainly the 'arquebuse' (an early form of musket).

1339-1392, civil war between Ashikaga court at Kyoto and rival court in Kyushu.

1460, by capturing these islands, Koreans restrict Japanese pirate raids.

663, Mimana, Tsushima Is., 1183 Dannoura, Inland Sea, Hakata, Yashima 1183, Nara, Kyoto, Edo, Kamakura, Songdo

KOGURYO, SILLA, KOREA, PAEKCHE, CHINESE, HOKKAIDO, AINU, HONSHU, SHIKOKU, KYUSHU, Tanegashima

BASIC JAPANESE CHRONOLOGY

?660 B.C.–A.D. 400		Early Period. First Emperor (Jimmu Tenno) in 660 B.C.
c.400	645 (coup d'état)	Yamato Period (Soga clan dominant).
710	784	Nara Period.
794	1184	Heian Period.
(672	1156)	(Fujiwara clan dominant).
(1156	1185)	(Taira: rivalry with Minamoto clan).
1185	1333	Kamakura Period (chiefly Hojo regency).
1338	1573	Ashikaga (Muromachi Period).
1573	1603	"Rules of Nobunaga, Hideyoshi, and Ieyasu."
1603	1868	Tokugawa (Edo) Period.
1868	1912	Meiji Period.
1912	1926	Taishō Period.
1926		Shōwa Period.

© Arthur Banks

JAPAN AND KUBLAI KHAN
1. *1274, FIRST INVASION BY MONGOLS. 30,000 MONGOLS AND KOREANS ATTACKED HAKATA AND TSUSHIMA BUT A STORM WRECKED THE FLEET. THE SURVIVORS THEN RETURNED TO KOREA.*
2. *1281, SECOND INVASION BY MONGOLS. A HUGE FORCE IN TWO DIVISIONS MET STRONG RESISTANCE IN JAPAN. THE INVASION ENDED IN CHAOS.*

Scale: 0 100 200 Miles

FOUR LATER VIEWS OF THE WORLD

❶ According to Idrisi 1154

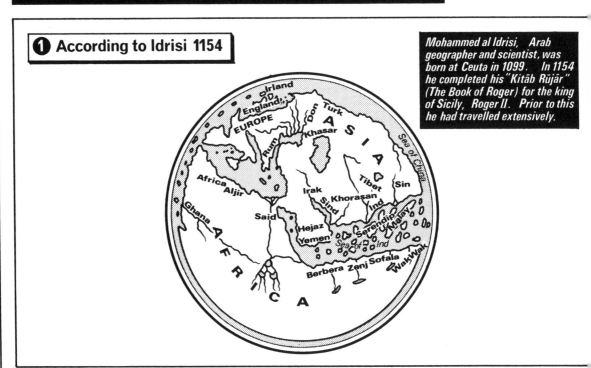

Mohammed al Idrisi, Arab geographer and scientist, was born at Ceuta in 1099. In 1154 he completed his "Kitāb Rūjār" (The Book of Roger) for the king of Sicily, Roger II. Prior to this he had travelled extensively.

❷ According to Fra Mauro 1450

Fra Mauro, a Venetian monk and cartographer, produced a world map from detail accumulated during the previous two centuries. His work was notable for details on Africa and Asia in particular.

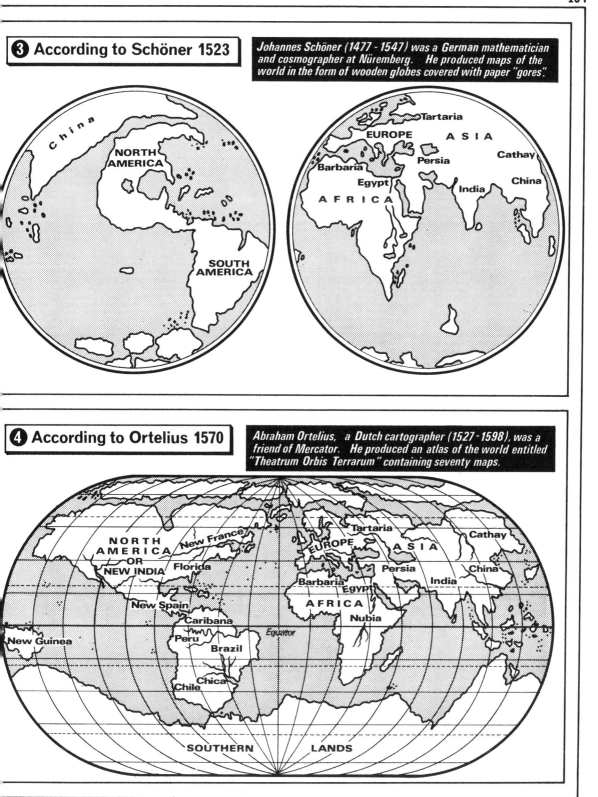

3 According to Schöner 1523

Johannes Schöner (1477 - 1547) was a German mathematician and cosmographer at Nüremberg. He produced maps of the world in the form of wooden globes covered with paper "gores".

China

NORTH AMERICA

SOUTH AMERICA

Tartaria

EUROPE   A S I A

Persia   Cathay

Barbaria   China

Egypt   India

A F R I C A

4 According to Ortelius 1570

Abraham Ortelius, a Dutch cartographer (1527-1598), was a friend of Mercator. He produced an atlas of the world entitled "Theatrum Orbis Terrarum" containing seventy maps.

NORTH AMERICA OR NEW INDIA

New France

Florida

New Spain

Caribana

Peru

Brazil

Chile   Chica

New Guinea

Tartaria   Cathay

EUROPE   A S I A

Persia   China

Barbaria   India

Egypt

A F R I C A   Nubia

Equator

SOUTHERN   LANDS

INDEX OF BATTLES, SIEGES, WARS, CAMPAIGNS, ETC

In the case of battles, only the place name is given. Dates are given only when necessary to distinguish between battles at the same site.

INDEX OF INDIVIDUALS

INDEX OF RACES, TRIBES,
AND ALL NAMED GROUPS OF PEOPLE

GEOGRAPHICAL INDEX